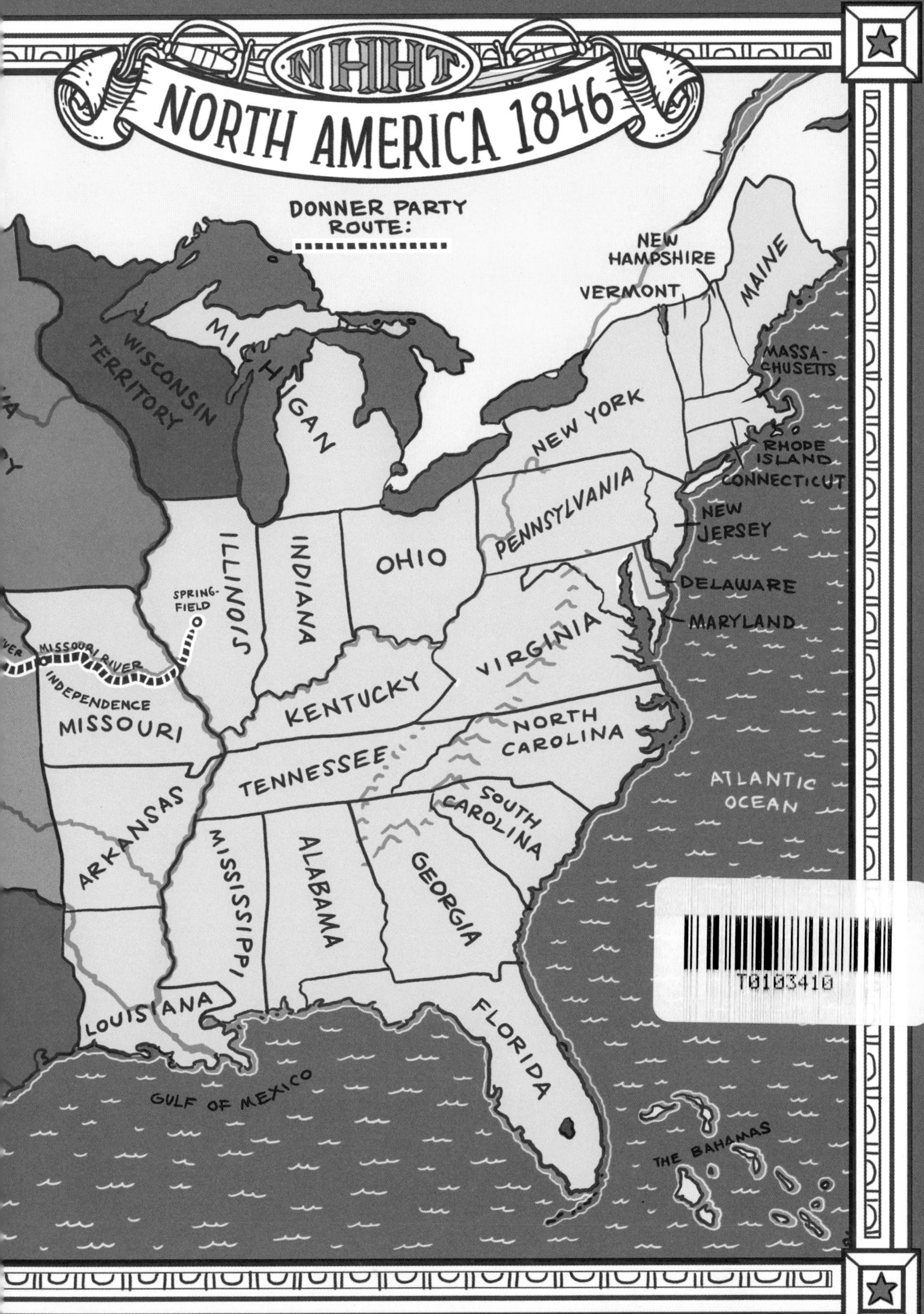
NHHT
NORTH AMERICA 1846
DONNER PARTY ROUTE:
NEW HAMPSHIRE
VERMONT
MAINE
MASSACHUSETTS
RHODE ISLAND
CONNECTICUT
NEW YORK
WISCONSIN TERRITORY
MICHIGAN
PENNSYLVANIA
NEW JERSEY
DELAWARE
MARYLAND
ILLINOIS
INDIANA
OHIO
SPRINGFIELD
MISSOURI RIVER
INDEPENDENCE
MISSOURI
KENTUCKY
VIRGINIA
NORTH CAROLINA
TENNESSEE
ATLANTIC OCEAN
SOUTH CAROLINA
ARKANSAS
MISSISSIPPI
ALABAMA
GEORGIA
LOUISIANA
FLORIDA
GULF OF MEXICO
THE BAHAMAS

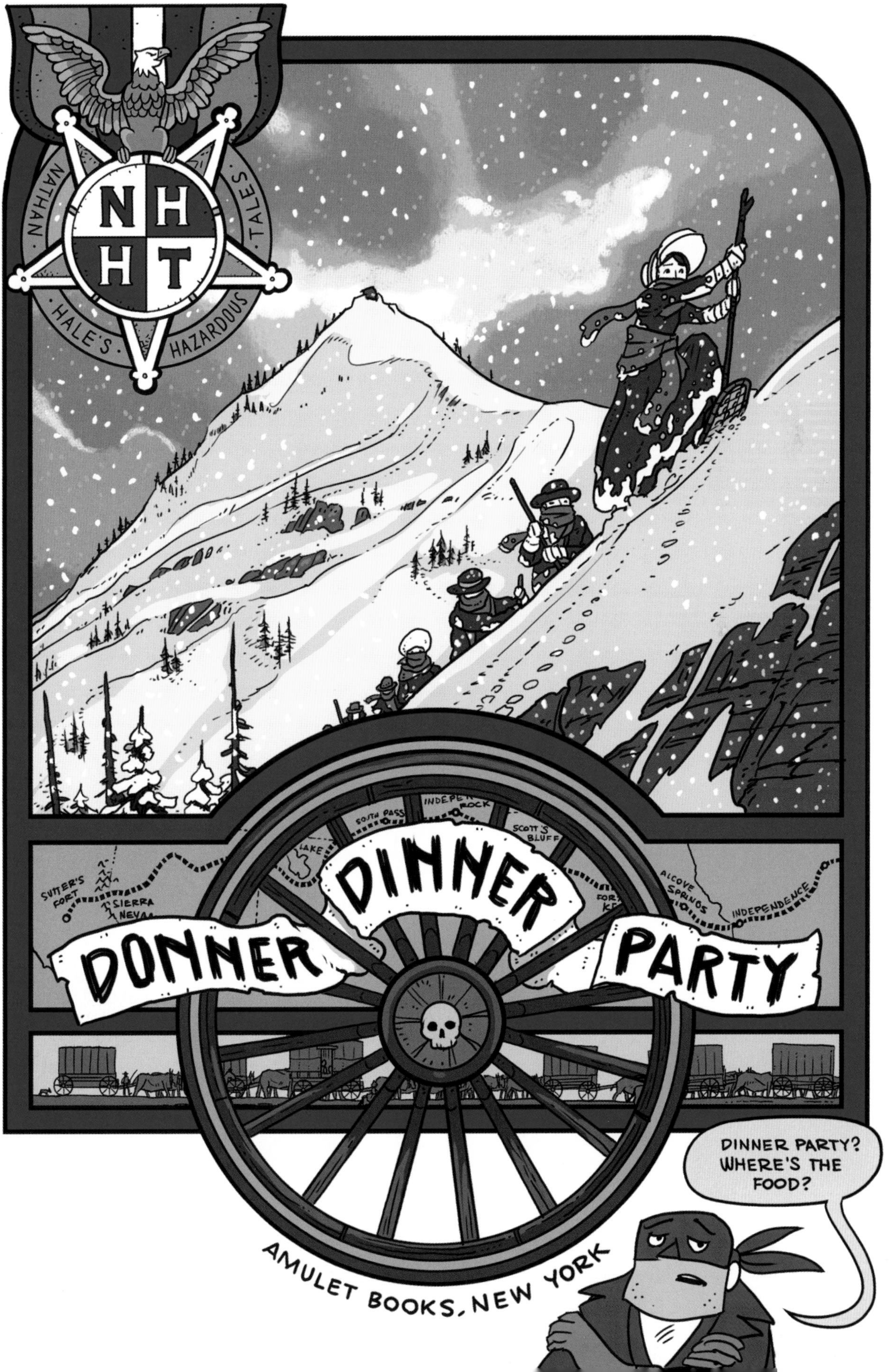
NATHAN HALE'S HAZARDOUS TALES
NH HT
SUTTER'S FORT
SOUTH PASS
SCOTT'S BLUFF
LAKE
ALCOVE SPRINGS
INDEPENDENCE
DONNER DINNER PARTY
AMULET BOOKS, NEW YORK
DINNER PARTY? WHERE'S THE FOOD?

LIBRARY OF CONGRESS CONTROL NUMBER FOR THE 2013 HARDCOVER: 2014378376
ISBN FOR THE 2013 HARDCOVER: 978-1-4197-0856-5
ISBN FOR THE 2020 BIGGER & BADDER EDITION: 978-1-4197-4907-0

TEXT AND ILLUSTRATIONS COPYRIGHT © 2013, 2020 NATHAN HALE
BOOK DESIGN BY NATHAN HALE AND MEGAN KELCHNER
ORIGINAL BOOK DESIGN BY NATHAN HALE AND CHAD W. BECKERMAN

THIS EDITION PUBLISHED IN 2020 BY AMULET BOOKS, AN IMPRINT OF ABRAMS.
ORIGINALLY PUBLISHED IN 2013 BY AMULET BOOKS. ALL RIGHTS RESERVED. NO PORTION
OF THIS BOOK MAY BE REPRODUCED, STORED IN A RETRIEVAL SYSTEM, OR TRANSMITTED
IN ANY FORM OR BY ANY MEANS, MECHANICAL, ELECTRONIC, PHOTOCOPYING, RECORDING,
OR OTHERWISE, WITHOUT WRITTEN PERMISSION FROM THE PUBLISHER.

PRINTED AND BOUND IN CHINA
10 9 8 7 6 5

AMULET BOOKS ARE AVAILABLE AT SPECIAL DISCOUNTS WHEN PURCHASED IN QUANTITY
FOR PREMIUMS AND PROMOTIONS AS WELL AS FUNDRAISING OR EDUCATIONAL USE.
SPECIAL EDITIONS CAN ALSO BE CREATED TO SPECIFICATION. FOR DETAILS, CONTACT
SPECIALSALES@ABRAMSBOOKS.COM OR THE ADDRESS BELOW.

AMULET BOOKS® IS A REGISTERED TRADEMARK OF HARRY N. ABRAMS, INC.

ABRAMS The Art of Books
195 Broadway, New York, NY 10007
abramsbooks.com

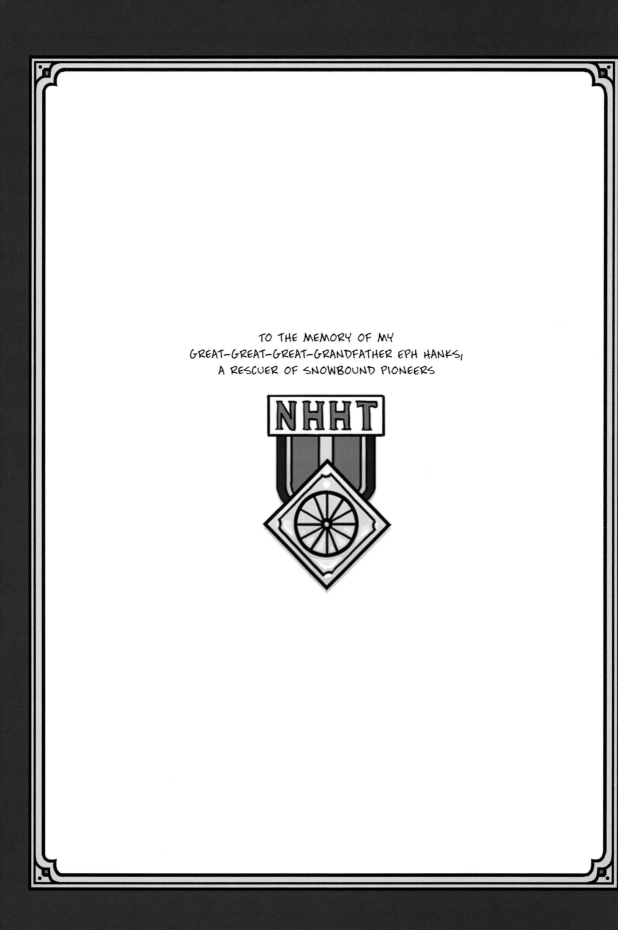

TO THE MEMORY OF MY
GREAT-GREAT-GREAT-GRANDFATHER EPH HANKS,
A RESCUER OF SNOWBOUND PIONEERS

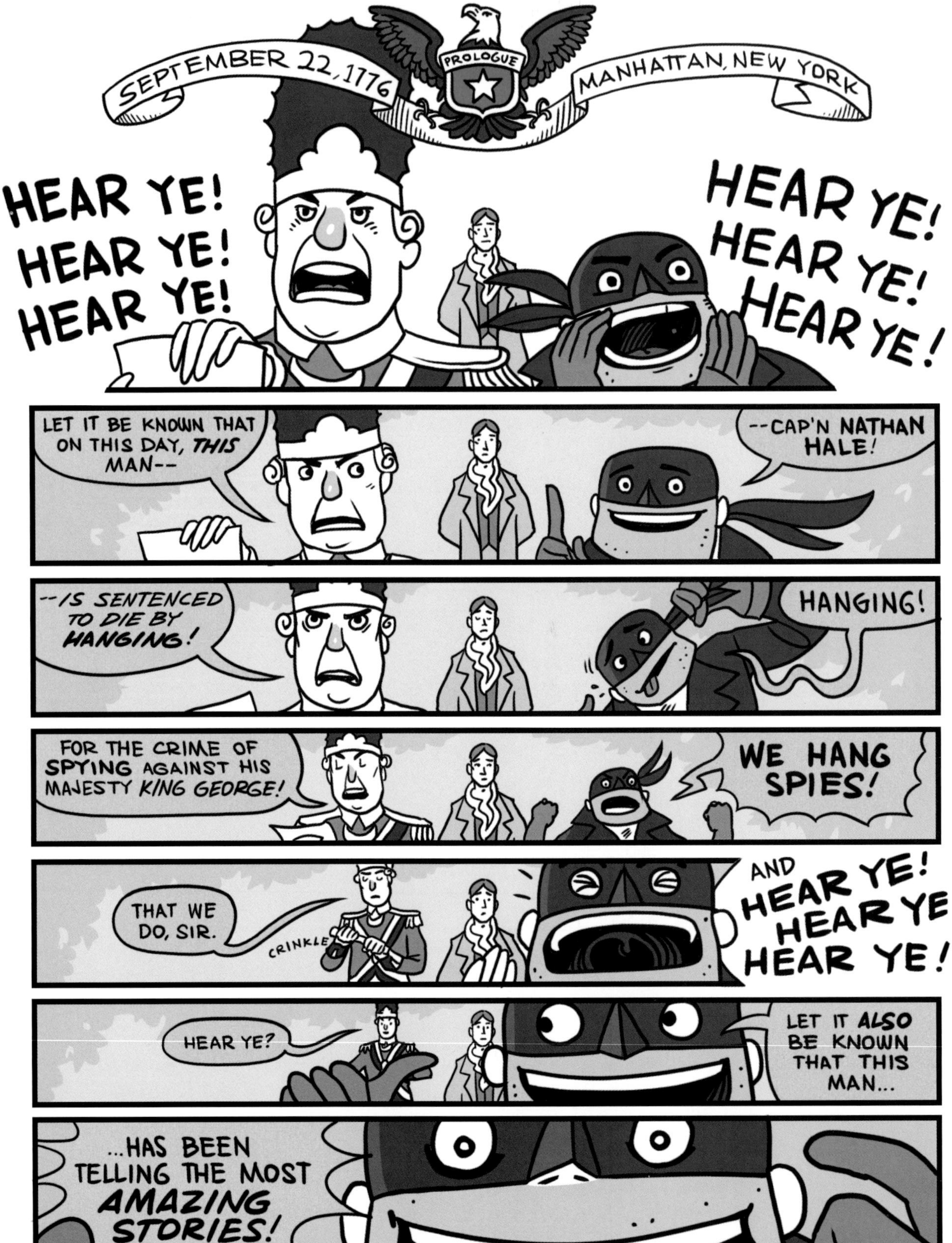
SEPTEMBER 22, 1776
PROLOGUE
MANHATTAN, NEW YORK
HEAR YE! HEAR YE! HEAR YE!
HEAR YE! HEAR YE! HEAR YE!
LET IT BE KNOWN THAT ON THIS DAY, THIS MAN--
--CAP'N NATHAN HALE!
--IS SENTENCED TO DIE BY HANGING!
HANGING!
FOR THE CRIME OF SPYING AGAINST HIS MAJESTY KING GEORGE!
WE HANG SPIES!
THAT WE DO, SIR.
CRINKLE
AND HEAR YE! HEAR YE! HEAR YE!
HEAR YE?
LET IT ALSO BE KNOWN THAT THIS MAN...
...HAS BEEN TELLING THE MOST AMAZING STORIES!

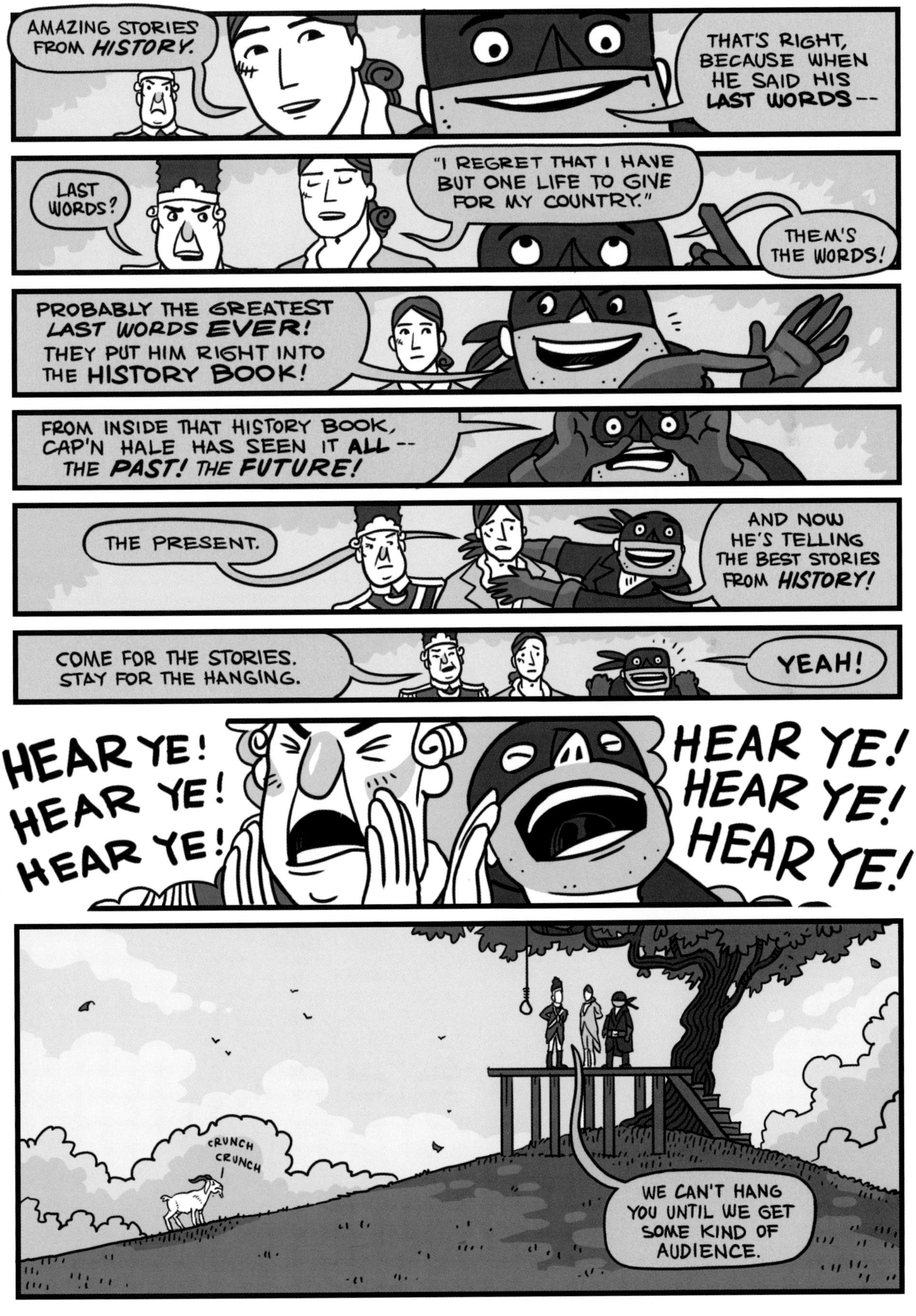
AMAZING STORIES FROM HISTORY.
THAT'S RIGHT, BECAUSE WHEN HE SAID HIS LAST WORDS--
LAST WORDS?
"I REGRET THAT I HAVE BUT ONE LIFE TO GIVE FOR MY COUNTRY."
THEM'S THE WORDS!
PROBABLY THE GREATEST LAST WORDS EVER! THEY PUT HIM RIGHT INTO THE HISTORY BOOK!
FROM INSIDE THAT HISTORY BOOK, CAP'N HALE HAS SEEN IT ALL-- THE PAST! THE FUTURE!
THE PRESENT.
AND NOW HE'S TELLING THE BEST STORIES FROM HISTORY!
COME FOR THE STORIES. STAY FOR THE HANGING.
YEAH!
HEAR YE! HEAR YE! HEAR YE!
HEAR YE! HEAR YE! HEAR YE!
CRUNCH CRUNCH
WE CAN'T HANG YOU UNTIL WE GET SOME KIND OF AUDIENCE.

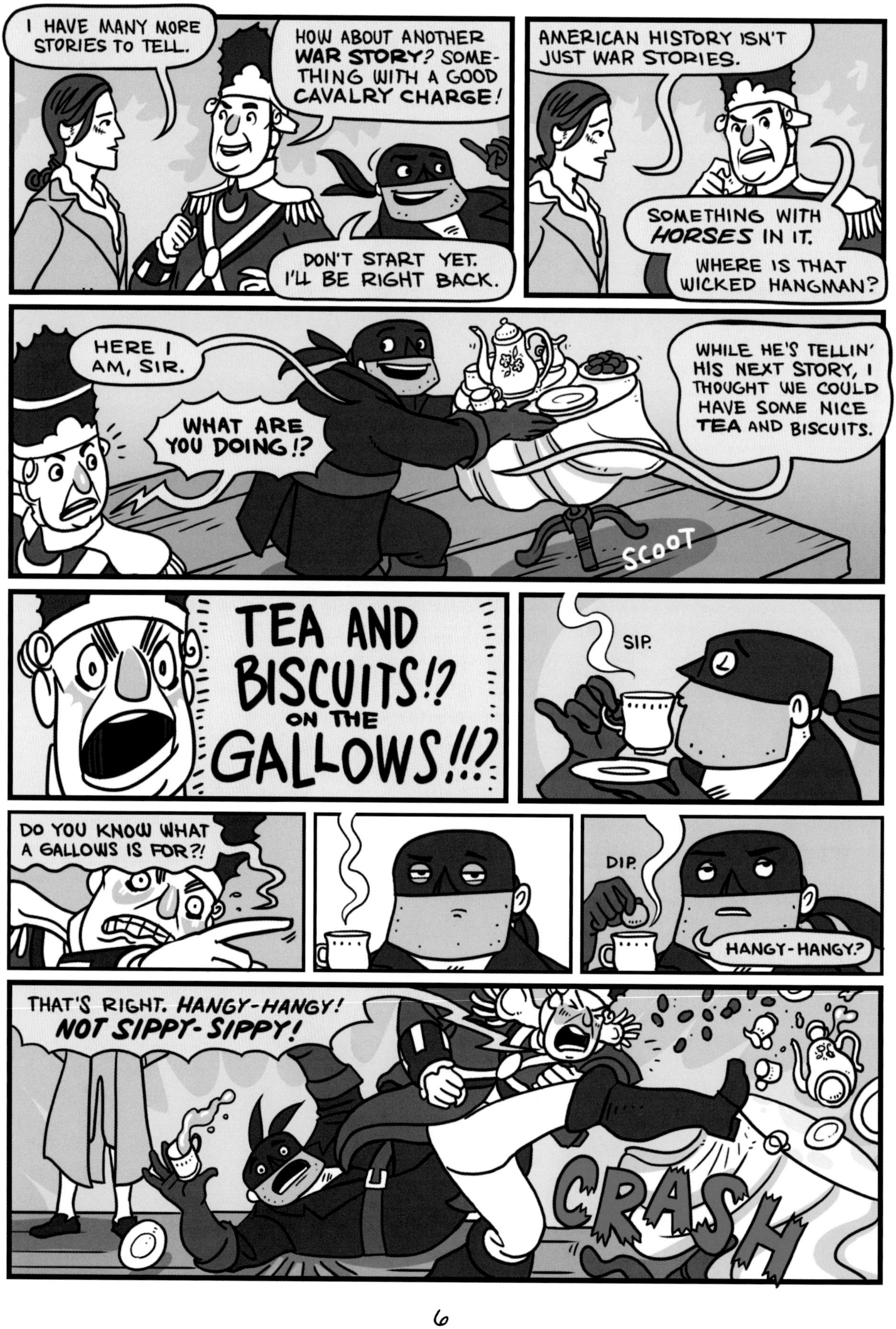
I HAVE MANY MORE STORIES TO TELL.
HOW ABOUT ANOTHER WAR STORY? SOMETHING WITH A GOOD CAVALRY CHARGE!
DON'T START YET. I'LL BE RIGHT BACK.
AMERICAN HISTORY ISN'T JUST WAR STORIES.
SOMETHING WITH HORSES IN IT.
WHERE IS THAT WICKED HANGMAN?
HERE I AM, SIR.
WHAT ARE YOU DOING!?
WHILE HE'S TELLIN' HIS NEXT STORY, I THOUGHT WE COULD HAVE SOME NICE TEA AND BISCUITS.
SCOOT
TEA AND BISCUITS!? ON THE GALLOWS!!?
SIP.
DO YOU KNOW WHAT A GALLOWS IS FOR?!
DIP.
HANGY-HANGY?
THAT'S RIGHT. HANGY-HANGY! NOT SIPPY-SIPPY!
CRASH

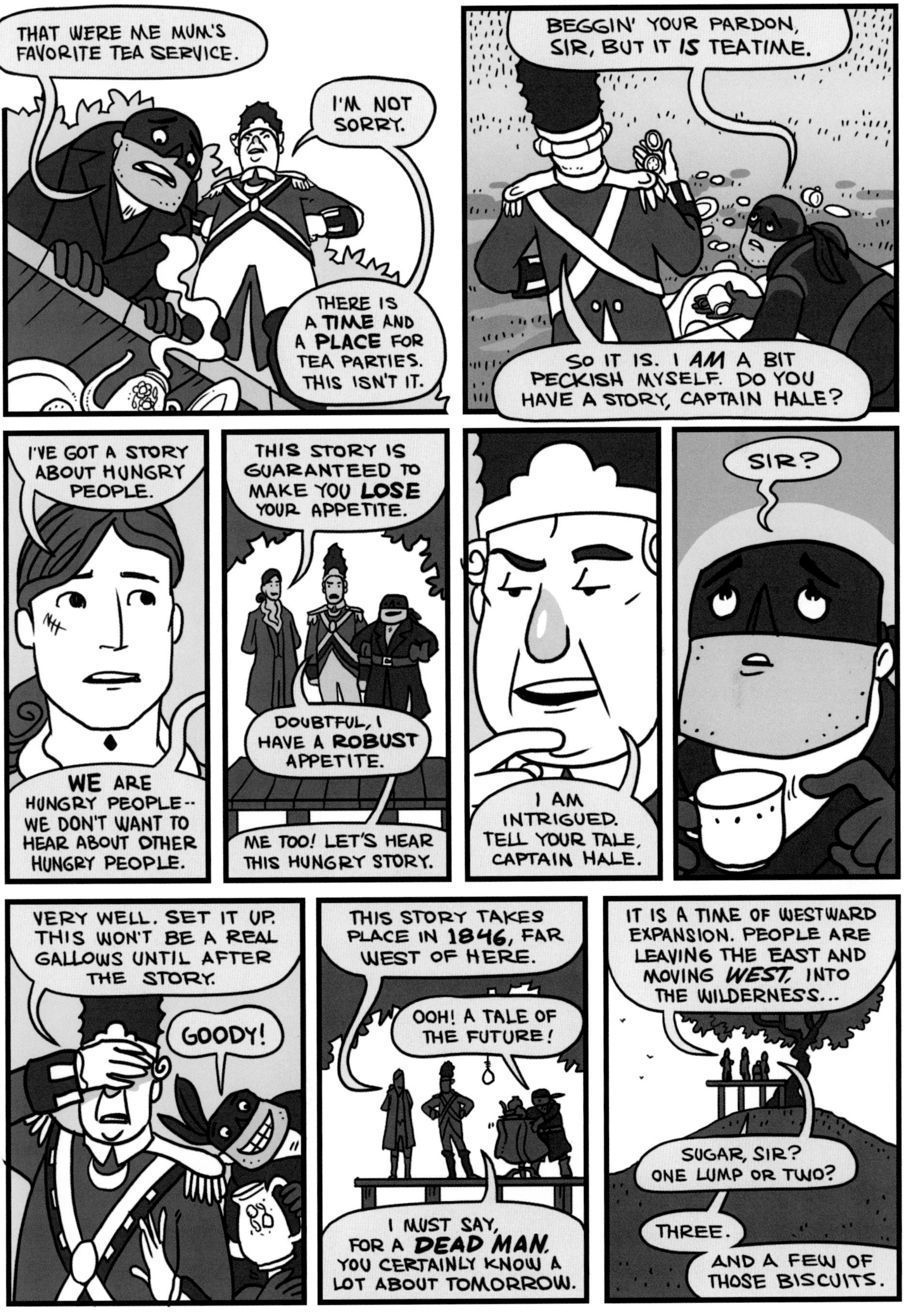
THAT WERE ME MUM'S FAVORITE TEA SERVICE.
I'M NOT SORRY.
THERE IS A TIME AND A PLACE FOR TEA PARTIES. THIS ISN'T IT.
BEGGIN' YOUR PARDON, SIR, BUT IT IS TEATIME.
SO IT IS. I AM A BIT PECKISH MYSELF. DO YOU HAVE A STORY, CAPTAIN HALE?
I'VE GOT A STORY ABOUT HUNGRY PEOPLE.
WE ARE HUNGRY PEOPLE-- WE DON'T WANT TO HEAR ABOUT OTHER HUNGRY PEOPLE.
THIS STORY IS GUARANTEED TO MAKE YOU LOSE YOUR APPETITE.
DOUBTFUL, I HAVE A ROBUST APPETITE.
ME TOO! LET'S HEAR THIS HUNGRY STORY.
I AM INTRIGUED. TELL YOUR TALE, CAPTAIN HALE.
SIR?
VERY WELL. SET IT UP. THIS WON'T BE A REAL GALLOWS UNTIL AFTER THE STORY.
GOODY!
THIS STORY TAKES PLACE IN 1846, FAR WEST OF HERE.
OOH! A TALE OF THE FUTURE!
I MUST SAY, FOR A DEAD MAN, YOU CERTAINLY KNOW A LOT ABOUT TOMORROW.
IT IS A TIME OF WESTWARD EXPANSION. PEOPLE ARE LEAVING THE EAST AND MOVING WEST, INTO THE WILDERNESS...
SUGAR, SIR? ONE LUMP OR TWO?
THREE.
AND A FEW OF THOSE BISCUITS.

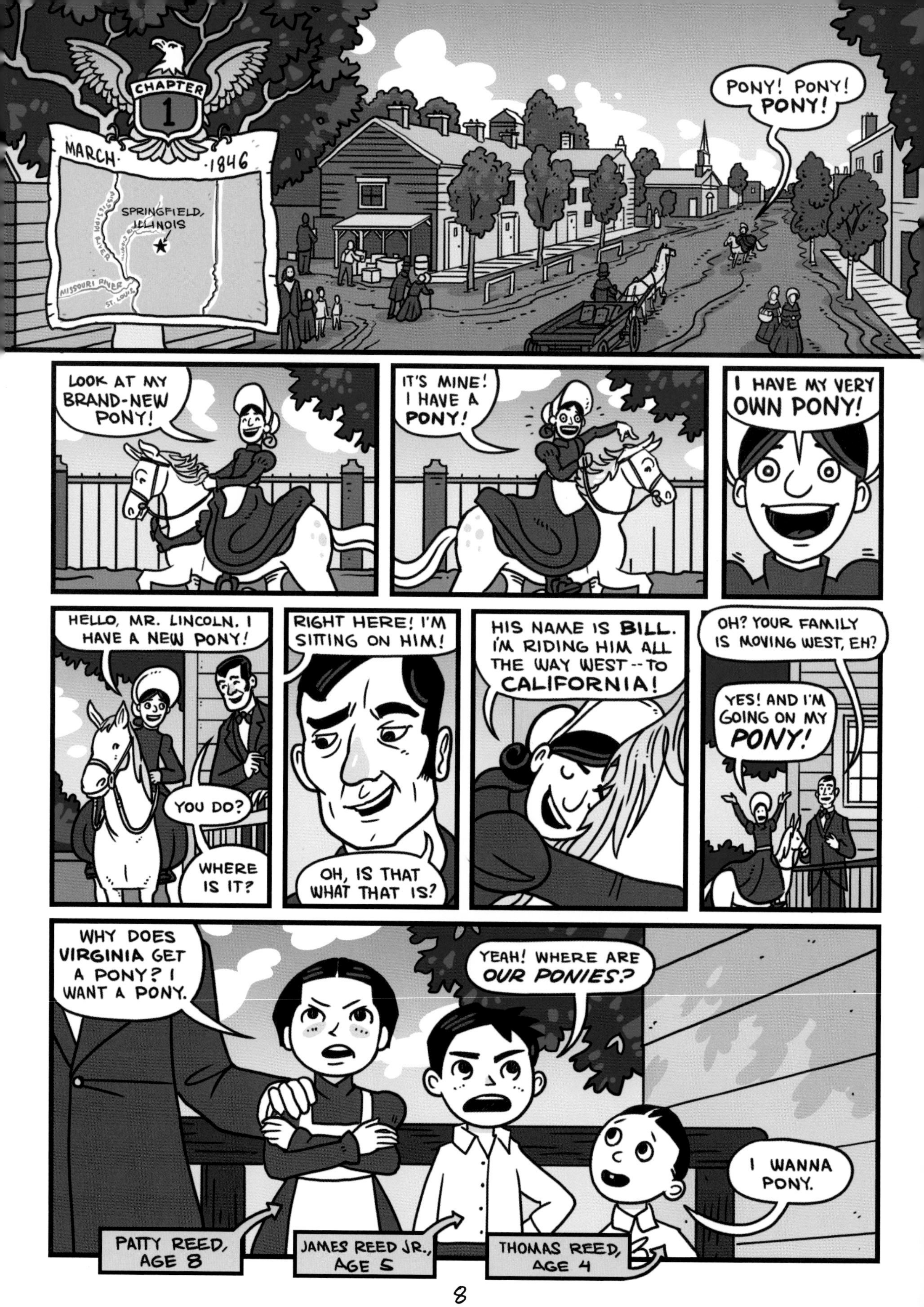
CHAPTER 1
MARCH 1846
MISSISSIPPI RIVER
SPRINGFIELD, ILLINOIS
ILLINOIS RIVER
MISSOURI RIVER
ST. LOUIS
PONY! PONY! PONY!
LOOK AT MY BRAND-NEW PONY!
IT'S MINE! I HAVE A PONY!
I HAVE MY VERY OWN PONY!
HELLO, MR. LINCOLN. I HAVE A NEW PONY!
YOU DO?
WHERE IS IT?
RIGHT HERE! I'M SITTING ON HIM!
OH, IS THAT WHAT THAT IS?
HIS NAME IS BILL. I'M RIDING HIM ALL THE WAY WEST--TO CALIFORNIA!
OH? YOUR FAMILY IS MOVING WEST, EH?
YES! AND I'M GOING ON MY PONY!
WHY DOES VIRGINIA GET A PONY? I WANT A PONY.
YEAH! WHERE ARE OUR PONIES?
I WANNA PONY.
PATTY REED, AGE 8
JAMES REED JR., AGE 5
THOMAS REED, AGE 4

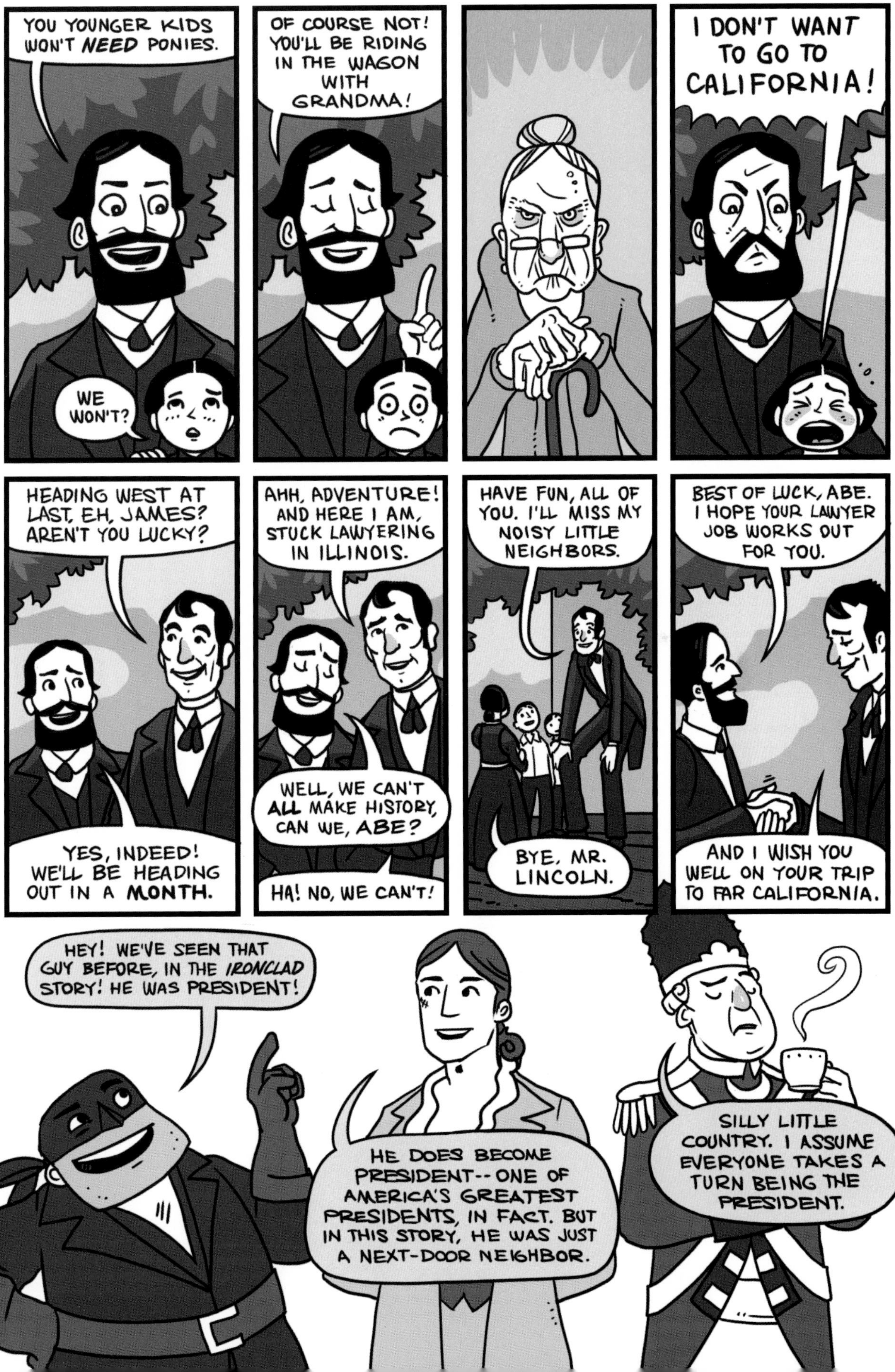
YOU YOUNGER KIDS WON'T NEED PONIES.
WE WON'T?
OF COURSE NOT! YOU'LL BE RIDING IN THE WAGON WITH GRANDMA!
I DON'T WANT TO GO TO CALIFORNIA!
HEADING WEST AT LAST, EH, JAMES? AREN'T YOU LUCKY?
YES, INDEED! WE'LL BE HEADING OUT IN A MONTH.
AHH, ADVENTURE! AND HERE I AM, STUCK LAWYERING IN ILLINOIS.
WELL, WE CAN'T ALL MAKE HISTORY, CAN WE, ABE?
HA! NO, WE CAN'T!
HAVE FUN, ALL OF YOU. I'LL MISS MY NOISY LITTLE NEIGHBORS.
BYE, MR. LINCOLN.
BEST OF LUCK, ABE. I HOPE YOUR LAWYER JOB WORKS OUT FOR YOU.
AND I WISH YOU WELL ON YOUR TRIP TO FAR CALIFORNIA.
HEY! WE'VE SEEN THAT GUY BEFORE, IN THE IRONCLAD STORY! HE WAS PRESIDENT!
HE DOES BECOME PRESIDENT--ONE OF AMERICA'S GREATEST PRESIDENTS, IN FACT. BUT IN THIS STORY, HE WAS JUST A NEXT-DOOR NEIGHBOR.
SILLY LITTLE COUNTRY. I ASSUME EVERYONE TAKES A TURN BEING THE PRESIDENT.

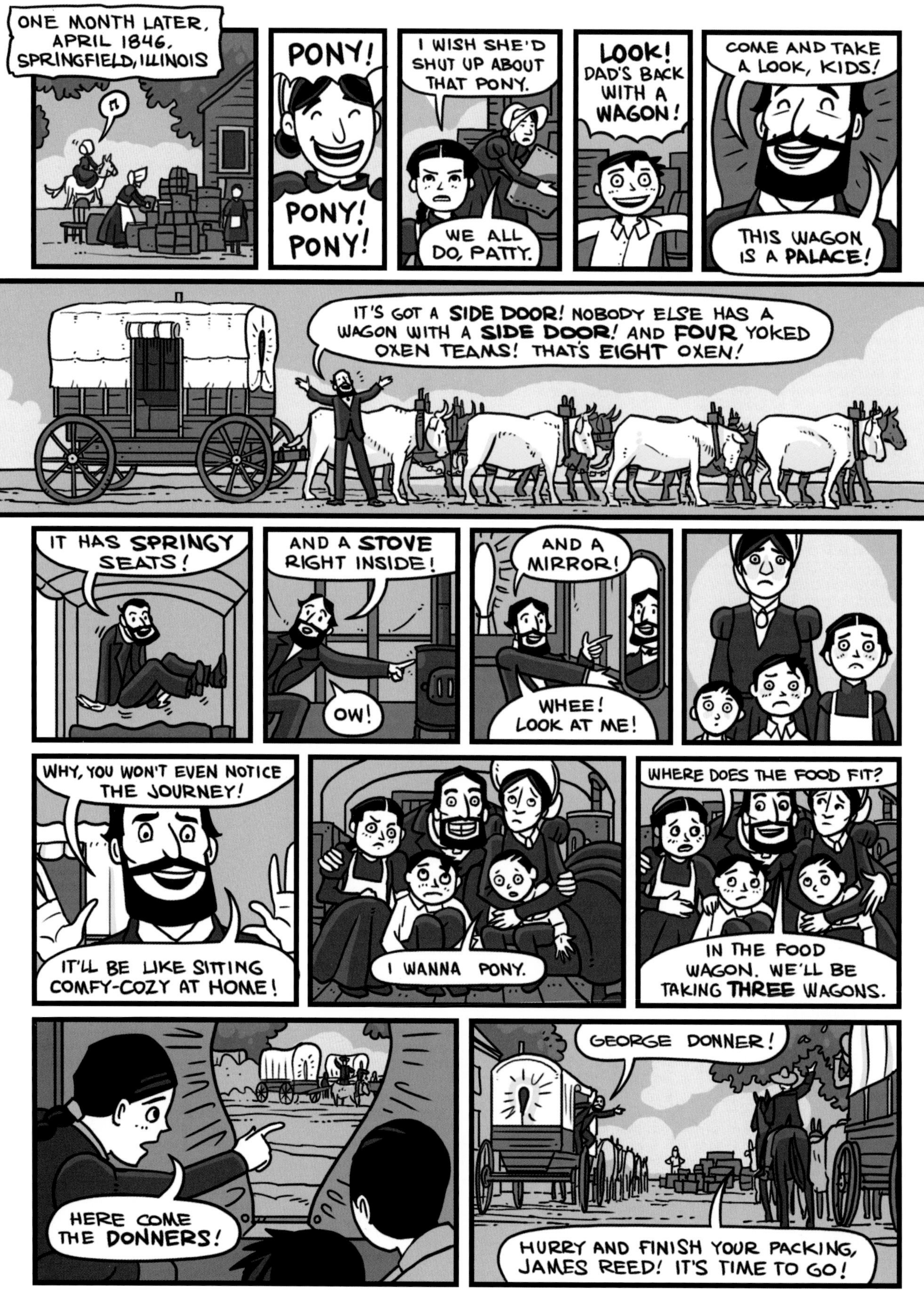
ONE MONTH LATER, APRIL 1846, SPRINGFIELD, ILLINOIS
PONY!
PONY! PONY!
I WISH SHE'D SHUT UP ABOUT THAT PONY.
WE ALL DO, PATTY.
LOOK! DAD'S BACK WITH A WAGON!
COME AND TAKE A LOOK, KIDS!
THIS WAGON IS A PALACE!
IT'S GOT A SIDE DOOR! NOBODY ELSE HAS A WAGON WITH A SIDE DOOR! AND FOUR YOKED OXEN TEAMS! THAT'S EIGHT OXEN!
IT HAS SPRINGY SEATS!
AND A STOVE RIGHT INSIDE!
OW!
AND A MIRROR!
WHEE! LOOK AT ME!
WHY, YOU WON'T EVEN NOTICE THE JOURNEY!
IT'LL BE LIKE SITTING COMFY-COZY AT HOME!
I WANNA PONY.
WHERE DOES THE FOOD FIT?
IN THE FOOD WAGON. WE'LL BE TAKING THREE WAGONS.
HERE COME THE DONNERS!
GEORGE DONNER!
HURRY AND FINISH YOUR PACKING, JAMES REED! IT'S TIME TO GO!

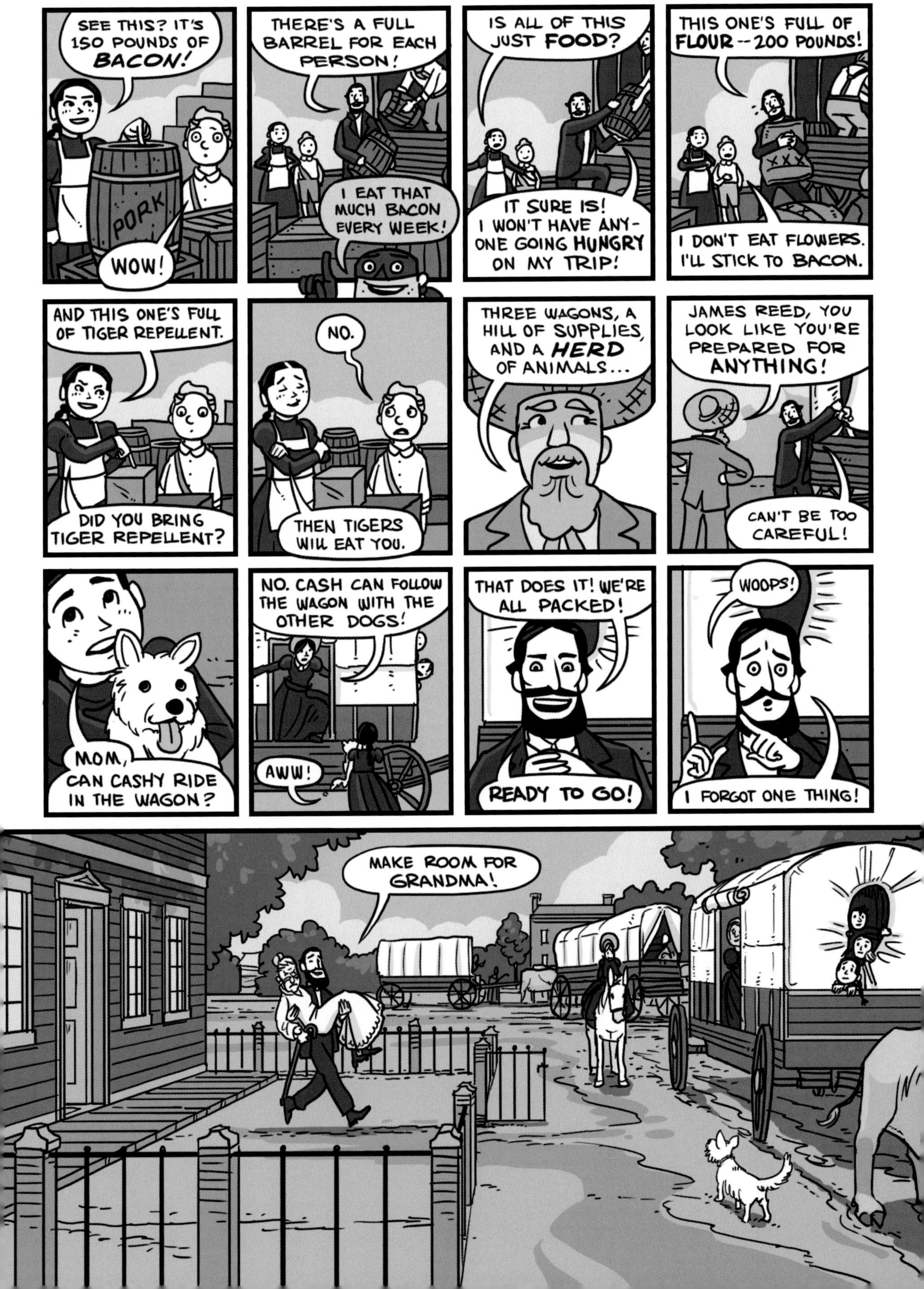
SEE THIS? IT'S 150 POUNDS OF BACON!
WOW!
THERE'S A FULL BARREL FOR EACH PERSON!
I EAT THAT MUCH BACON EVERY WEEK!
IS ALL OF THIS JUST FOOD?
IT SURE IS! I WON'T HAVE ANY-ONE GOING HUNGRY ON MY TRIP!
THIS ONE'S FULL OF FLOUR--200 POUNDS!
I DON'T EAT FLOWERS. I'LL STICK TO BACON.
AND THIS ONE'S FULL OF TIGER REPELLENT.
DID YOU BRING TIGER REPELLENT?
NO.
THEN TIGERS WILL EAT YOU.
THREE WAGONS, A HILL OF SUPPLIES, AND A HERD OF ANIMALS...
JAMES REED, YOU LOOK LIKE YOU'RE PREPARED FOR ANYTHING!
CAN'T BE TOO CAREFUL!
MOM, CAN CASHY RIDE IN THE WAGON?
NO. CASH CAN FOLLOW THE WAGON WITH THE OTHER DOGS!
AWW!
THAT DOES IT! WE'RE ALL PACKED!
READY TO GO!
WOOPS!
I FORGOT ONE THING!
MAKE ROOM FOR GRANDMA!
PORK

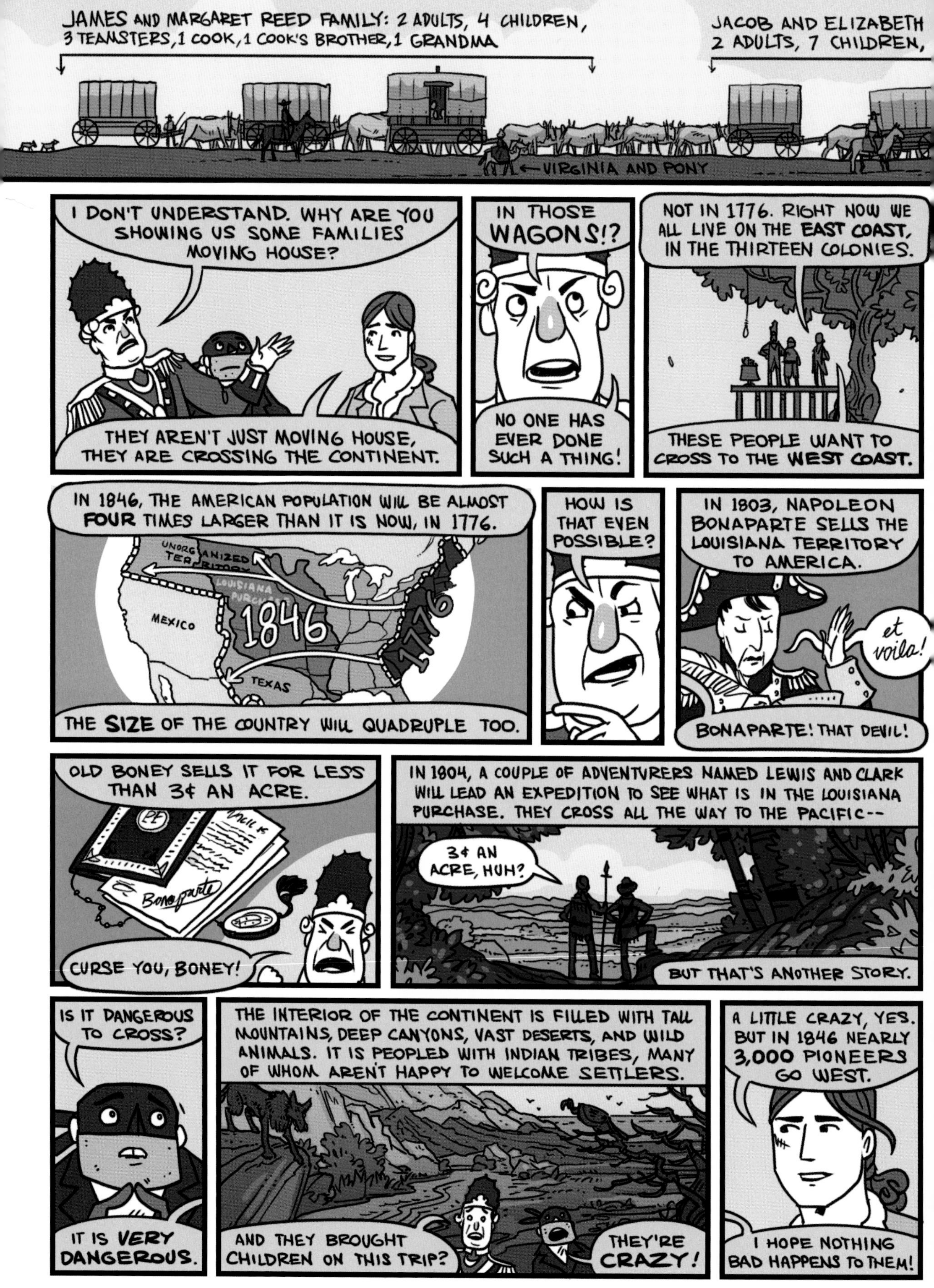
JAMES AND MARGARET REED FAMILY: 2 ADULTS, 4 CHILDREN, 3 TEAMSTERS, 1 COOK, 1 COOK'S BROTHER, 1 GRANDMA
JACOB AND ELIZABETH
2 ADULTS, 7 CHILDREN,
VIRGINIA AND PONY
I DON'T UNDERSTAND. WHY ARE YOU SHOWING US SOME FAMILIES MOVING HOUSE?
THEY AREN'T JUST MOVING HOUSE, THEY ARE CROSSING THE CONTINENT.
IN THOSE WAGONS!?
NO ONE HAS EVER DONE SUCH A THING!
NOT IN 1776. RIGHT NOW WE ALL LIVE ON THE EAST COAST, IN THE THIRTEEN COLONIES.
THESE PEOPLE WANT TO CROSS TO THE WEST COAST.
IN 1846, THE AMERICAN POPULATION WILL BE ALMOST FOUR TIMES LARGER THAN IT IS NOW, IN 1776.
UNORGANIZED TERRITORY
LOUISIANA PURCHASE
MEXICO
1846
1776
TEXAS
THE SIZE OF THE COUNTRY WILL QUADRUPLE TOO.
HOW IS THAT EVEN POSSIBLE?
IN 1803, NAPOLEON BONAPARTE SELLS THE LOUISIANA TERRITORY TO AMERICA.
et voila!
BONAPARTE! THAT DEVIL!
OLD BONEY SELLS IT FOR LESS THAN 3¢ AN ACRE.
Bonaparte
CURSE YOU, BONEY!
IN 1804, A COUPLE OF ADVENTURERS NAMED LEWIS AND CLARK WILL LEAD AN EXPEDITION TO SEE WHAT IS IN THE LOUISIANA PURCHASE. THEY CROSS ALL THE WAY TO THE PACIFIC--
3¢ AN ACRE, HUH?
BUT THAT'S ANOTHER STORY.
IS IT DANGEROUS TO CROSS?
IT IS VERY DANGEROUS.
THE INTERIOR OF THE CONTINENT IS FILLED WITH TALL MOUNTAINS, DEEP CANYONS, VAST DESERTS, AND WILD ANIMALS. IT IS PEOPLED WITH INDIAN TRIBES, MANY OF WHOM AREN'T HAPPY TO WELCOME SETTLERS.
AND THEY BROUGHT CHILDREN ON THIS TRIP?
THEY'RE CRAZY!
A LITTLE CRAZY, YES. BUT IN 1846 NEARLY 3,000 PIONEERS GO WEST.
I HOPE NOTHING BAD HAPPENS TO THEM!

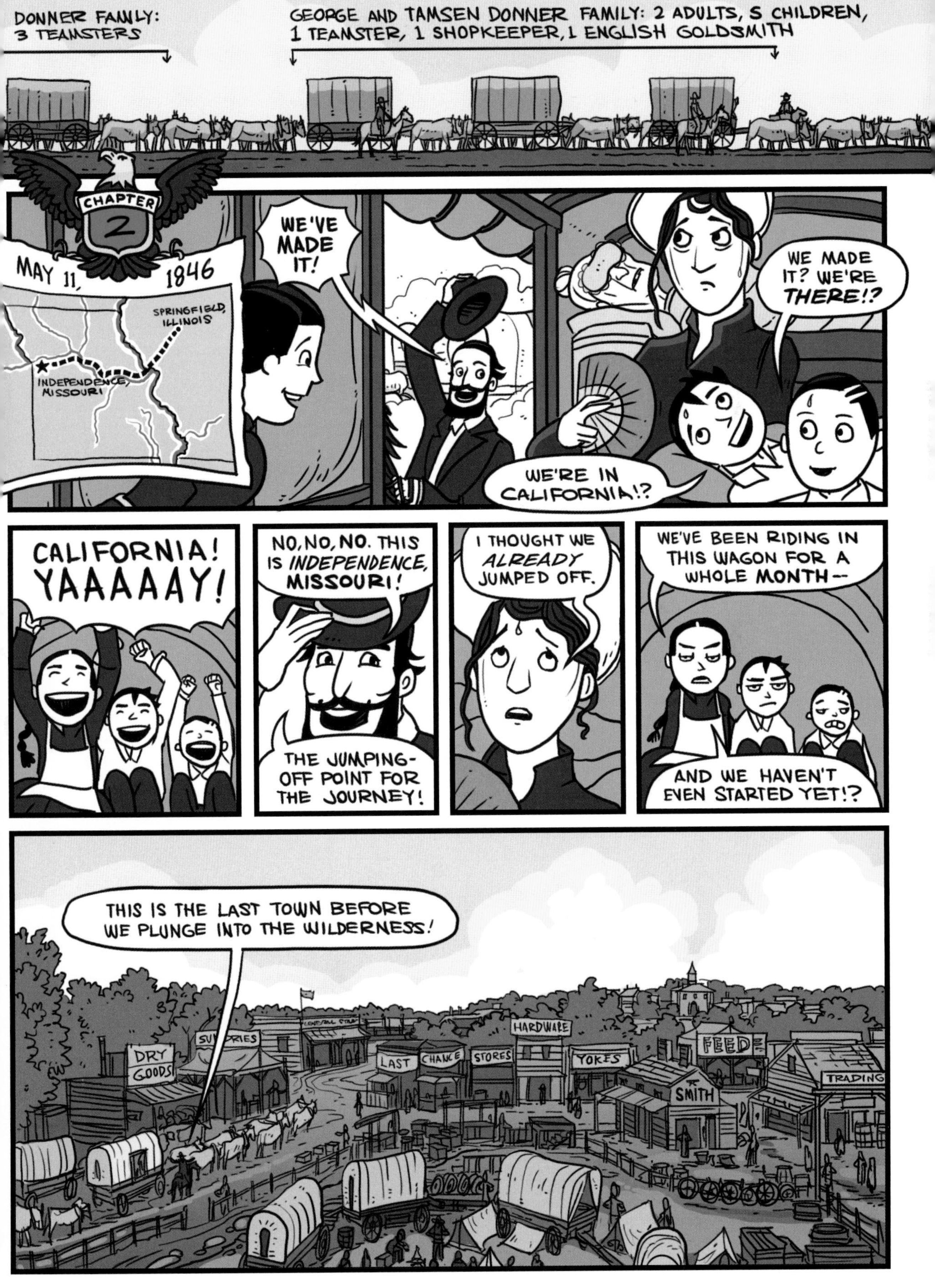
DONNER FAMILY: 3 TEAMSTERS
GEORGE AND TAMSEN DONNER FAMILY: 2 ADULTS, 5 CHILDREN, 1 TEAMSTER, 1 SHOPKEEPER, 1 ENGLISH GOLDSMITH
CHAPTER 2
MAY 11, 1846
SPRINGFIELD, ILLINOIS
INDEPENDENCE, MISSOURI
WE'VE MADE IT!
WE MADE IT? WE'RE THERE!?
WE'RE IN CALIFORNIA!?
CALIFORNIA! YAAAAAY!
NO, NO, NO. THIS IS INDEPENDENCE, MISSOURI!
THE JUMPING-OFF POINT FOR THE JOURNEY!
I THOUGHT WE ALREADY JUMPED OFF.
WE'VE BEEN RIDING IN THIS WAGON FOR A WHOLE MONTH--
AND WE HAVEN'T EVEN STARTED YET!?
THIS IS THE LAST TOWN BEFORE WE PLUNGE INTO THE WILDERNESS!
DRY GOODS
SUPPLIES
HARDWARE
LAST CHANCE STORES
YOKES
FEED
SMITH
TRADING

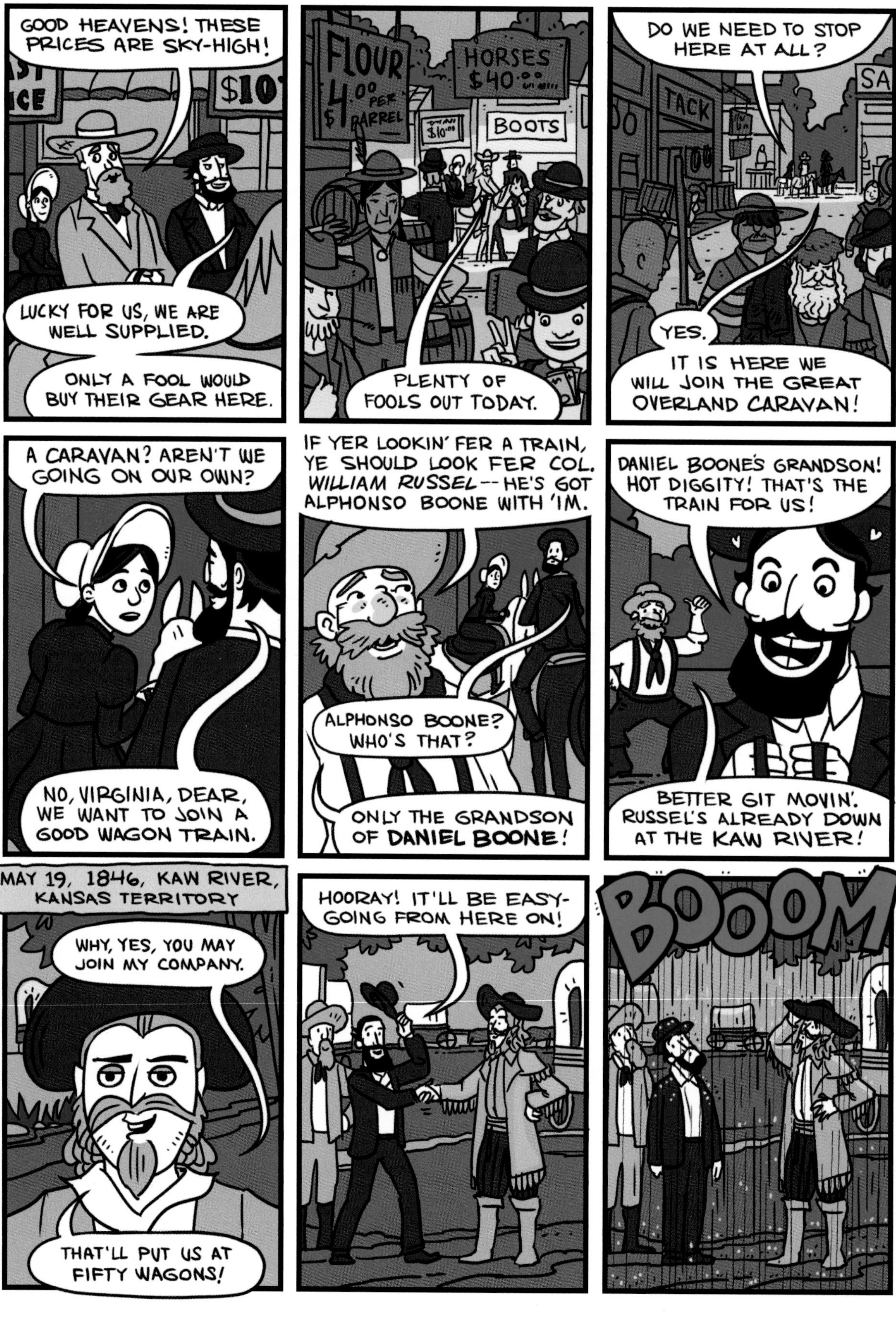
GOOD HEAVENS! THESE PRICES ARE SKY-HIGH!
$10
LUCKY FOR US, WE ARE WELL SUPPLIED.
ONLY A FOOL WOULD BUY THEIR GEAR HERE.
FLOUR $4.00 PER BARREL
HORSES $40.00
BOOTS
PLENTY OF FOOLS OUT TODAY.
DO WE NEED TO STOP HERE AT ALL?
TACK
YES.
IT IS HERE WE WILL JOIN THE GREAT OVERLAND CARAVAN!
A CARAVAN? AREN'T WE GOING ON OUR OWN?
NO, VIRGINIA, DEAR, WE WANT TO JOIN A GOOD WAGON TRAIN.
IF YER LOOKIN' FER A TRAIN, YE SHOULD LOOK FER COL. *WILLIAM RUSSEL*--HE'S GOT ALPHONSO BOONE WITH 'IM.
ALPHONSO BOONE? WHO'S THAT?
ONLY THE GRANDSON OF **DANIEL BOONE**!
DANIEL BOONE'S GRANDSON! HOT DIGGITY! THAT'S THE TRAIN FOR US!
BETTER GIT MOVIN'. RUSSEL'S ALREADY DOWN AT THE KAW RIVER!
MAY 19, 1846, KAW RIVER, KANSAS TERRITORY
WHY, YES, YOU MAY JOIN MY COMPANY.
THAT'LL PUT US AT FIFTY WAGONS!
HOORAY! IT'LL BE EASY-GOING FROM HERE ON!
BOOOM

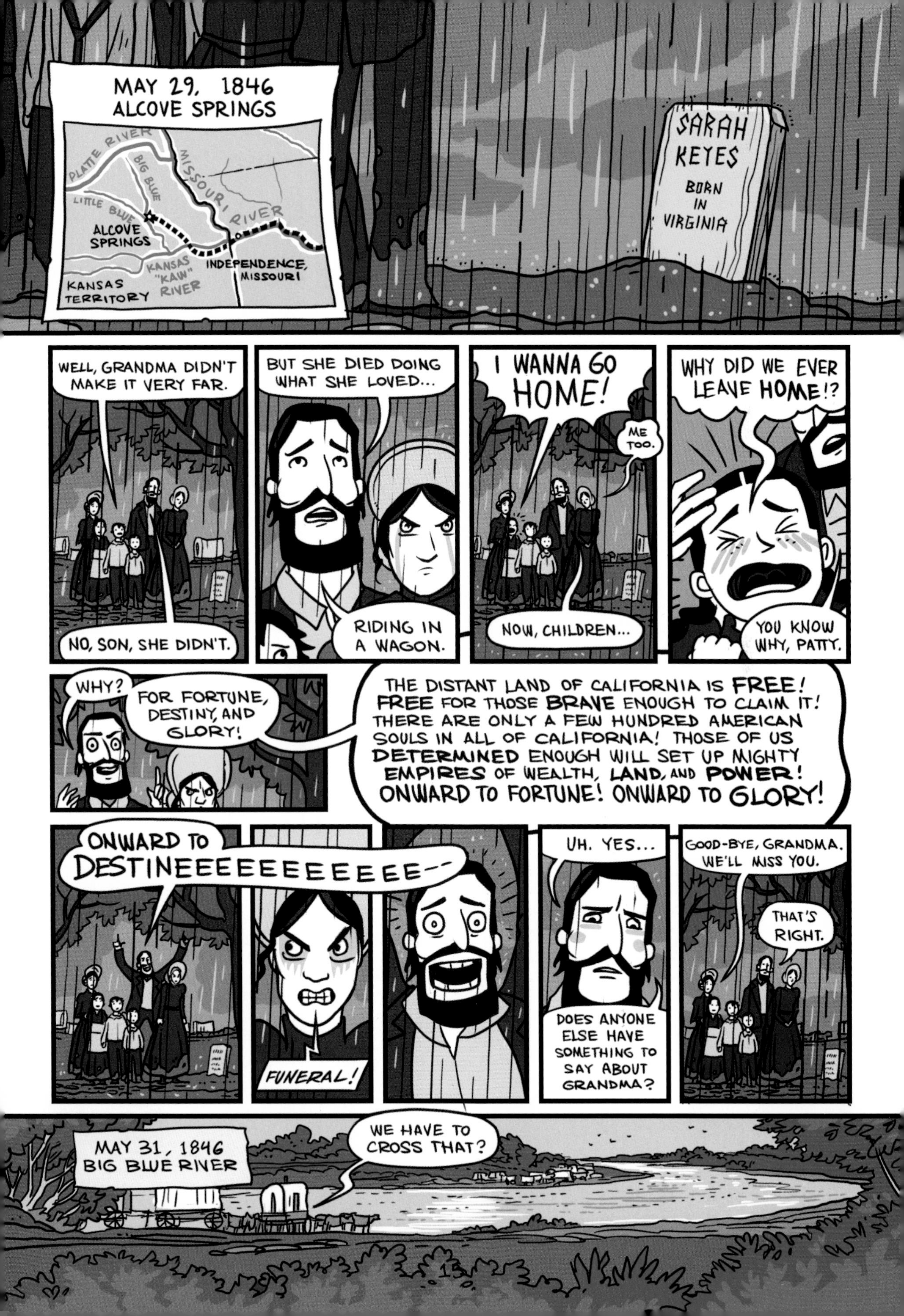

MAY 29, 1846
ALCOVE SPRINGS
PLATTE RIVER
BIG BLUE
MISSOURI RIVER
LITTLE BLUE
ALCOVE SPRINGS
KANSAS "KAW" RIVER
INDEPENDENCE, MISSOURI
KANSAS TERRITORY
SARAH KEYES
BORN IN VIRGINIA
WELL, GRANDMA DIDN'T MAKE IT VERY FAR.
NO, SON, SHE DIDN'T.
BUT SHE DIED DOING WHAT SHE LOVED...
RIDING IN A WAGON.
I WANNA GO HOME!
ME TOO.
NOW, CHILDREN...
WHY DID WE EVER LEAVE HOME!?
YOU KNOW WHY, PATTY.
WHY?
FOR FORTUNE, DESTINY, AND GLORY!
THE DISTANT LAND OF CALIFORNIA IS FREE! FREE FOR THOSE BRAVE ENOUGH TO CLAIM IT! THERE ARE ONLY A FEW HUNDRED AMERICAN SOULS IN ALL OF CALIFORNIA! THOSE OF US DETERMINED ENOUGH WILL SET UP MIGHTY EMPIRES OF WEALTH, LAND, AND POWER! ONWARD TO FORTUNE! ONWARD TO GLORY!
ONWARD TO DESTINEEEEEEEEEEEE--
FUNERAL!
UH. YES...
DOES ANYONE ELSE HAVE SOMETHING TO SAY ABOUT GRANDMA?
GOOD-BYE, GRANDMA. WE'LL MISS YOU.
THAT'S RIGHT.
MAY 31, 1846
BIG BLUE RIVER
WE HAVE TO CROSS THAT?

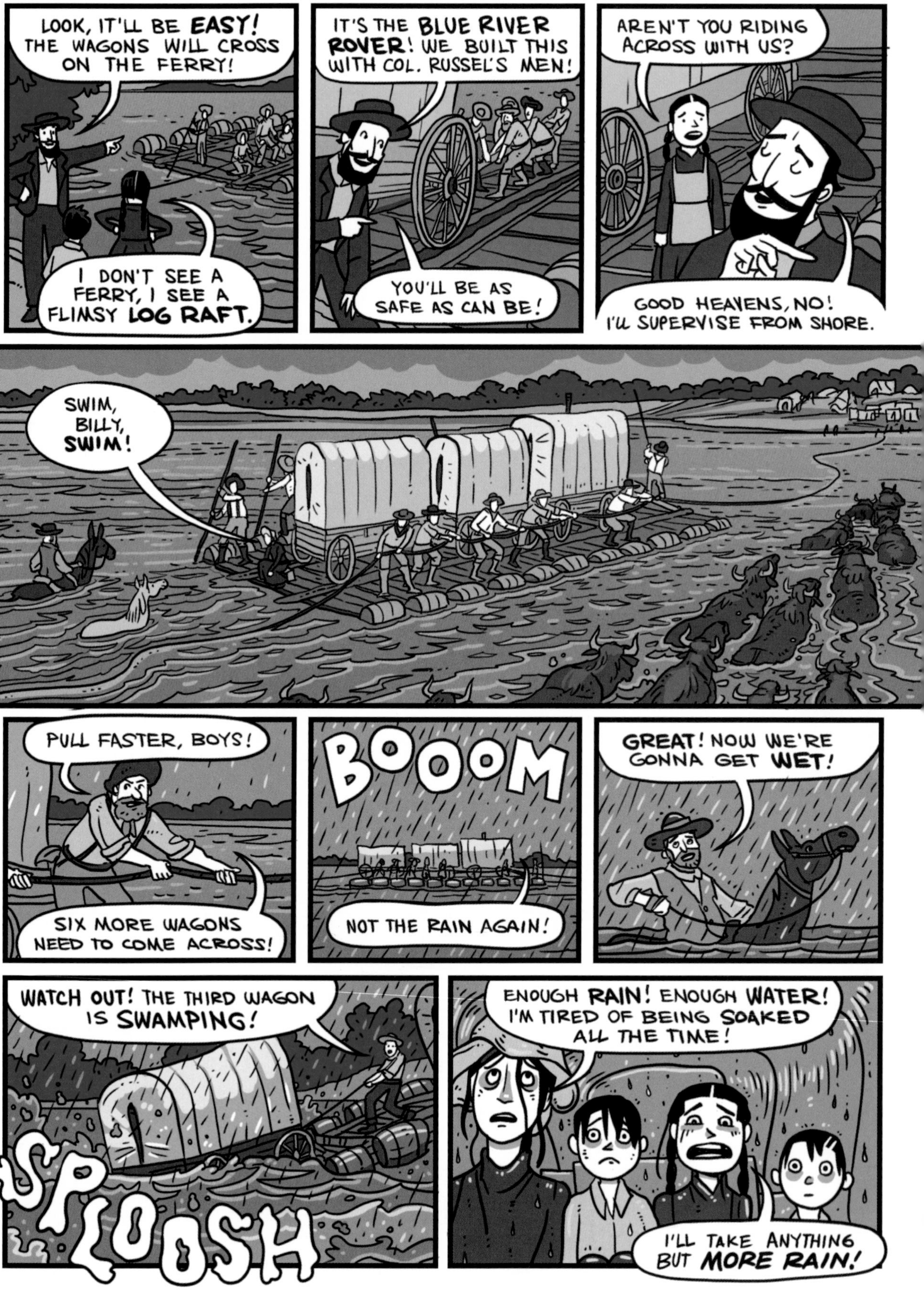
LOOK, IT'LL BE EASY! THE WAGONS WILL CROSS ON THE FERRY!
I DON'T SEE A FERRY, I SEE A FLIMSY LOG RAFT.
IT'S THE BLUE RIVER ROVER! WE BUILT THIS WITH COL. RUSSEL'S MEN!
YOU'LL BE AS SAFE AS CAN BE!
AREN'T YOU RIDING ACROSS WITH US?
GOOD HEAVENS, NO! I'LL SUPERVISE FROM SHORE.
SWIM, BILLY, SWIM!
PULL FASTER, BOYS!
SIX MORE WAGONS NEED TO COME ACROSS!
BOOOM
NOT THE RAIN AGAIN!
GREAT! NOW WE'RE GONNA GET WET!
WATCH OUT! THE THIRD WAGON IS SWAMPING!
SPLOOSH
ENOUGH RAIN! ENOUGH WATER! I'M TIRED OF BEING SOAKED ALL THE TIME!
I'LL TAKE ANYTHING BUT MORE RAIN!

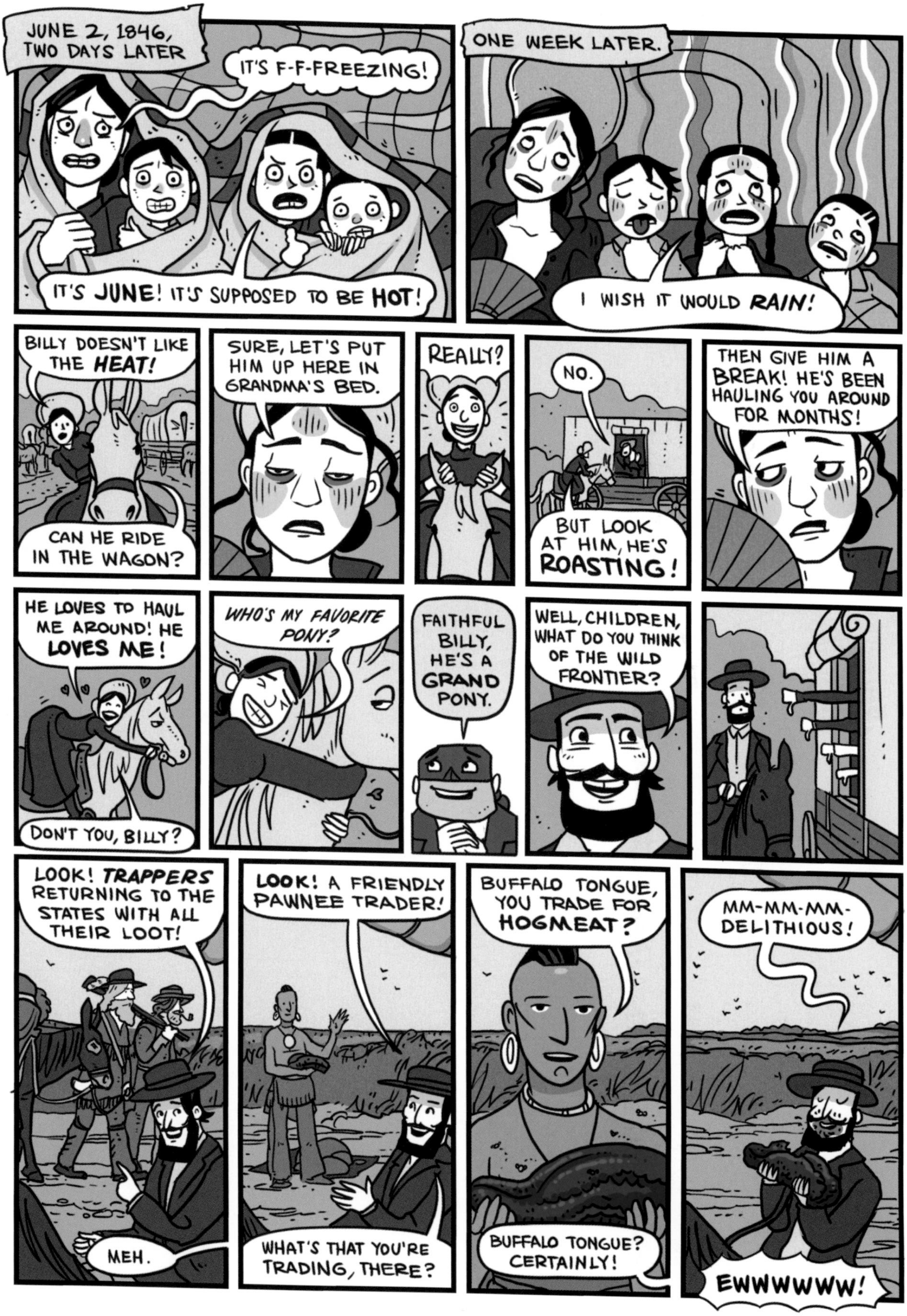
JUNE 2, 1846, TWO DAYS LATER
IT'S F-F-FREEZING!
IT'S JUNE! IT'S SUPPOSED TO BE HOT!
ONE WEEK LATER.
I WISH IT WOULD RAIN!
BILLY DOESN'T LIKE THE HEAT!
CAN HE RIDE IN THE WAGON?
SURE, LET'S PUT HIM UP HERE IN GRANDMA'S BED.
REALLY?
NO.
BUT LOOK AT HIM, HE'S ROASTING!
THEN GIVE HIM A BREAK! HE'S BEEN HAULING YOU AROUND FOR MONTHS!
HE LOVES TO HAUL ME AROUND! HE LOVES ME!
DON'T YOU, BILLY?
WHO'S MY FAVORITE PONY?
FAITHFUL BILLY, HE'S A GRAND PONY.
WELL, CHILDREN, WHAT DO YOU THINK OF THE WILD FRONTIER?
LOOK! TRAPPERS RETURNING TO THE STATES WITH ALL THEIR LOOT!
MEH.
LOOK! A FRIENDLY PAWNEE TRADER!
WHAT'S THAT YOU'RE TRADING, THERE?
BUFFALO TONGUE, YOU TRADE FOR HOGMEAT?
BUFFALO TONGUE? CERTAINLY!
MM-MM-MM-DELITHIOUS!
EWWWWWW!

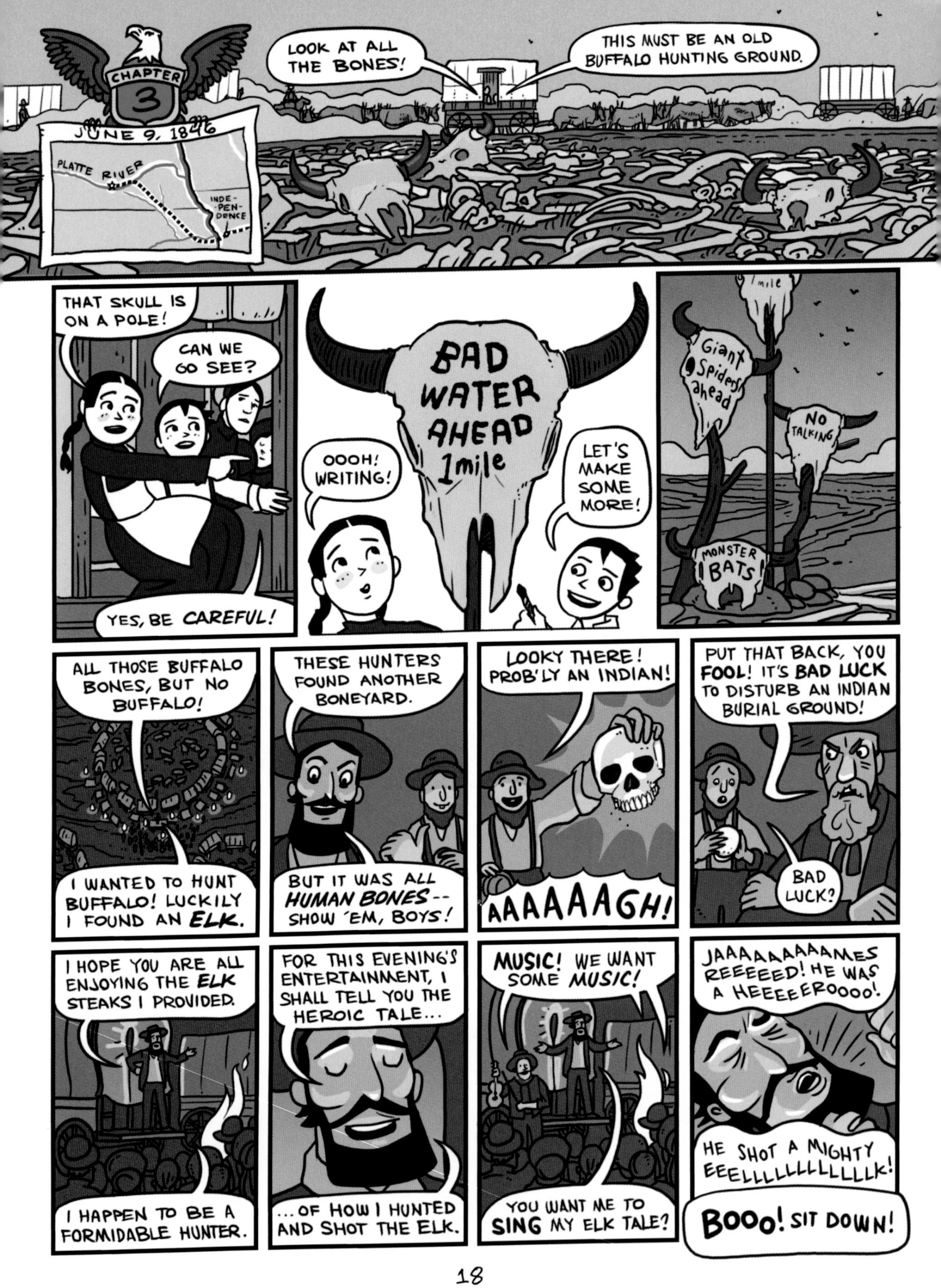
CHAPTER 3
JUNE 9, 1846
PLATTE RIVER
INDE-PEN-DENCE
LOOK AT ALL THE BONES!
THIS MUST BE AN OLD BUFFALO HUNTING GROUND.
THAT SKULL IS ON A POLE!
CAN WE GO SEE?
YES, BE CAREFUL!
BAD WATER AHEAD 1mile
OOOH! WRITING!
LET'S MAKE SOME MORE!
1mile
Giant Spiders ahead
NO TALKING
MONSTER BATS!
ALL THOSE BUFFALO BONES, BUT NO BUFFALO!
I WANTED TO HUNT BUFFALO! LUCKILY I FOUND AN ELK.
THESE HUNTERS FOUND ANOTHER BONEYARD.
BUT IT WAS ALL HUMAN BONES-- SHOW 'EM, BOYS!
LOOKY THERE! PROB'LY AN INDIAN!
AAAAAAGH!
PUT THAT BACK, YOU FOOL! IT'S BAD LUCK TO DISTURB AN INDIAN BURIAL GROUND!
BAD LUCK?
I HOPE YOU ARE ALL ENJOYING THE ELK STEAKS I PROVIDED.
I HAPPEN TO BE A FORMIDABLE HUNTER.
FOR THIS EVENING'S ENTERTAINMENT, I SHALL TELL YOU THE HEROIC TALE...
...OF HOW I HUNTED AND SHOT THE ELK.
MUSIC! WE WANT SOME MUSIC!
YOU WANT ME TO SING MY ELK TALE?
JAAAAAAAAAMES REEEEED! HE WAS A HEEEEEROOOO!
HE SHOT A MIGHTY EEELLLLLLLLLLLLK!
BOOO! SIT DOWN!

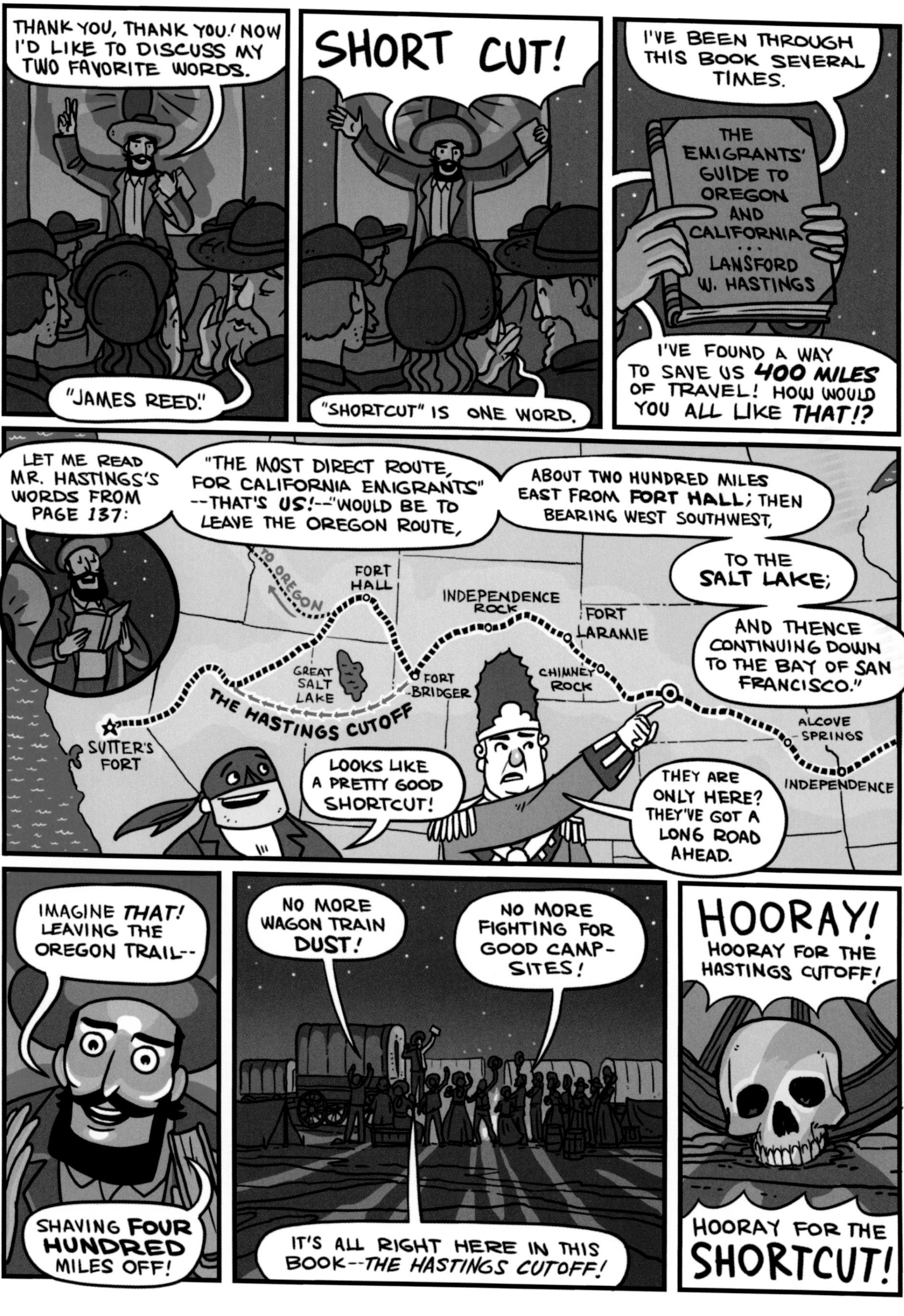
THANK YOU, THANK YOU! NOW I'D LIKE TO DISCUSS MY TWO FAVORITE WORDS.
"JAMES REED."
SHORT CUT!
"SHORTCUT" IS ONE WORD.
I'VE BEEN THROUGH THIS BOOK SEVERAL TIMES.
THE EMIGRANTS' GUIDE TO OREGON AND CALIFORNIA ... LANSFORD W. HASTINGS
I'VE FOUND A WAY TO SAVE US 400 MILES OF TRAVEL! HOW WOULD YOU ALL LIKE THAT!?
LET ME READ MR. HASTINGS'S WORDS FROM PAGE 137:
"THE MOST DIRECT ROUTE, FOR CALIFORNIA EMIGRANTS" --THAT'S US!--"WOULD BE TO LEAVE THE OREGON ROUTE,
ABOUT TWO HUNDRED MILES EAST FROM FORT HALL; THEN BEARING WEST SOUTHWEST,
TO THE SALT LAKE;
AND THENCE CONTINUING DOWN TO THE BAY OF SAN FRANCISCO."
TO OREGON
FORT HALL
INDEPENDENCE ROCK
FORT LARAMIE
GREAT SALT LAKE
FORT BRIDGER
CHIMNEY ROCK
THE HASTINGS CUTOFF
SUTTER'S FORT
ALCOVE SPRINGS
INDEPENDENCE
LOOKS LIKE A PRETTY GOOD SHORTCUT!
THEY ARE ONLY HERE? THEY'VE GOT A LONG ROAD AHEAD.
IMAGINE THAT! LEAVING THE OREGON TRAIL--
SHAVING FOUR HUNDRED MILES OFF!
NO MORE WAGON TRAIN DUST!
NO MORE FIGHTING FOR GOOD CAMP-SITES!
IT'S ALL RIGHT HERE IN THIS BOOK--THE HASTINGS CUTOFF!
HOORAY!
HOORAY FOR THE HASTINGS CUTOFF!
HOORAY FOR THE SHORTCUT!

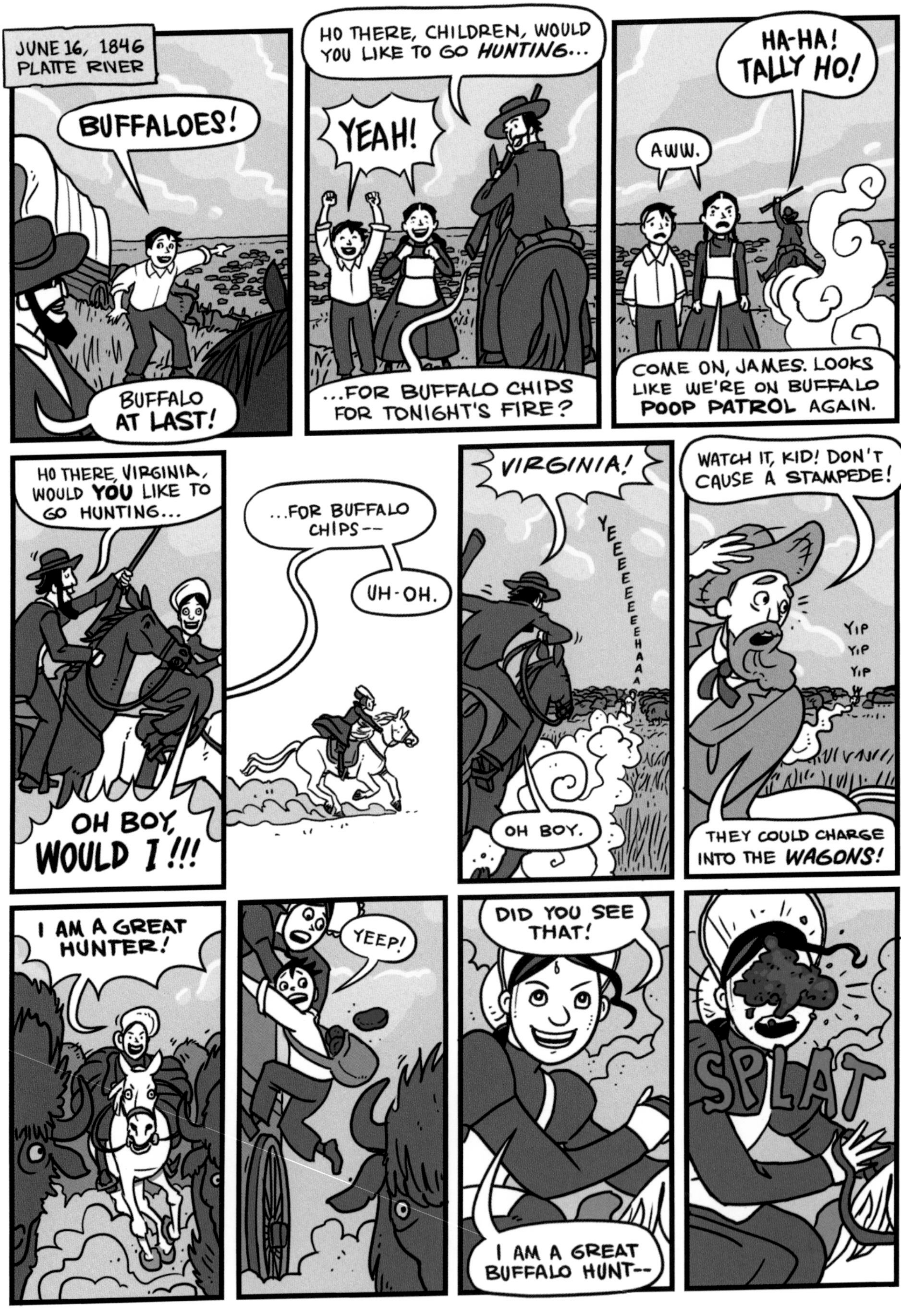
JUNE 16, 1846
PLATTE RIVER
BUFFALOES!
BUFFALO AT LAST!
HO THERE, CHILDREN, WOULD YOU LIKE TO GO HUNTING...
YEAH!
...FOR BUFFALO CHIPS FOR TONIGHT'S FIRE?
HA-HA! TALLY HO!
AWW.
COME ON, JAMES. LOOKS LIKE WE'RE ON BUFFALO POOP PATROL AGAIN.
HO THERE, VIRGINIA, WOULD YOU LIKE TO GO HUNTING...
OH BOY, WOULD I!!!
...FOR BUFFALO CHIPS--
UH-OH.
VIRGINIA!
YEEEEEEEEEHAAA
OH BOY.
WATCH IT, KID! DON'T CAUSE A STAMPEDE!
YIP YIP YIP
THEY COULD CHARGE INTO THE WAGONS!
I AM A GREAT HUNTER!
YEEP!
DID YOU SEE THAT!
I AM A GREAT BUFFALO HUNT--
SPLAT

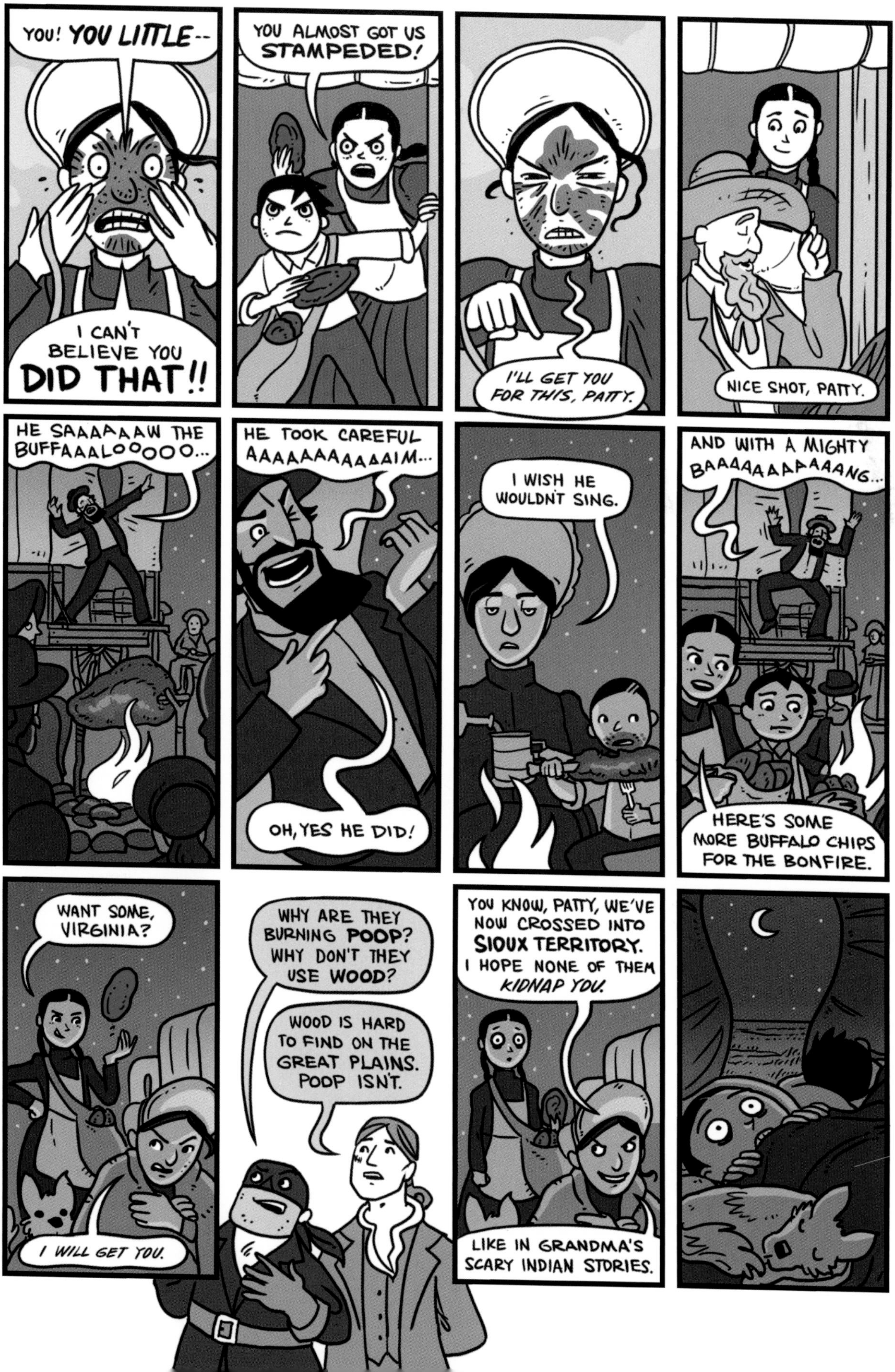
YOU! YOU LITTLE--
I CAN'T BELIEVE YOU DID THAT!!
YOU ALMOST GOT US STAMPEDED!
I'LL GET YOU FOR THIS, PATTY.
NICE SHOT, PATTY.
HE SAAAAAAW THE BUFFAAALOOOOO...
HE TOOK CAREFUL AAAAAAAAAAAIM...
OH, YES HE DID!
I WISH HE WOULDN'T SING.
AND WITH A MIGHTY BAAAAAAAAAAANG...
HERE'S SOME MORE BUFFALO CHIPS FOR THE BONFIRE.
WANT SOME, VIRGINIA?
I WILL GET YOU.
WHY ARE THEY BURNING POOP? WHY DON'T THEY USE WOOD?
WOOD IS HARD TO FIND ON THE GREAT PLAINS. POOP ISN'T.
YOU KNOW, PATTY, WE'VE NOW CROSSED INTO SIOUX TERRITORY. I HOPE NONE OF THEM KIDNAP YOU.
LIKE IN GRANDMA'S SCARY INDIAN STORIES.

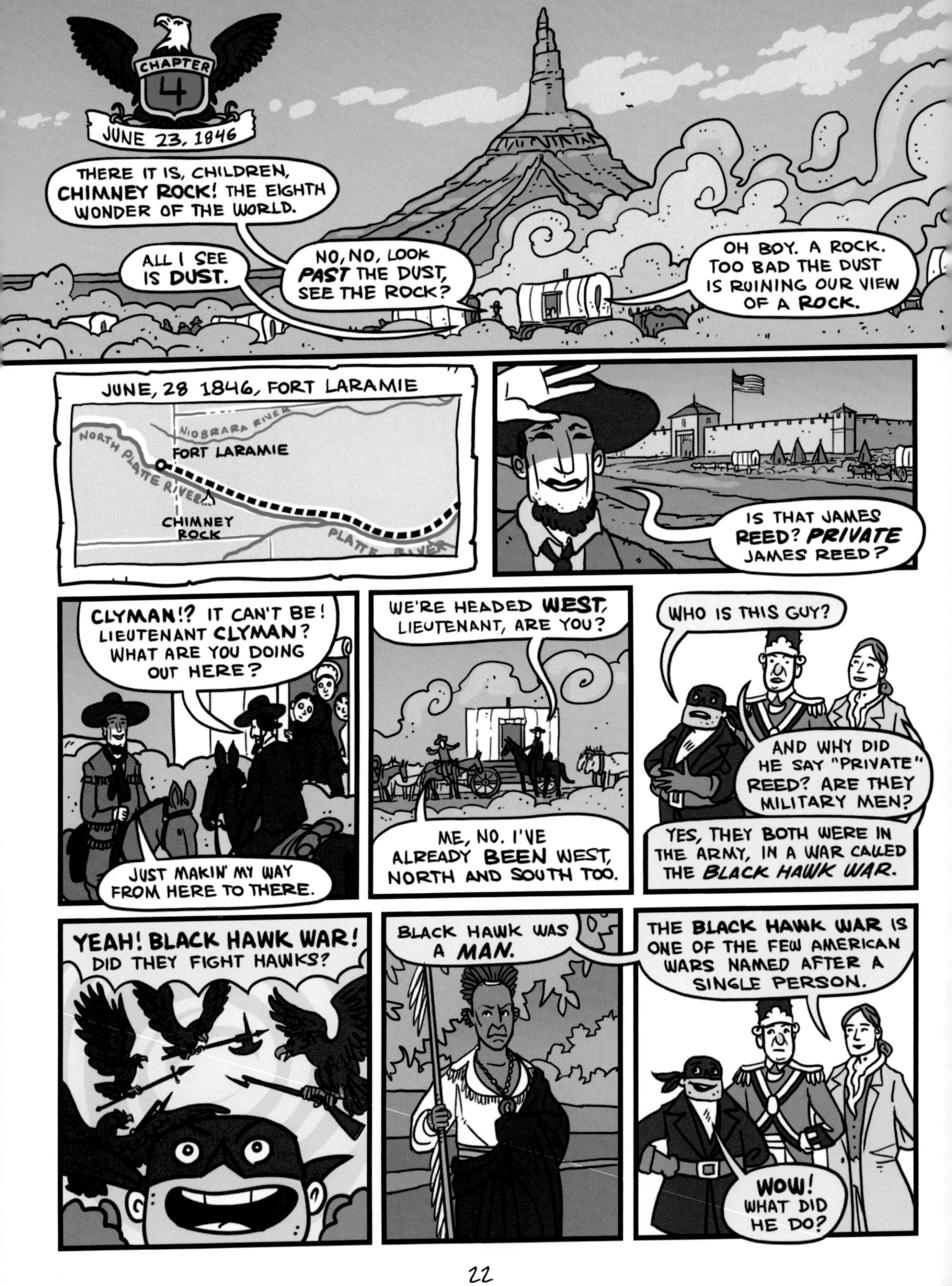
CHAPTER 4
JUNE 23, 1846
THERE IT IS, CHILDREN, CHIMNEY ROCK! THE EIGHTH WONDER OF THE WORLD.
ALL I SEE IS DUST.
NO, NO, LOOK PAST THE DUST, SEE THE ROCK?
OH BOY. A ROCK. TOO BAD THE DUST IS RUINING OUR VIEW OF A ROCK.
JUNE, 28 1846, FORT LARAMIE
NIOBRARA RIVER
NORTH PLATTE RIVER
FORT LARAMIE
CHIMNEY ROCK
PLATTE RIVER
IS THAT JAMES REED? PRIVATE JAMES REED?
CLYMAN!? IT CAN'T BE! LIEUTENANT CLYMAN? WHAT ARE YOU DOING OUT HERE?
JUST MAKIN' MY WAY FROM HERE TO THERE.
WE'RE HEADED WEST, LIEUTENANT, ARE YOU?
ME, NO. I'VE ALREADY BEEN WEST, NORTH AND SOUTH TOO.
WHO IS THIS GUY?
AND WHY DID HE SAY "PRIVATE" REED? ARE THEY MILITARY MEN?
YES, THEY BOTH WERE IN THE ARMY, IN A WAR CALLED THE BLACK HAWK WAR.
YEAH! BLACK HAWK WAR! DID THEY FIGHT HAWKS?
BLACK HAWK WAS A MAN.
THE BLACK HAWK WAR IS ONE OF THE FEW AMERICAN WARS NAMED AFTER A SINGLE PERSON.
WOW! WHAT DID HE DO?

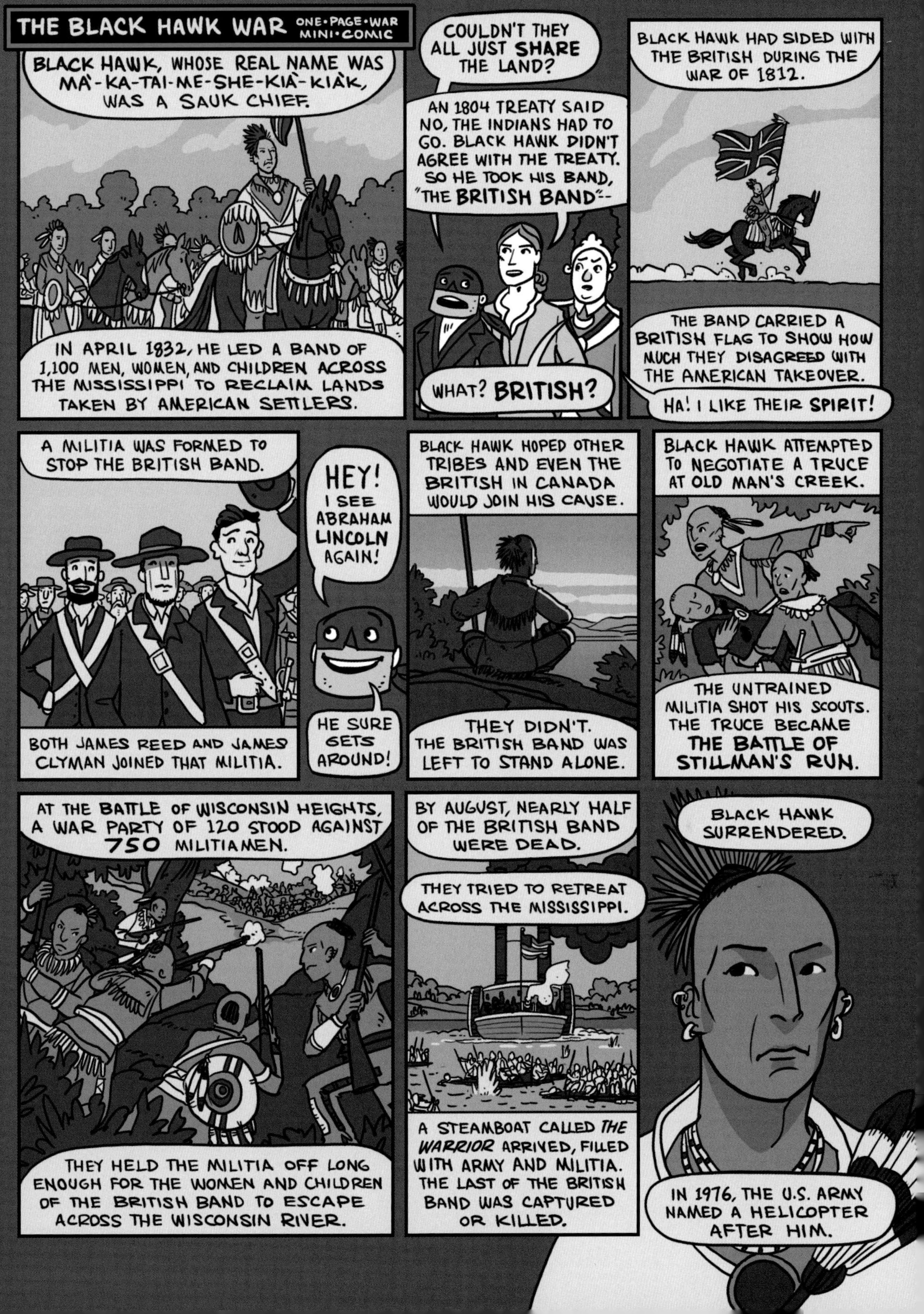
THE BLACK HAWK WAR
ONE•PAGE•WAR MINI•COMIC
BLACK HAWK, WHOSE REAL NAME WAS MÀ-KA-TAI-ME-SHE-KIÀ-KIÀK, WAS A SAUK CHIEF.
IN APRIL 1832, HE LED A BAND OF 1,100 MEN, WOMEN, AND CHILDREN ACROSS THE MISSISSIPPI TO RECLAIM LANDS TAKEN BY AMERICAN SETTLERS.
COULDN'T THEY ALL JUST SHARE THE LAND?
AN 1804 TREATY SAID NO, THE INDIANS HAD TO GO. BLACK HAWK DIDN'T AGREE WITH THE TREATY. SO HE TOOK HIS BAND, "THE BRITISH BAND"--
WHAT? BRITISH?
BLACK HAWK HAD SIDED WITH THE BRITISH DURING THE WAR OF 1812.
THE BAND CARRIED A BRITISH FLAG TO SHOW HOW MUCH THEY DISAGREED WITH THE AMERICAN TAKEOVER.
HA! I LIKE THEIR SPIRIT!
A MILITIA WAS FORMED TO STOP THE BRITISH BAND.
BOTH JAMES REED AND JAMES CLYMAN JOINED THAT MILITIA.
HEY! I SEE ABRAHAM LINCOLN AGAIN!
HE SURE GETS AROUND!
BLACK HAWK HOPED OTHER TRIBES AND EVEN THE BRITISH IN CANADA WOULD JOIN HIS CAUSE.
THEY DIDN'T. THE BRITISH BAND WAS LEFT TO STAND ALONE.
BLACK HAWK ATTEMPTED TO NEGOTIATE A TRUCE AT OLD MAN'S CREEK.
THE UNTRAINED MILITIA SHOT HIS SCOUTS. THE TRUCE BECAME THE BATTLE OF STILLMAN'S RUN.
AT THE BATTLE OF WISCONSIN HEIGHTS, A WAR PARTY OF 120 STOOD AGAINST 750 MILITIAMEN.
THEY HELD THE MILITIA OFF LONG ENOUGH FOR THE WOMEN AND CHILDREN OF THE BRITISH BAND TO ESCAPE ACROSS THE WISCONSIN RIVER.
BY AUGUST, NEARLY HALF OF THE BRITISH BAND WERE DEAD.
THEY TRIED TO RETREAT ACROSS THE MISSISSIPPI.
A STEAMBOAT CALLED THE WARRIOR ARRIVED, FILLED WITH ARMY AND MILITIA. THE LAST OF THE BRITISH BAND WAS CAPTURED OR KILLED.
BLACK HAWK SURRENDERED.
IN 1976, THE U.S. ARMY NAMED A HELICOPTER AFTER HIM.

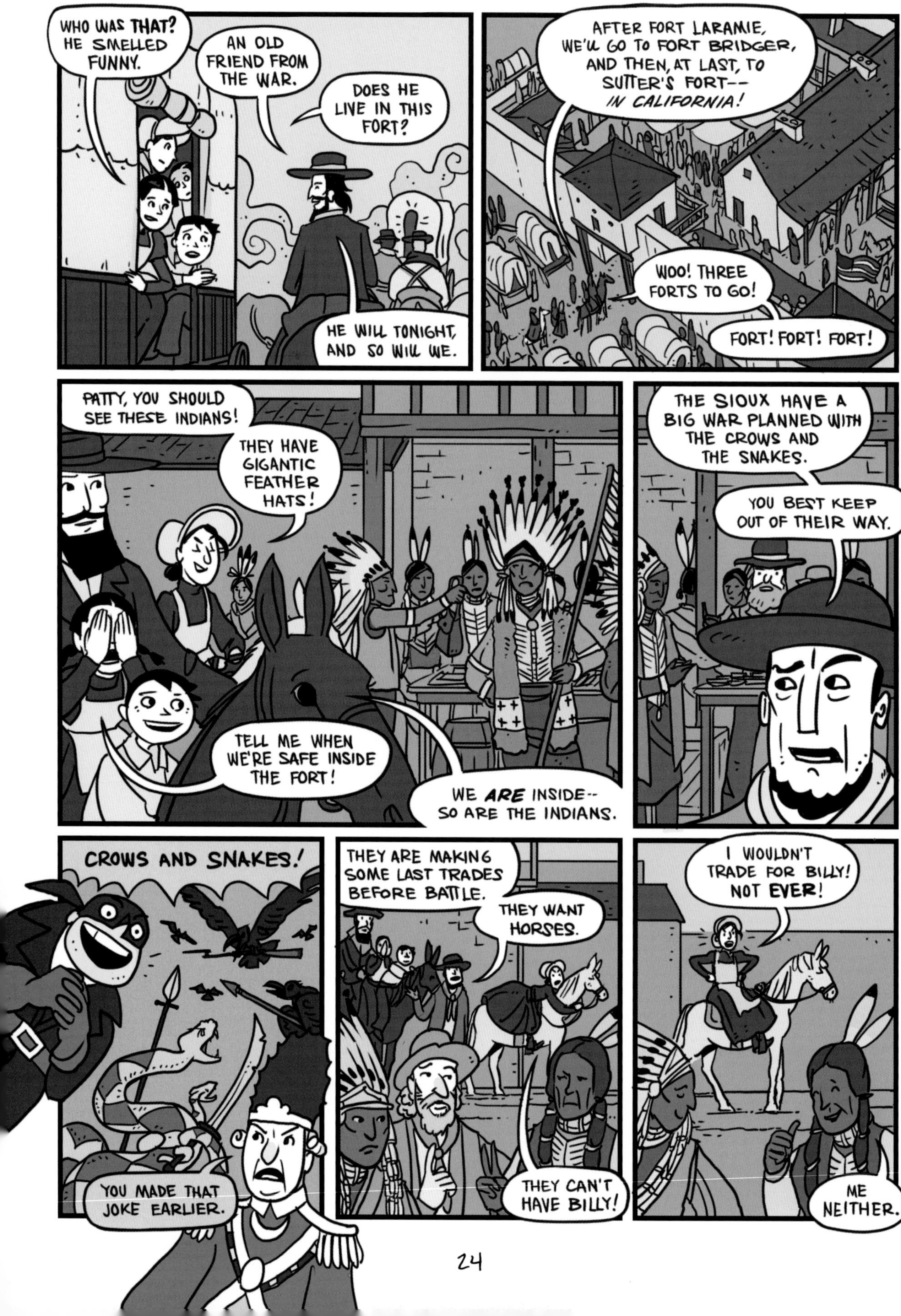
WHO WAS THAT? HE SMELLED FUNNY.
AN OLD FRIEND FROM THE WAR.
DOES HE LIVE IN THIS FORT?
HE WILL TONIGHT, AND SO WILL WE.
AFTER FORT LARAMIE, WE'LL GO TO FORT BRIDGER, AND THEN, AT LAST, TO SUTTER'S FORT-- IN CALIFORNIA!
WOO! THREE FORTS TO GO!
FORT! FORT! FORT!
PATTY, YOU SHOULD SEE THESE INDIANS!
THEY HAVE GIGANTIC FEATHER HATS!
TELL ME WHEN WE'RE SAFE INSIDE THE FORT!
WE ARE INSIDE-- SO ARE THE INDIANS.
THE SIOUX HAVE A BIG WAR PLANNED WITH THE CROWS AND THE SNAKES.
YOU BEST KEEP OUT OF THEIR WAY.
CROWS AND SNAKES!
YOU MADE THAT JOKE EARLIER.
THEY ARE MAKING SOME LAST TRADES BEFORE BATTLE.
THEY WANT HORSES.
THEY CAN'T HAVE BILLY!
I WOULDN'T TRADE FOR BILLY! NOT EVER!
ME NEITHER.

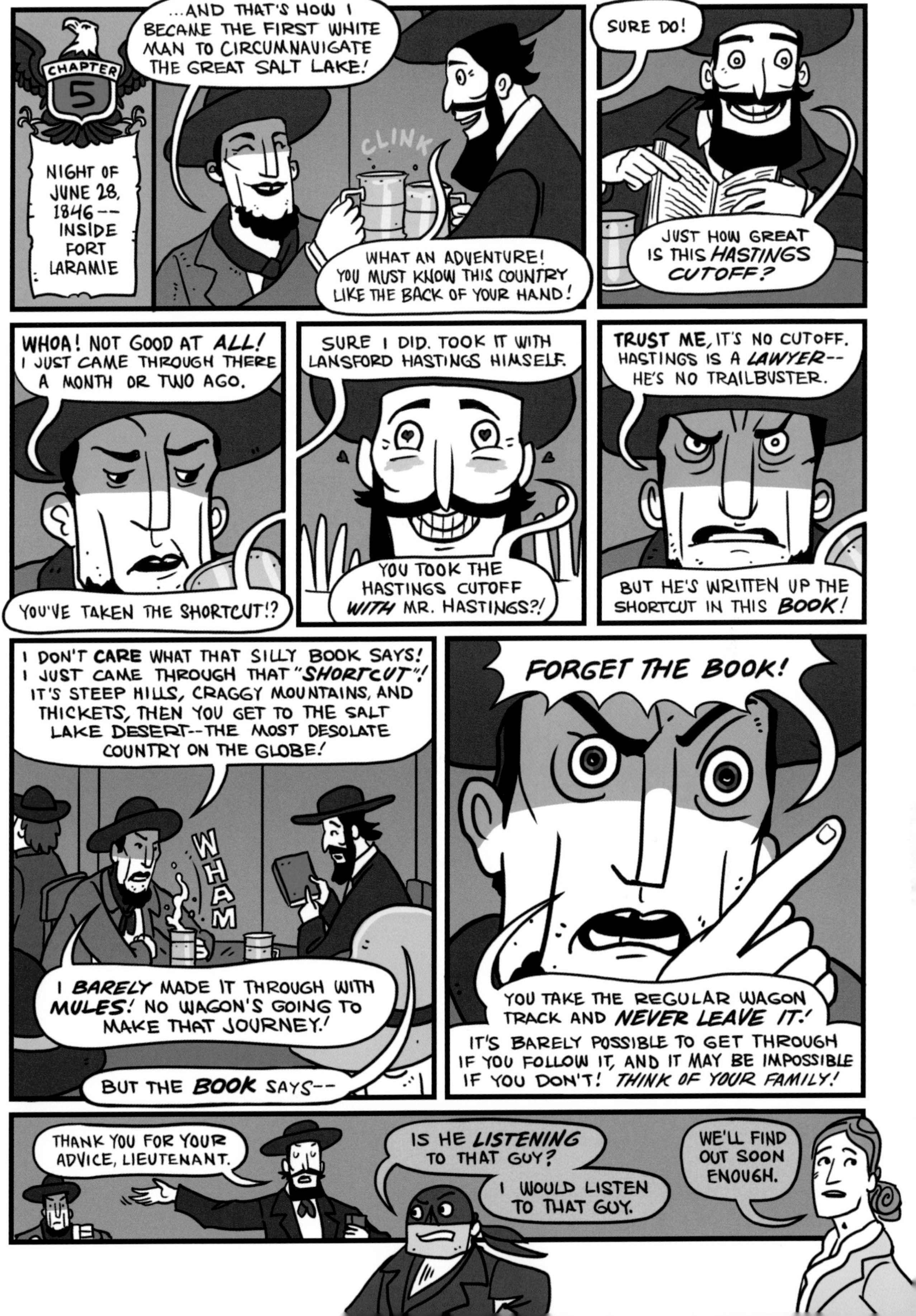
CHAPTER 5
NIGHT OF JUNE 28, 1846-- INSIDE FORT LARAMIE
...AND THAT'S HOW I BECAME THE FIRST WHITE MAN TO CIRCUMNAVIGATE THE GREAT SALT LAKE!
CLINK
WHAT AN ADVENTURE! YOU MUST KNOW THIS COUNTRY LIKE THE BACK OF YOUR HAND!
SURE DO!
JUST HOW GREAT IS THIS HASTINGS CUTOFF?
WHOA! NOT GOOD AT ALL! I JUST CAME THROUGH THERE A MONTH OR TWO AGO.
YOU'VE TAKEN THE SHORTCUT!?
SURE I DID. TOOK IT WITH LANSFORD HASTINGS HIMSELF.
YOU TOOK THE HASTINGS CUTOFF WITH MR. HASTINGS?!
TRUST ME, IT'S NO CUTOFF. HASTINGS IS A LAWYER-- HE'S NO TRAILBUSTER.
BUT HE'S WRITTEN UP THE SHORTCUT IN THIS BOOK!
I DON'T CARE WHAT THAT SILLY BOOK SAYS! I JUST CAME THROUGH THAT "SHORTCUT"! IT'S STEEP HILLS, CRAGGY MOUNTAINS, AND THICKETS, THEN YOU GET TO THE SALT LAKE DESERT--THE MOST DESOLATE COUNTRY ON THE GLOBE!
WHAM
I BARELY MADE IT THROUGH WITH MULES! NO WAGON'S GOING TO MAKE THAT JOURNEY!
BUT THE BOOK SAYS--
FORGET THE BOOK!
YOU TAKE THE REGULAR WAGON TRACK AND NEVER LEAVE IT!
IT'S BARELY POSSIBLE TO GET THROUGH IF YOU FOLLOW IT, AND IT MAY BE IMPOSSIBLE IF YOU DON'T! THINK OF YOUR FAMILY!
THANK YOU FOR YOUR ADVICE, LIEUTENANT.
IS HE LISTENING TO THAT GUY?
I WOULD LISTEN TO THAT GUY.
WE'LL FIND OUT SOON ENOUGH.

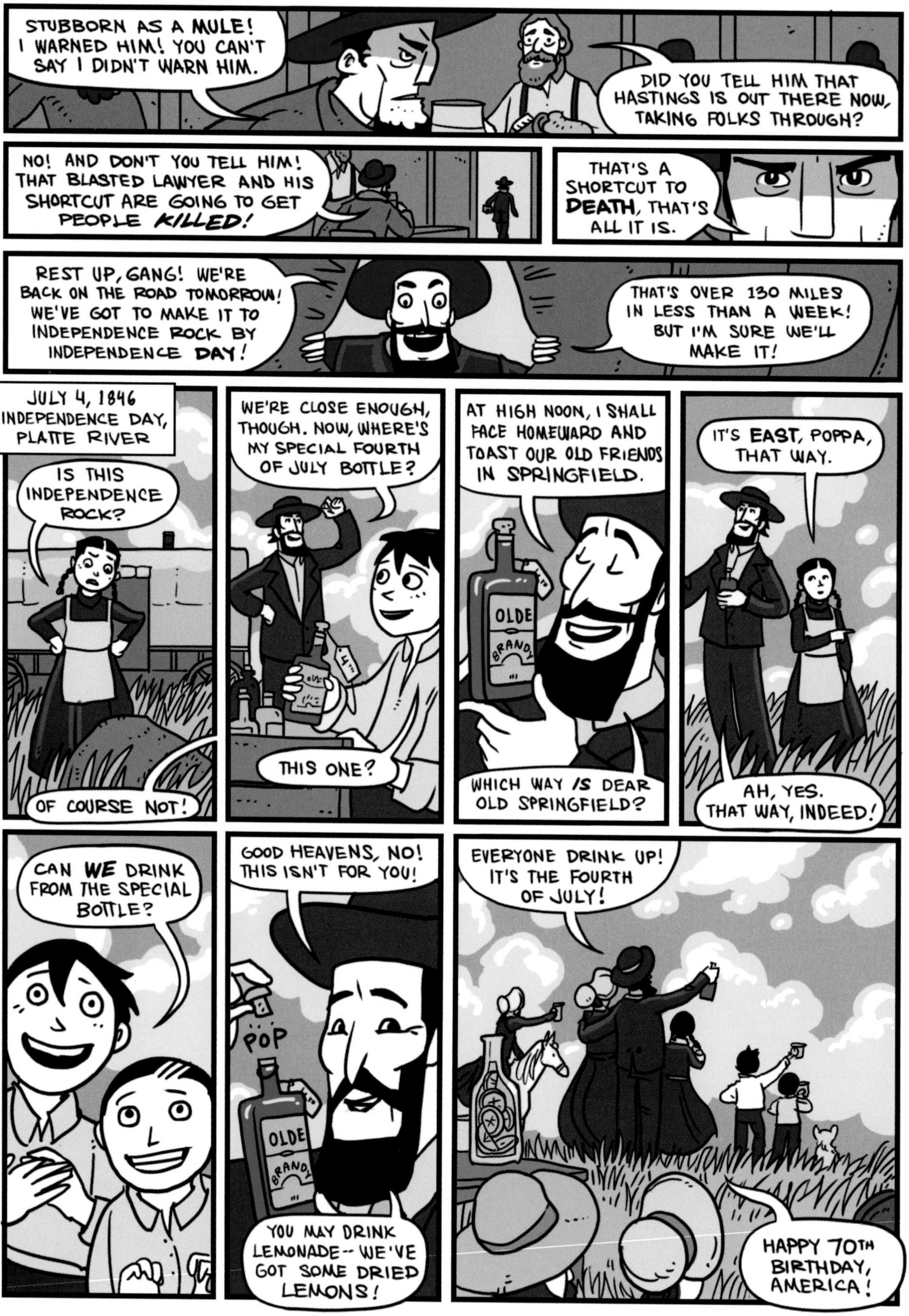
STUBBORN AS A MULE! I WARNED HIM! YOU CAN'T SAY I DIDN'T WARN HIM.
DID YOU TELL HIM THAT HASTINGS IS OUT THERE NOW, TAKING FOLKS THROUGH?
NO! AND DON'T YOU TELL HIM! THAT BLASTED LAWYER AND HIS SHORTCUT ARE GOING TO GET PEOPLE KILLED!
THAT'S A SHORTCUT TO DEATH, THAT'S ALL IT IS.
REST UP, GANG! WE'RE BACK ON THE ROAD TOMORROW! WE'VE GOT TO MAKE IT TO INDEPENDENCE ROCK BY INDEPENDENCE DAY!
THAT'S OVER 130 MILES IN LESS THAN A WEEK! BUT I'M SURE WE'LL MAKE IT!
JULY 4, 1846 INDEPENDENCE DAY, PLATTE RIVER
IS THIS INDEPENDENCE ROCK?
OF COURSE NOT!
WE'RE CLOSE ENOUGH, THOUGH. NOW, WHERE'S MY SPECIAL FOURTH OF JULY BOTTLE?
THIS ONE?
AT HIGH NOON, I SHALL FACE HOMEWARD AND TOAST OUR OLD FRIENDS IN SPRINGFIELD.
OLDE BRANDY
WHICH WAY IS DEAR OLD SPRINGFIELD?
IT'S EAST, POPPA, THAT WAY.
AH, YES. THAT WAY, INDEED!
CAN WE DRINK FROM THE SPECIAL BOTTLE?
GOOD HEAVENS, NO! THIS ISN'T FOR YOU!
POP
OLDE BRANDY
YOU MAY DRINK LEMONADE-- WE'VE GOT SOME DRIED LEMONS!
EVERYONE DRINK UP! IT'S THE FOURTH OF JULY!
HAPPY 70TH BIRTHDAY, AMERICA!

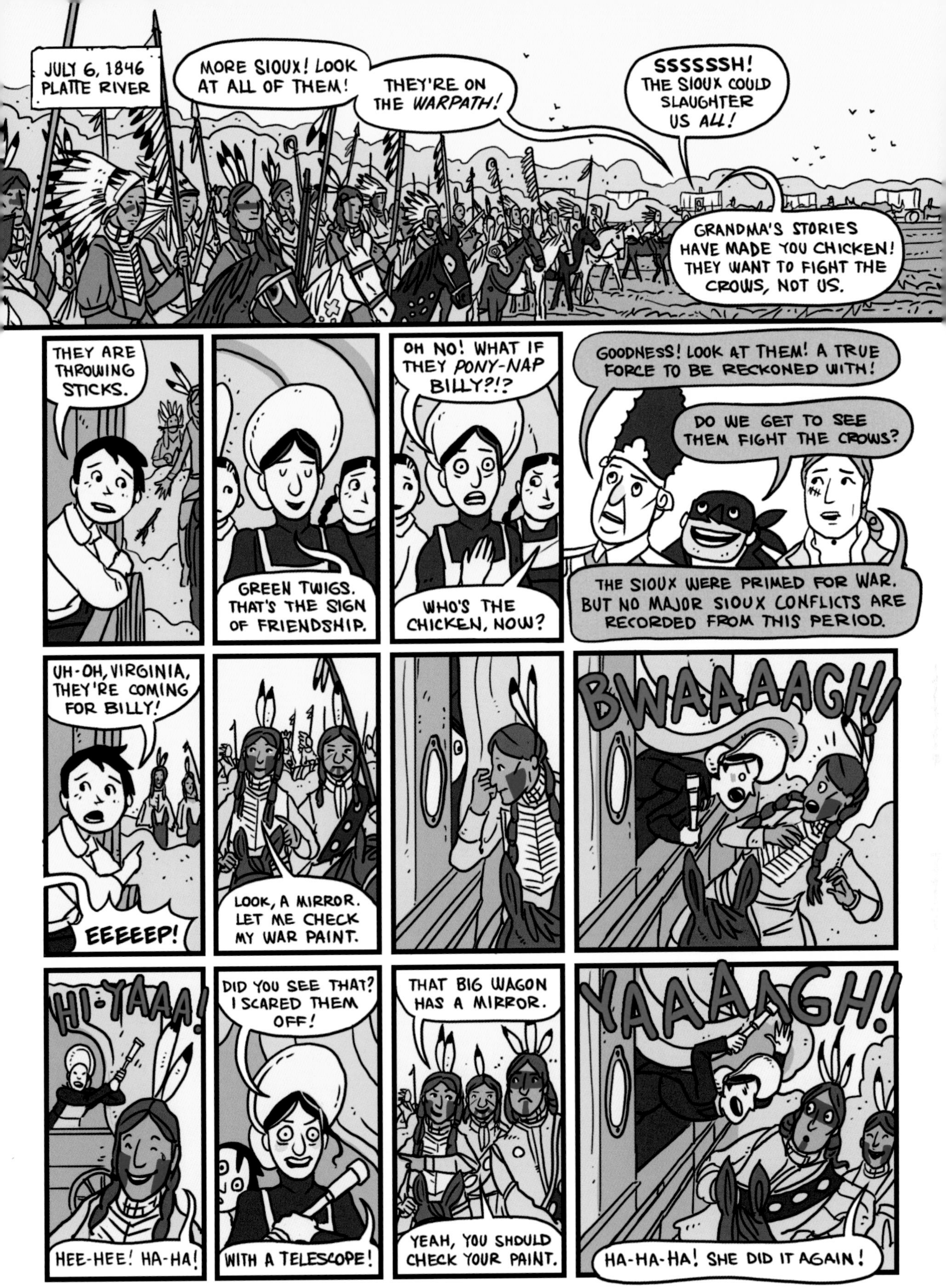
JULY 6, 1846
PLATTE RIVER
MORE SIOUX! LOOK AT ALL OF THEM!
THEY'RE ON THE *WARPATH*!
SSSSSSH! THE SIOUX COULD SLAUGHTER US *ALL*!
GRANDMA'S STORIES HAVE MADE YOU CHICKEN! THEY WANT TO FIGHT THE CROWS, NOT US.
THEY ARE THROWING STICKS.
GREEN TWIGS. THAT'S THE SIGN OF FRIENDSHIP.
OH NO! WHAT IF THEY *PONY-NAP* BILLY?!?
WHO'S THE CHICKEN, NOW?
GOODNESS! LOOK AT THEM! A TRUE FORCE TO BE RECKONED WITH!
DO WE GET TO SEE THEM FIGHT THE CROWS?
THE SIOUX WERE PRIMED FOR WAR. BUT NO MAJOR SIOUX CONFLICTS ARE RECORDED FROM THIS PERIOD.
UH-OH, VIRGINIA, THEY'RE COMING FOR BILLY!
EEEEEP!
LOOK, A MIRROR. LET ME CHECK MY WAR PAINT.
BWAAAAGH!
HI-YAAA!
HEE-HEE! HA-HA!
DID YOU SEE THAT? I SCARED THEM OFF!
WITH A TELESCOPE!
THAT BIG WAGON HAS A MIRROR.
YEAH, YOU SHOULD CHECK YOUR PAINT.
YAAAAGH!
HA-HA-HA! SHE DID IT AGAIN!

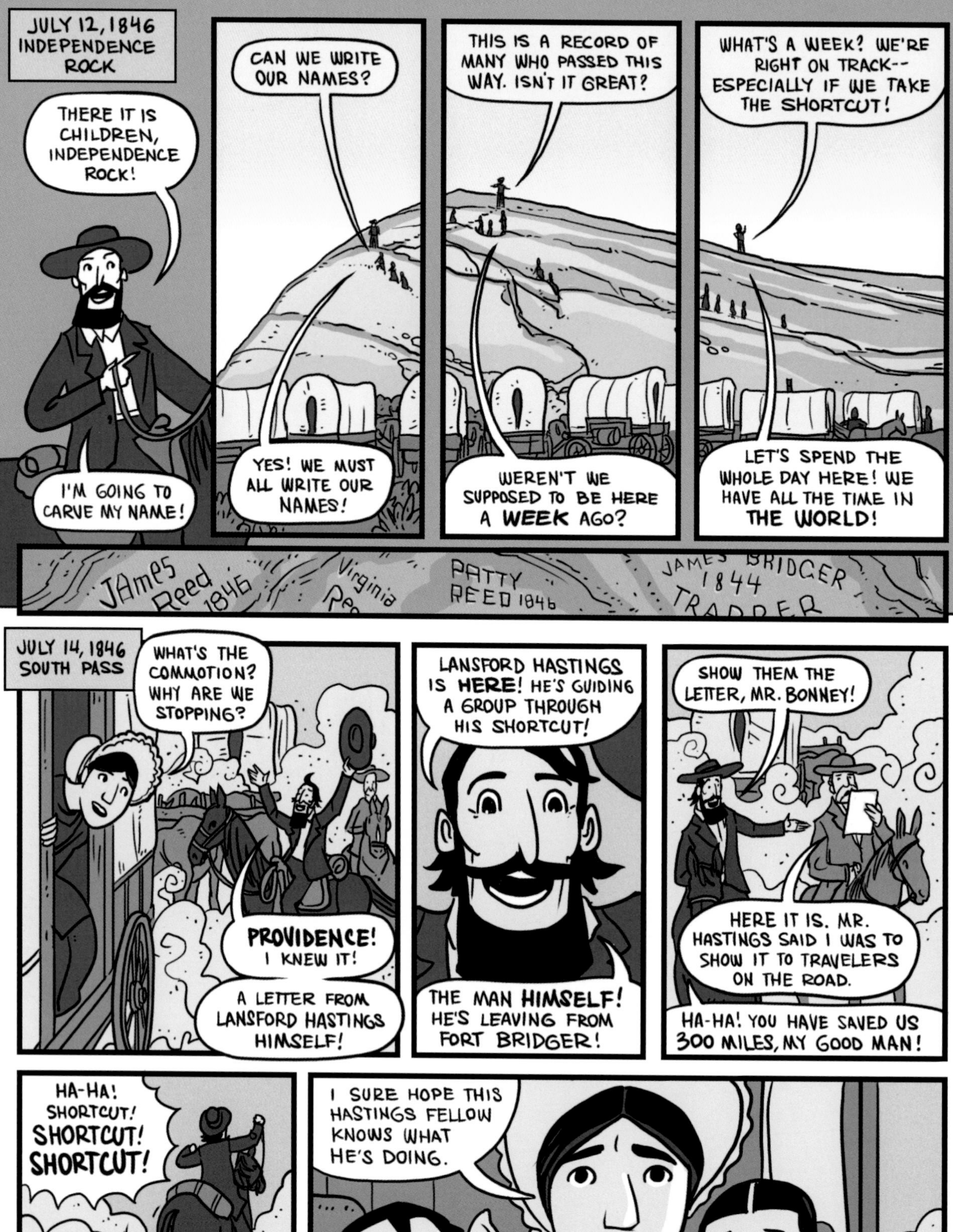

JULY 12, 1846
INDEPENDENCE ROCK
THERE IT IS CHILDREN, INDEPENDENCE ROCK!
I'M GOING TO CARVE MY NAME!
CAN WE WRITE OUR NAMES?
YES! WE MUST ALL WRITE OUR NAMES!
THIS IS A RECORD OF MANY WHO PASSED THIS WAY. ISN'T IT GREAT?
WEREN'T WE SUPPOSED TO BE HERE A **WEEK** AGO?
WHAT'S A WEEK? WE'RE RIGHT ON TRACK--ESPECIALLY IF WE TAKE THE SHORTCUT!
LET'S SPEND THE WHOLE DAY HERE! WE HAVE ALL THE TIME IN **THE WORLD**!
JAmes Reed 1846
Virginia
PATTY REED 1846
JAMES BRIDGER 1844 TRAPPER
JULY 14, 1846
SOUTH PASS
WHAT'S THE COMMOTION? WHY ARE WE STOPPING?
PROVIDENCE! I KNEW IT!
A LETTER FROM LANSFORD HASTINGS HIMSELF!
LANSFORD HASTINGS IS **HERE**! HE'S GUIDING A GROUP THROUGH HIS SHORTCUT!
THE MAN **HIMSELF**! HE'S LEAVING FROM FORT BRIDGER!
SHOW THEM THE LETTER, MR. BONNEY!
HERE IT IS. MR. HASTINGS SAID I WAS TO SHOW IT TO TRAVELERS ON THE ROAD.
HA-HA! YOU HAVE SAVED US 300 MILES, MY GOOD MAN!
HA-HA! SHORTCUT! **SHORTCUT! SHORTCUT!**
I SURE HOPE THIS HASTINGS FELLOW KNOWS WHAT HE'S DOING.
ME TOO.

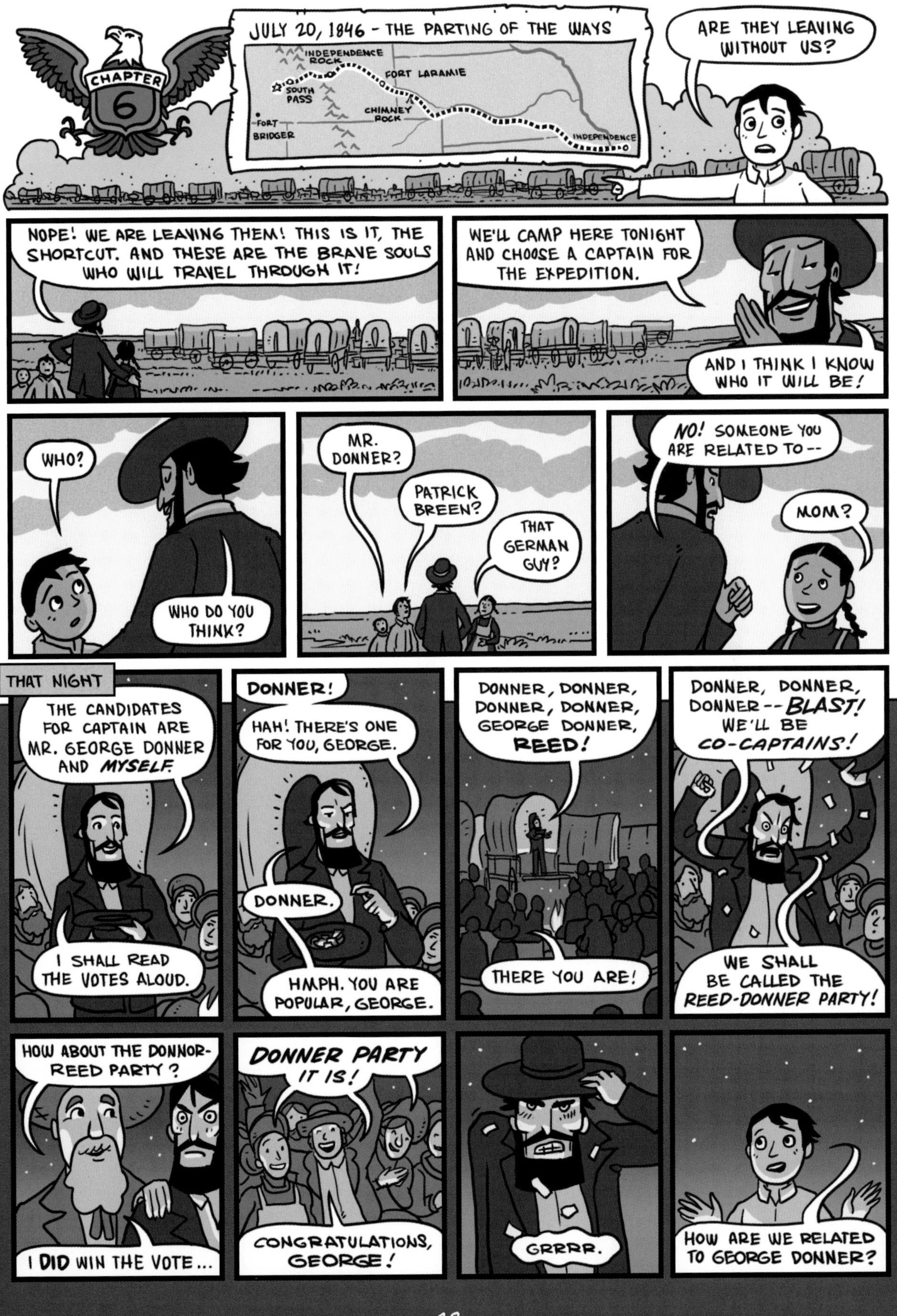
CHAPTER 6
JULY 20, 1846 - THE PARTING OF THE WAYS
INDEPENDENCE ROCK
FORT LARAMIE
SOUTH PASS
CHIMNEY ROCK
FORT BRIDGER
INDEPENDENCE
ARE THEY LEAVING WITHOUT US?
NOPE! WE ARE LEAVING THEM! THIS IS IT, THE SHORTCUT. AND THESE ARE THE BRAVE SOULS WHO WILL TRAVEL THROUGH IT!
WE'LL CAMP HERE TONIGHT AND CHOOSE A CAPTAIN FOR THE EXPEDITION.
AND I THINK I KNOW WHO IT WILL BE!
WHO?
WHO DO YOU THINK?
MR. DONNER?
PATRICK BREEN?
THAT GERMAN GUY?
NO! SOMEONE YOU ARE RELATED TO--
MOM?
THAT NIGHT
THE CANDIDATES FOR CAPTAIN ARE MR. GEORGE DONNER AND MYSELF.
I SHALL READ THE VOTES ALOUD.
DONNER!
HAH! THERE'S ONE FOR YOU, GEORGE.
DONNER.
HMPH. YOU ARE POPULAR, GEORGE.
DONNER, DONNER, DONNER, DONNER, GEORGE DONNER, REED!
THERE YOU ARE!
DONNER, DONNER, DONNER--BLAST! WE'LL BE CO-CAPTAINS!
WE SHALL BE CALLED THE REED-DONNER PARTY!
HOW ABOUT THE DONNOR-REED PARTY?
I DID WIN THE VOTE...
DONNER PARTY IT IS!
CONGRATULATIONS, GEORGE!
GRRRR.
HOW ARE WE RELATED TO GEORGE DONNER?

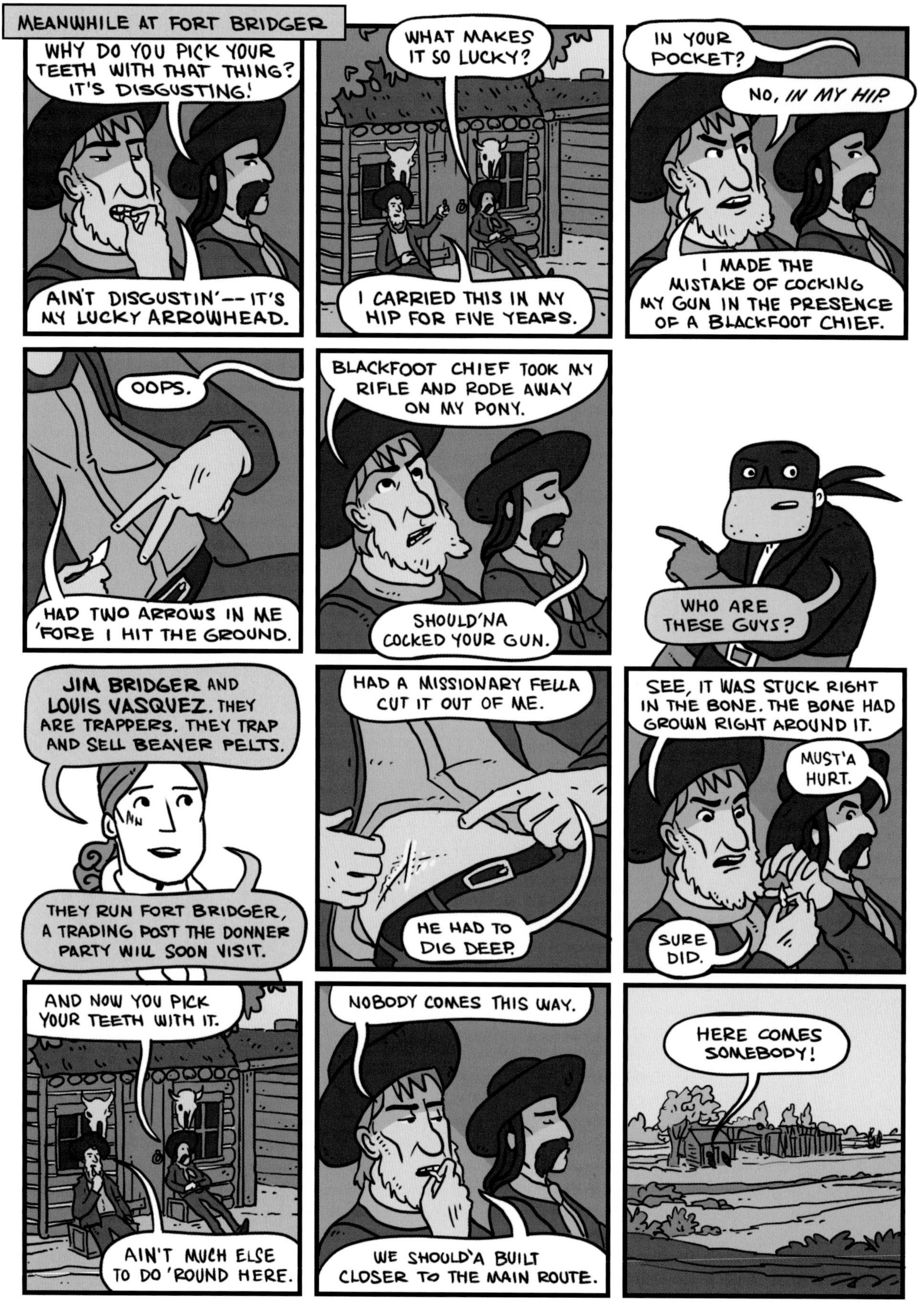
MEANWHILE AT FORT BRIDGER
WHY DO YOU PICK YOUR TEETH WITH THAT THING? IT'S DISGUSTING!
AIN'T DISGUSTIN'-- IT'S MY LUCKY ARROWHEAD.
WHAT MAKES IT SO LUCKY?
I CARRIED THIS IN MY HIP FOR FIVE YEARS.
IN YOUR POCKET?
NO, IN MY HIP.
I MADE THE MISTAKE OF COCKING MY GUN IN THE PRESENCE OF A BLACKFOOT CHIEF.
OOPS.
HAD TWO ARROWS IN ME 'FORE I HIT THE GROUND.
BLACKFOOT CHIEF TOOK MY RIFLE AND RODE AWAY ON MY PONY.
SHOULD'NA COCKED YOUR GUN.
WHO ARE THESE GUYS?
JIM BRIDGER AND LOUIS VASQUEZ. THEY ARE TRAPPERS. THEY TRAP AND SELL BEAVER PELTS.
THEY RUN FORT BRIDGER, A TRADING POST THE DONNER PARTY WILL SOON VISIT.
HAD A MISSIONARY FELLA CUT IT OUT OF ME.
HE HAD TO DIG DEEP.
SEE, IT WAS STUCK RIGHT IN THE BONE. THE BONE HAD GROWN RIGHT AROUND IT.
MUST'A HURT.
SURE DID.
AND NOW YOU PICK YOUR TEETH WITH IT.
AIN'T MUCH ELSE TO DO 'ROUND HERE.
NOBODY COMES THIS WAY.
WE SHOULD'A BUILT CLOSER TO THE MAIN ROUTE.
HERE COMES SOMEBODY!

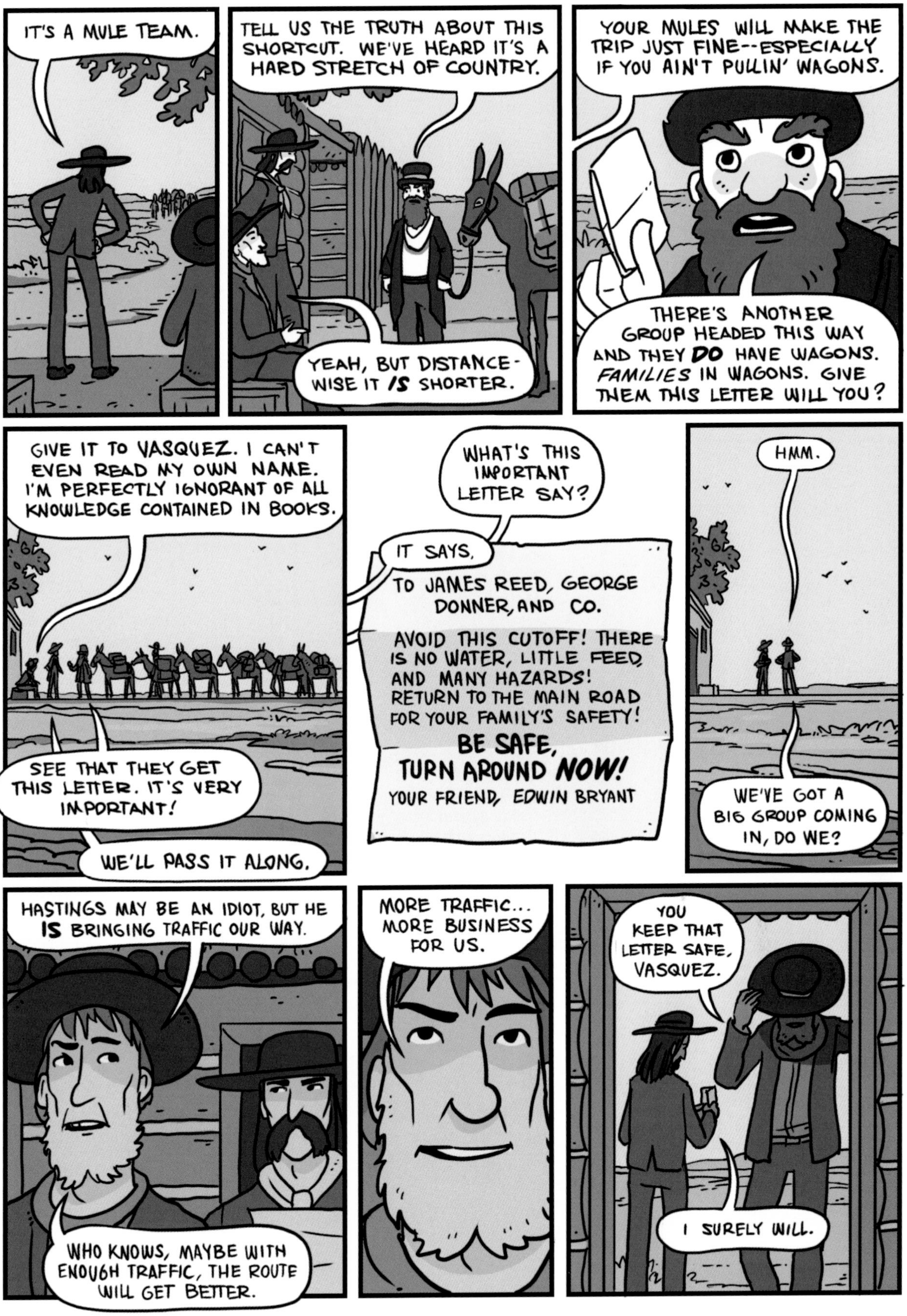
IT'S A MULE TEAM.
TELL US THE TRUTH ABOUT THIS SHORTCUT. WE'VE HEARD IT'S A HARD STRETCH OF COUNTRY.
YEAH, BUT DISTANCE-WISE IT IS SHORTER.
YOUR MULES WILL MAKE THE TRIP JUST FINE--ESPECIALLY IF YOU AIN'T PULLIN' WAGONS.
THERE'S ANOTHER GROUP HEADED THIS WAY AND THEY DO HAVE WAGONS. FAMILIES IN WAGONS. GIVE THEM THIS LETTER WILL YOU?
GIVE IT TO VASQUEZ. I CAN'T EVEN READ MY OWN NAME. I'M PERFECTLY IGNORANT OF ALL KNOWLEDGE CONTAINED IN BOOKS.
SEE THAT THEY GET THIS LETTER. IT'S VERY IMPORTANT!
WE'LL PASS IT ALONG.
WHAT'S THIS IMPORTANT LETTER SAY?
IT SAYS,
TO JAMES REED, GEORGE DONNER, AND CO.
AVOID THIS CUTOFF! THERE IS NO WATER, LITTLE FEED, AND MANY HAZARDS! RETURN TO THE MAIN ROAD FOR YOUR FAMILY'S SAFETY!
BE SAFE, TURN AROUND NOW!
YOUR FRIEND, EDWIN BRYANT
HMM.
WE'VE GOT A BIG GROUP COMING IN, DO WE?
HASTINGS MAY BE AN IDIOT, BUT HE IS BRINGING TRAFFIC OUR WAY.
WHO KNOWS, MAYBE WITH ENOUGH TRAFFIC, THE ROUTE WILL GET BETTER.
MORE TRAFFIC... MORE BUSINESS FOR US.
YOU KEEP THAT LETTER SAFE, VASQUEZ.
I SURELY WILL.

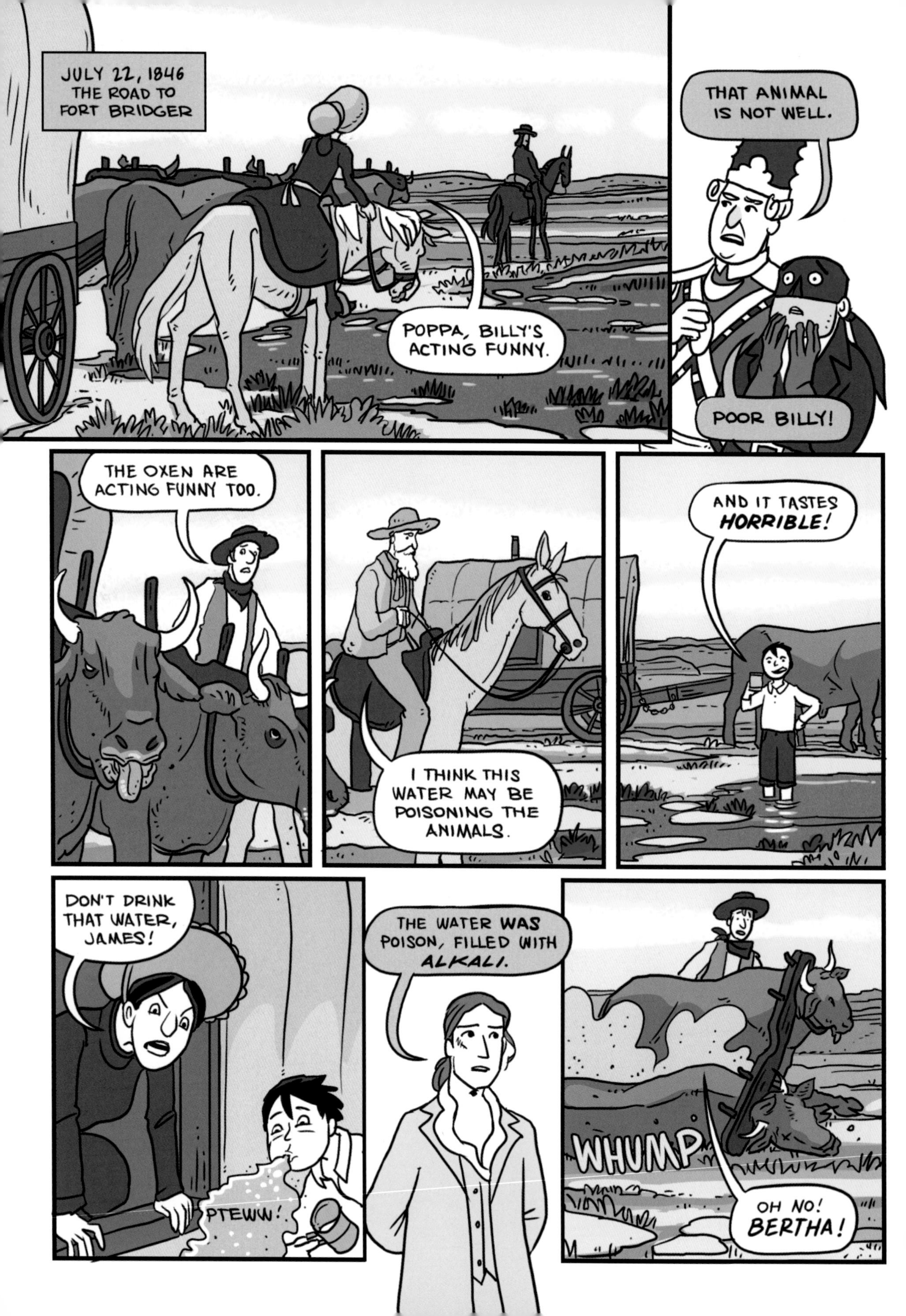
JULY 22, 1846
THE ROAD TO FORT BRIDGER
POPPA, BILLY'S ACTING FUNNY.
THAT ANIMAL IS NOT WELL.
POOR BILLY!
THE OXEN ARE ACTING FUNNY TOO.
I THINK THIS WATER MAY BE POISONING THE ANIMALS.
AND IT TASTES HORRIBLE!
DON'T DRINK THAT WATER, JAMES!
PTEWW!
THE WATER WAS POISON, FILLED WITH ALKALI.
WHUMP
OH NO! BERTHA!

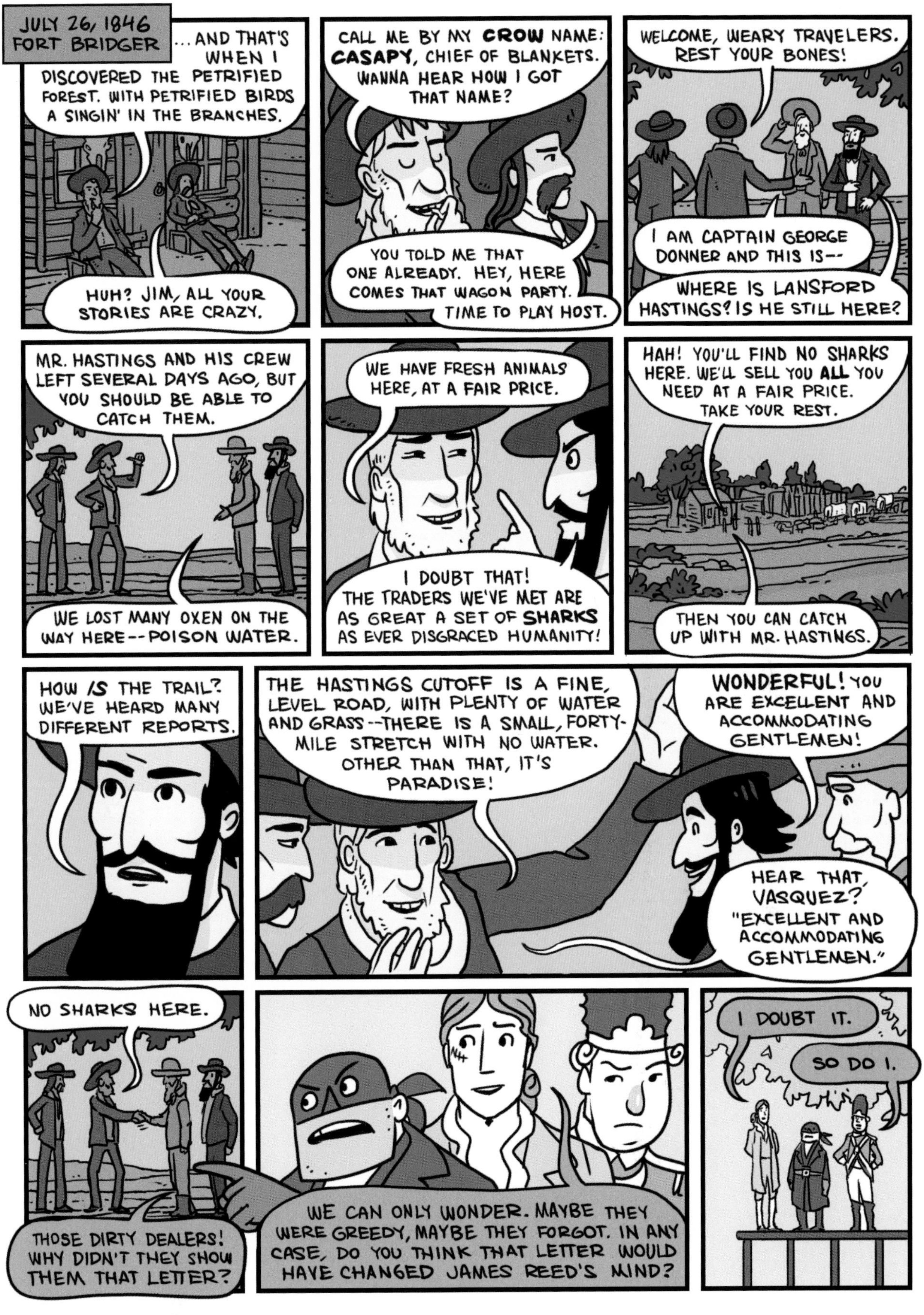

JULY 26, 1846
FORT BRIDGER
...AND THAT'S WHEN I DISCOVERED THE PETRIFIED FOREST. WITH PETRIFIED BIRDS A SINGIN' IN THE BRANCHES.
HUH? JIM, ALL YOUR STORIES ARE CRAZY.
CALL ME BY MY CROW NAME: CASAPY, CHIEF OF BLANKETS. WANNA HEAR HOW I GOT THAT NAME?
YOU TOLD ME THAT ONE ALREADY. HEY, HERE COMES THAT WAGON PARTY.
TIME TO PLAY HOST.
WELCOME, WEARY TRAVELERS. REST YOUR BONES!
I AM CAPTAIN GEORGE DONNER AND THIS IS--
WHERE IS LANSFORD HASTINGS? IS HE STILL HERE?
MR. HASTINGS AND HIS CREW LEFT SEVERAL DAYS AGO, BUT YOU SHOULD BE ABLE TO CATCH THEM.
WE LOST MANY OXEN ON THE WAY HERE--POISON WATER.
WE HAVE FRESH ANIMALS HERE, AT A FAIR PRICE.
I DOUBT THAT! THE TRADERS WE'VE MET ARE AS GREAT A SET OF SHARKS AS EVER DISGRACED HUMANITY!
HAH! YOU'LL FIND NO SHARKS HERE. WE'LL SELL YOU ALL YOU NEED AT A FAIR PRICE. TAKE YOUR REST.
THEN YOU CAN CATCH UP WITH MR. HASTINGS.
HOW IS THE TRAIL? WE'VE HEARD MANY DIFFERENT REPORTS.
THE HASTINGS CUTOFF IS A FINE, LEVEL ROAD, WITH PLENTY OF WATER AND GRASS--THERE IS A SMALL, FORTY-MILE STRETCH WITH NO WATER. OTHER THAN THAT, IT'S PARADISE!
WONDERFUL! YOU ARE EXCELLENT AND ACCOMMODATING GENTLEMEN!
HEAR THAT, VASQUEZ? "EXCELLENT AND ACCOMMODATING GENTLEMEN."
NO SHARKS HERE.
THOSE DIRTY DEALERS! WHY DIDN'T THEY SHOW THEM THAT LETTER?
WE CAN ONLY WONDER. MAYBE THEY WERE GREEDY, MAYBE THEY FORGOT. IN ANY CASE, DO YOU THINK THAT LETTER WOULD HAVE CHANGED JAMES REED'S MIND?
I DOUBT IT.
SO DO I.

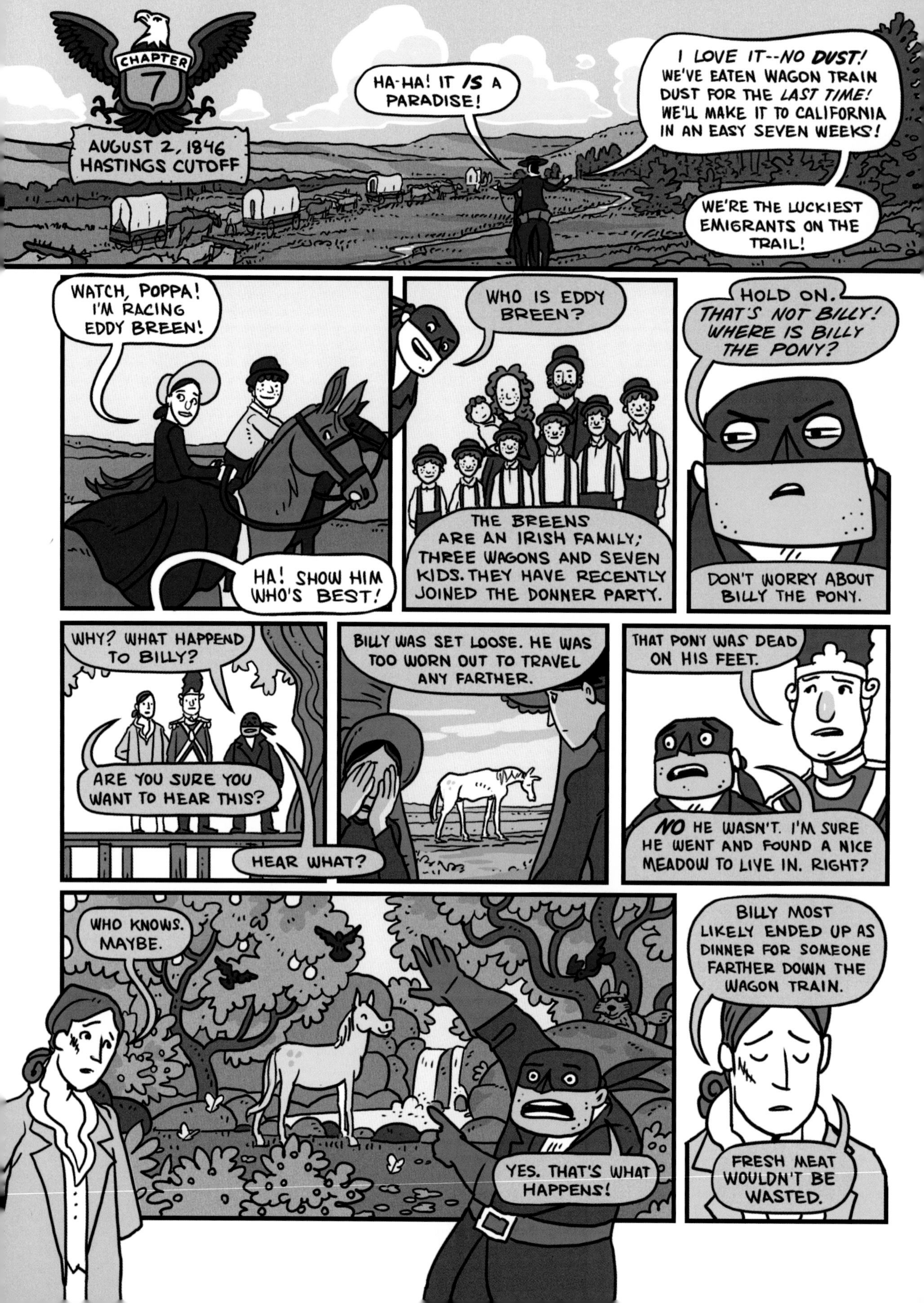
CHAPTER 7
AUGUST 2, 1846 HASTINGS CUTOFF
HA-HA! IT *IS* A PARADISE!
I LOVE IT--NO *DUST!* WE'VE EATEN WAGON TRAIN DUST FOR THE *LAST TIME!* WE'LL MAKE IT TO CALIFORNIA IN AN EASY SEVEN WEEKS!
WE'RE THE LUCKIEST EMIGRANTS ON THE TRAIL!
WATCH, POPPA! I'M RACING EDDY BREEN!
HA! SHOW HIM WHO'S BEST!
WHO IS EDDY BREEN?
THE BREENS ARE AN IRISH FAMILY; THREE WAGONS AND SEVEN KIDS. THEY HAVE RECENTLY JOINED THE DONNER PARTY.
HOLD ON. *THAT'S NOT BILLY! WHERE IS BILLY THE PONY?*
DON'T WORRY ABOUT BILLY THE PONY.
WHY? WHAT HAPPEND TO BILLY?
ARE YOU SURE YOU WANT TO HEAR THIS?
HEAR WHAT?
BILLY WAS SET LOOSE. HE WAS TOO WORN OUT TO TRAVEL ANY FARTHER.
THAT PONY WAS DEAD ON HIS FEET.
NO HE WASN'T. I'M SURE HE WENT AND FOUND A NICE MEADOW TO LIVE IN. RIGHT?
WHO KNOWS. MAYBE.
YES. THAT'S WHAT HAPPENS!
BILLY MOST LIKELY ENDED UP AS DINNER FOR SOMEONE FARTHER DOWN THE WAGON TRAIN.
FRESH MEAT WOULDN'T BE WASTED.

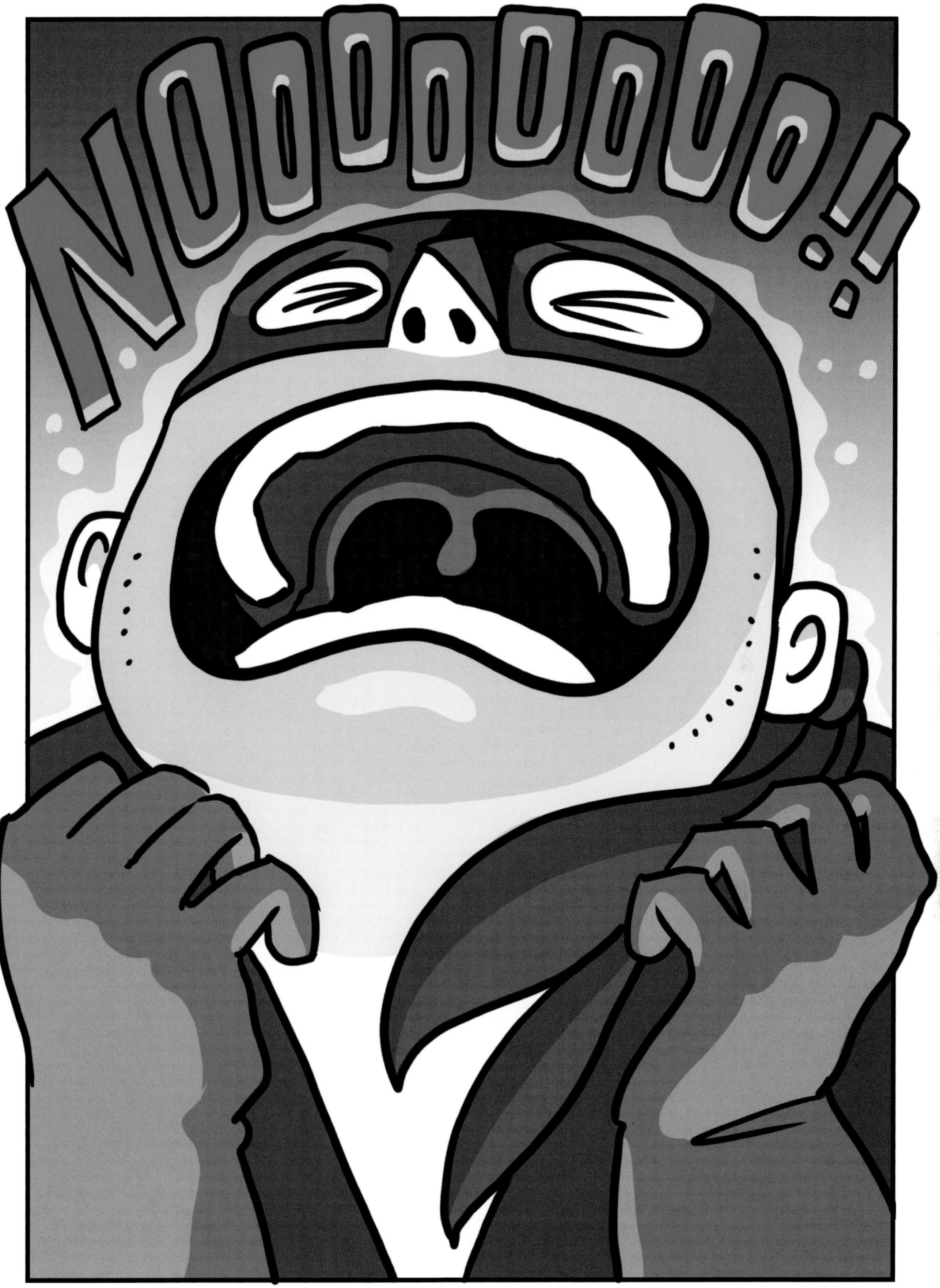
NOOOOOOOOO!!

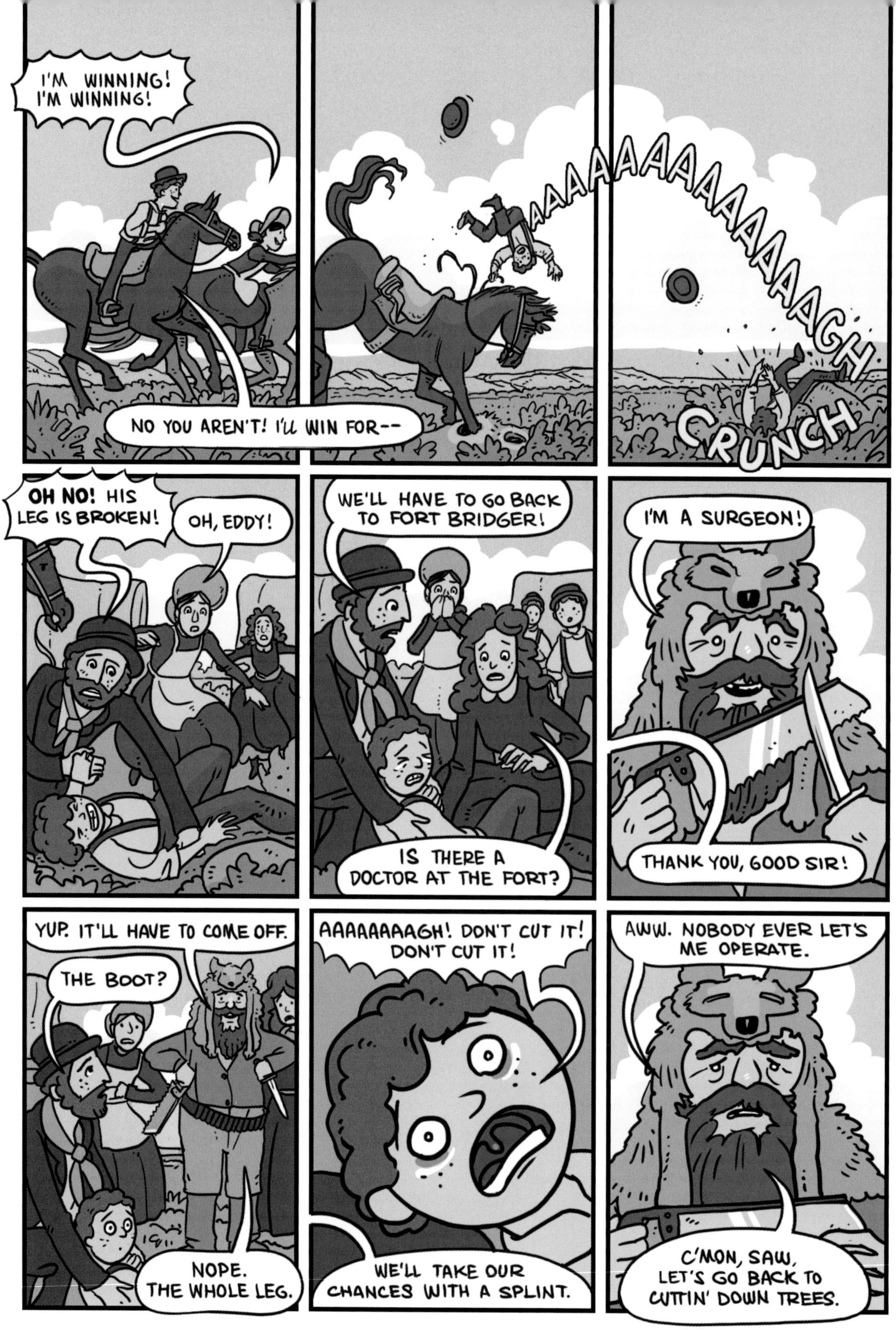

I'M WINNING! I'M WINNING!
NO YOU AREN'T! I'LL WIN FOR--
AAAAAAAAAAAAAAAAAAAGH
CRUNCH
OH NO! HIS LEG IS BROKEN!
OH, EDDY!
WE'LL HAVE TO GO BACK TO FORT BRIDGER!
IS THERE A DOCTOR AT THE FORT?
I'M A SURGEON!
THANK YOU, GOOD SIR!
YUP. IT'LL HAVE TO COME OFF.
THE BOOT?
NOPE. THE WHOLE LEG.
AAAAAAAAGH! DON'T CUT IT! DON'T CUT IT!
WE'LL TAKE OUR CHANCES WITH A SPLINT.
AWW. NOBODY EVER LET'S ME OPERATE.
C'MON, SAW, LET'S GO BACK TO CUTTIN' DOWN TREES.

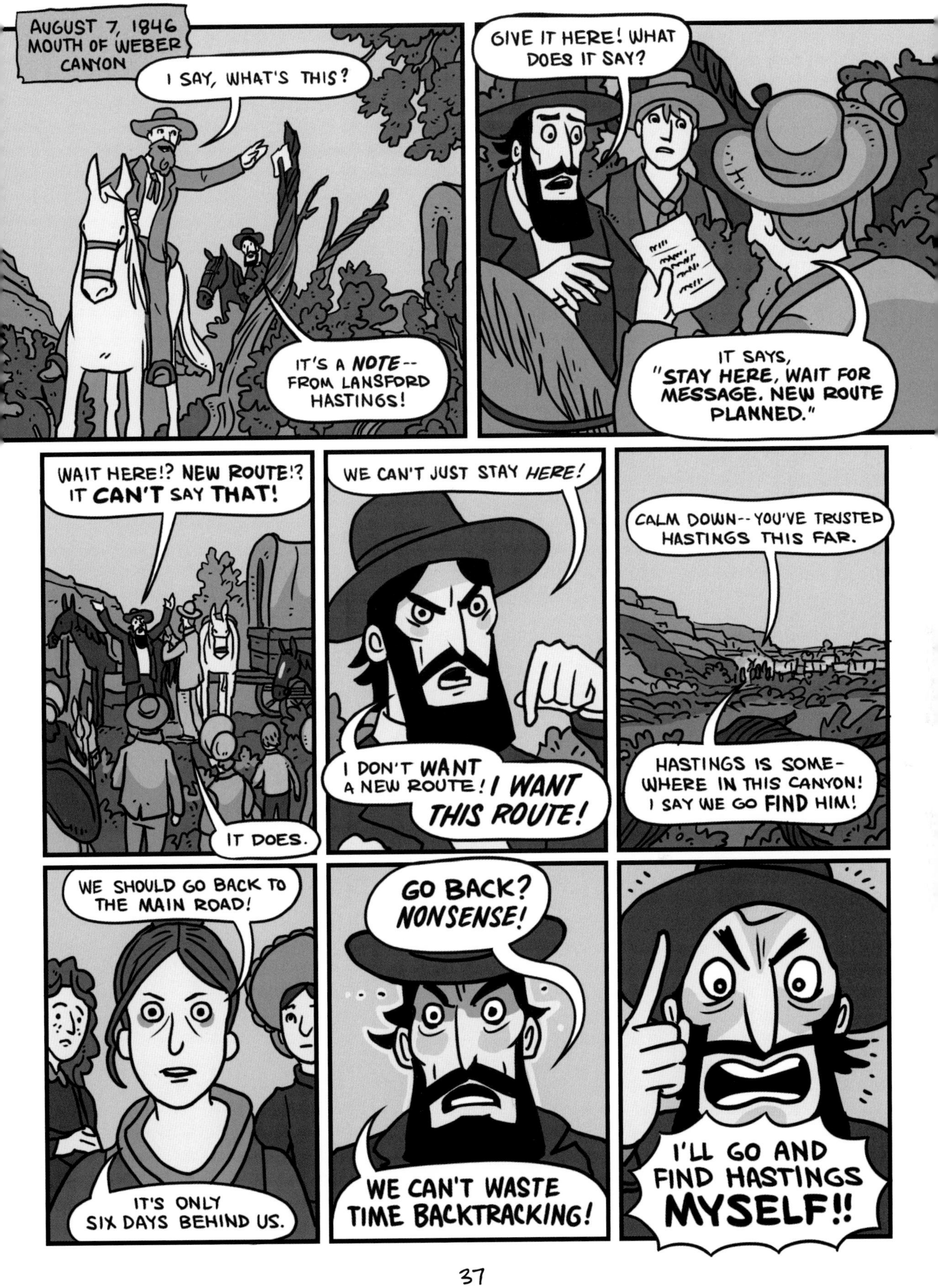
AUGUST 7, 1846 MOUTH OF WEBER CANYON
I SAY, WHAT'S THIS?
IT'S A NOTE-- FROM LANSFORD HASTINGS!
GIVE IT HERE! WHAT DOES IT SAY?
IT SAYS, "STAY HERE, WAIT FOR MESSAGE. NEW ROUTE PLANNED."
WAIT HERE!? NEW ROUTE!? IT CAN'T SAY THAT!
IT DOES.
WE CAN'T JUST STAY HERE!
I DON'T WANT A NEW ROUTE! I WANT THIS ROUTE!
CALM DOWN--YOU'VE TRUSTED HASTINGS THIS FAR.
HASTINGS IS SOMEWHERE IN THIS CANYON! I SAY WE GO FIND HIM!
WE SHOULD GO BACK TO THE MAIN ROAD!
IT'S ONLY SIX DAYS BEHIND US.
GO BACK? NONSENSE!
WE CAN'T WASTE TIME BACKTRACKING!
I'LL GO AND FIND HASTINGS MYSELF!!

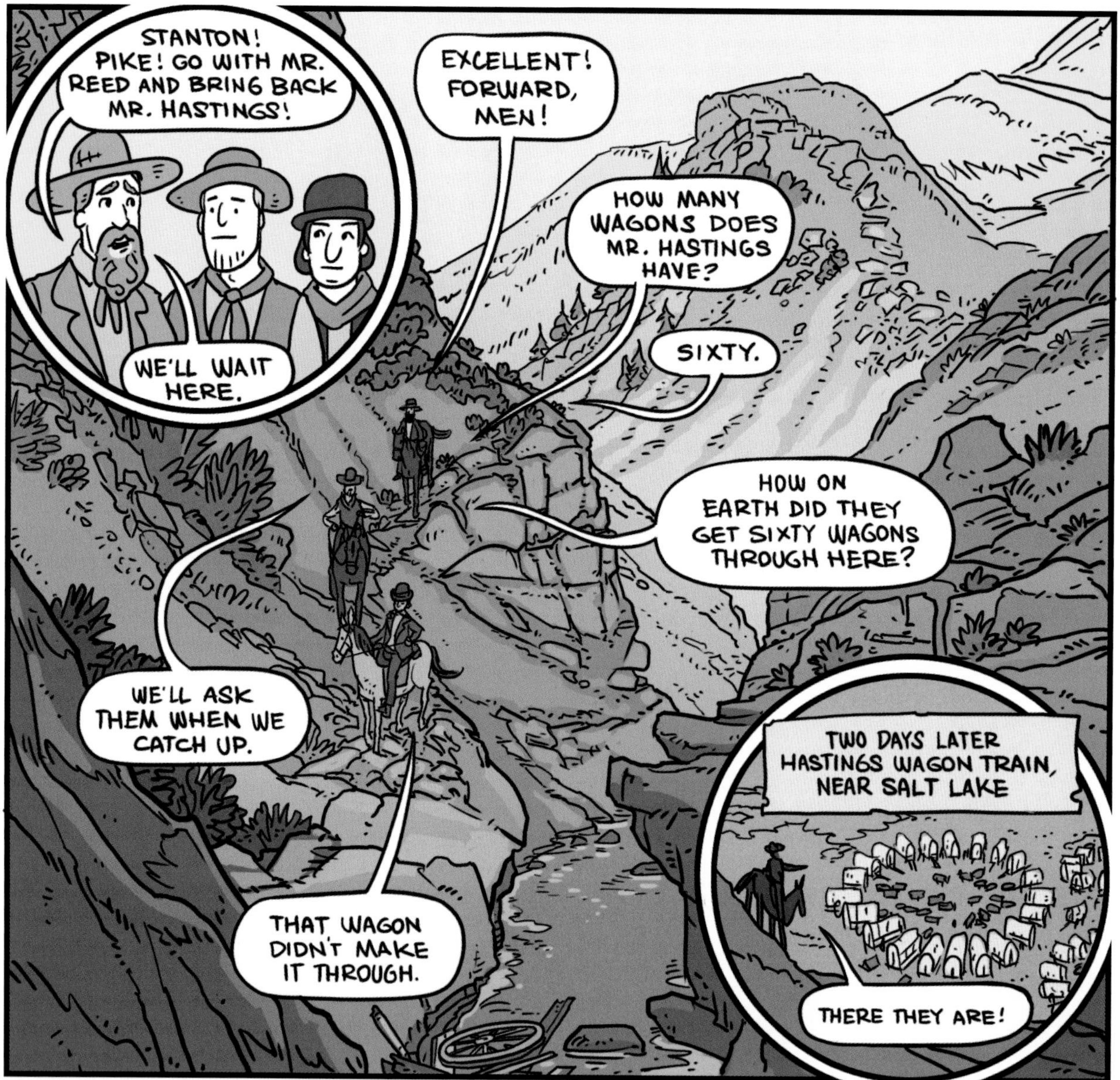
STANTON! PIKE! GO WITH MR. REED AND BRING BACK MR. HASTINGS!
WE'LL WAIT HERE.
EXCELLENT! FORWARD, MEN!
HOW MANY WAGONS DOES MR. HASTINGS HAVE?
SIXTY.
HOW ON EARTH DID THEY GET SIXTY WAGONS THROUGH HERE?
WE'LL ASK THEM WHEN WE CATCH UP.
THAT WAGON DIDN'T MAKE IT THROUGH.
TWO DAYS LATER HASTINGS WAGON TRAIN, NEAR SALT LAKE
THERE THEY ARE!

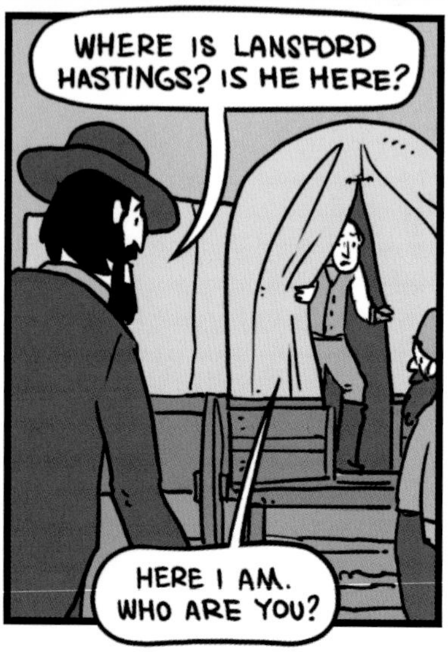
WHERE IS LANSFORD HASTINGS? IS HE HERE?
HERE I AM. WHO ARE YOU?

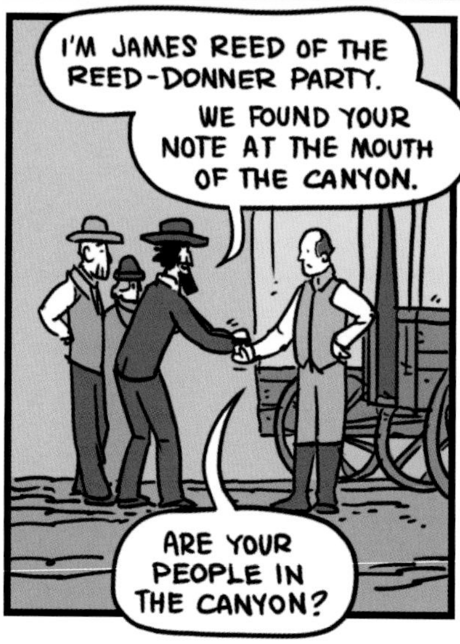
I'M JAMES REED OF THE REED-DONNER PARTY.
WE FOUND YOUR NOTE AT THE MOUTH OF THE CANYON.
ARE YOUR PEOPLE IN THE CANYON?

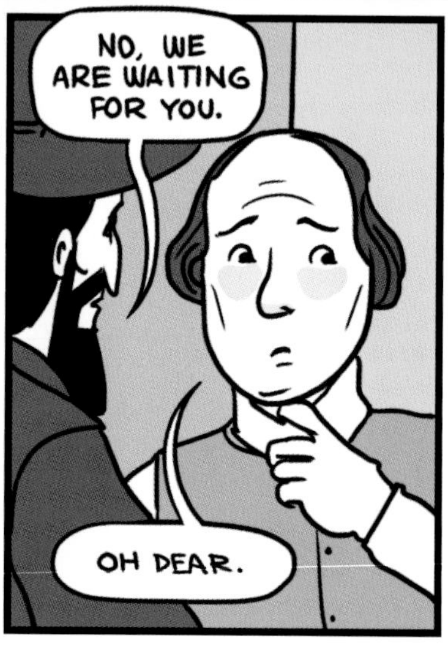
NO, WE ARE WAITING FOR YOU.
OH DEAR.

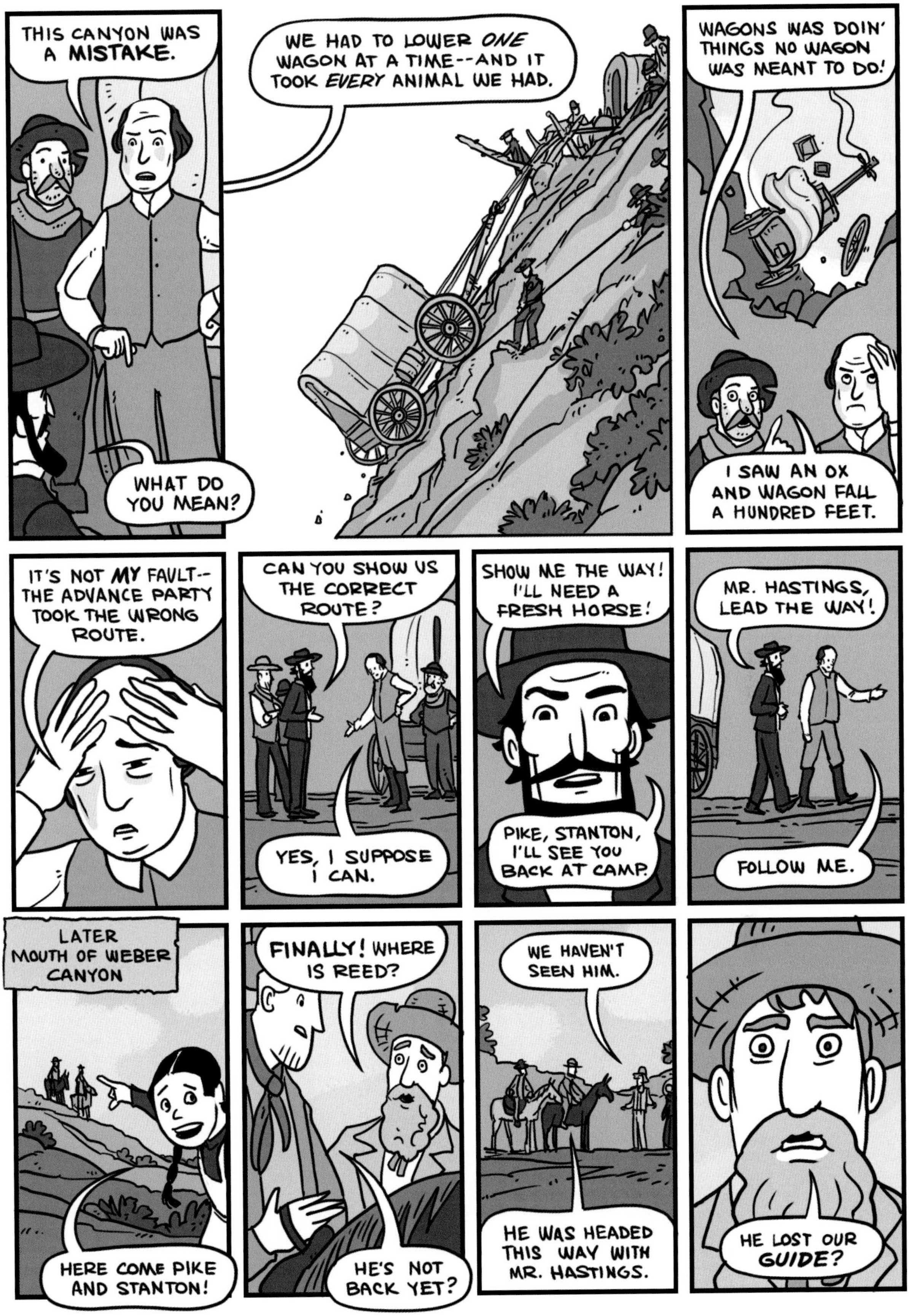
THIS CANYON WAS A MISTAKE.
WHAT DO YOU MEAN?
WE HAD TO LOWER ONE WAGON AT A TIME--AND IT TOOK EVERY ANIMAL WE HAD.
WAGONS WAS DOIN' THINGS NO WAGON WAS MEANT TO DO!
I SAW AN OX AND WAGON FALL A HUNDRED FEET.
IT'S NOT MY FAULT--THE ADVANCE PARTY TOOK THE WRONG ROUTE.
CAN YOU SHOW US THE CORRECT ROUTE?
YES, I SUPPOSE I CAN.
SHOW ME THE WAY! I'LL NEED A FRESH HORSE!
PIKE, STANTON, I'LL SEE YOU BACK AT CAMP.
MR. HASTINGS, LEAD THE WAY!
FOLLOW ME.
LATER
MOUTH OF WEBER CANYON
HERE COME PIKE AND STANTON!
FINALLY! WHERE IS REED?
HE'S NOT BACK YET?
WE HAVEN'T SEEN HIM.
HE WAS HEADED THIS WAY WITH MR. HASTINGS.
HE LOST OUR GUIDE?

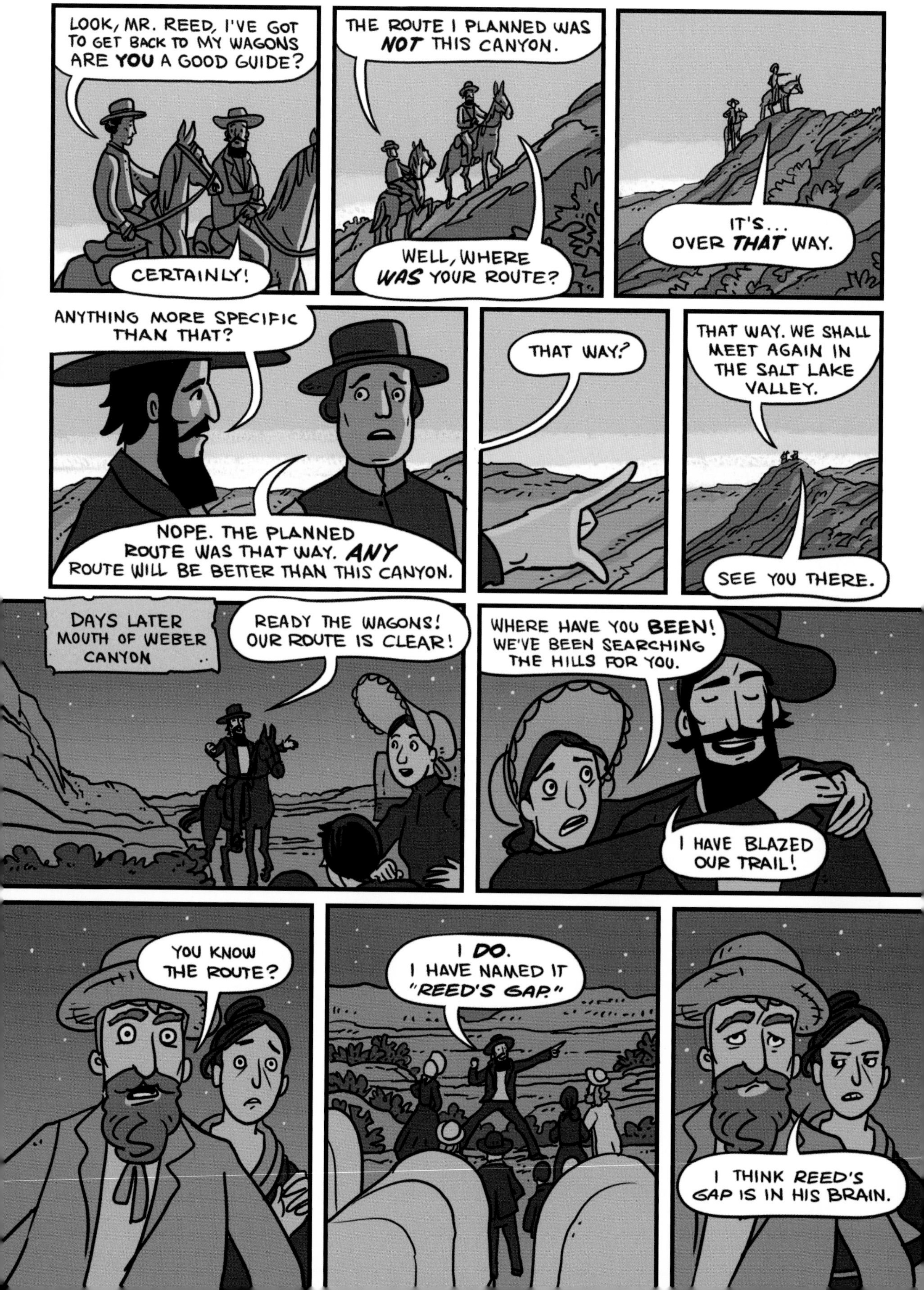

LOOK, MR. REED, I'VE GOT TO GET BACK TO MY WAGONS. ARE YOU A GOOD GUIDE?
CERTAINLY!
THE ROUTE I PLANNED WAS NOT THIS CANYON.
WELL, WHERE WAS YOUR ROUTE?
IT'S... OVER THAT WAY.
ANYTHING MORE SPECIFIC THAN THAT?
NOPE. THE PLANNED ROUTE WAS THAT WAY. ANY ROUTE WILL BE BETTER THAN THIS CANYON.
THAT WAY?
THAT WAY. WE SHALL MEET AGAIN IN THE SALT LAKE VALLEY.
SEE YOU THERE.
DAYS LATER MOUTH OF WEBER CANYON
READY THE WAGONS! OUR ROUTE IS CLEAR!
WHERE HAVE YOU BEEN! WE'VE BEEN SEARCHING THE HILLS FOR YOU.
I HAVE BLAZED OUR TRAIL!
YOU KNOW THE ROUTE?
I DO. I HAVE NAMED IT "REED'S GAP."
I THINK REED'S GAP IS IN HIS BRAIN.

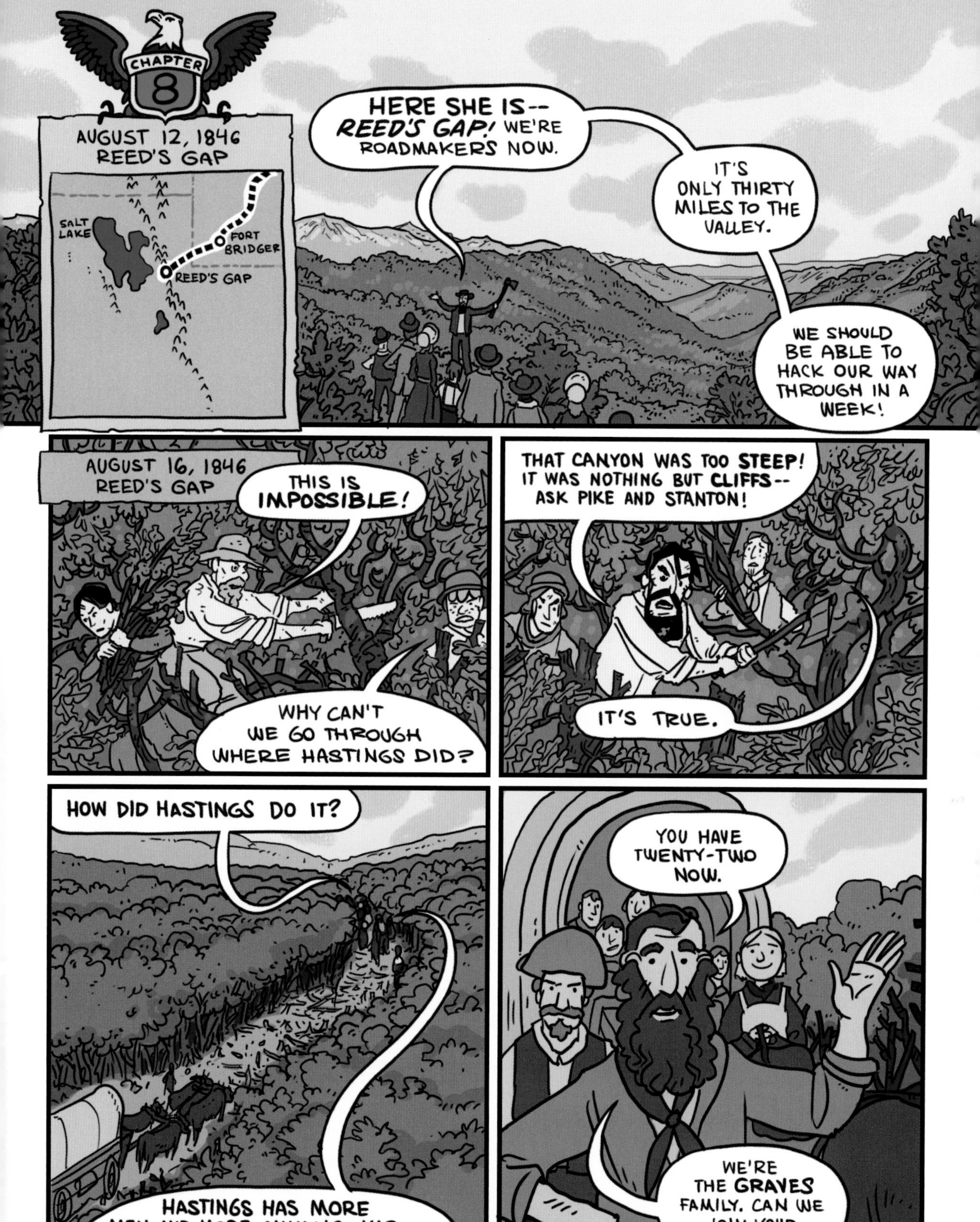
CHAPTER 8
AUGUST 12, 1846
REED'S GAP
SALT LAKE
FORT BRIDGER
REED'S GAP
HERE SHE IS-- REED'S GAP! WE'RE ROADMAKERS NOW.
IT'S ONLY THIRTY MILES TO THE VALLEY.
WE SHOULD BE ABLE TO HACK OUR WAY THROUGH IN A WEEK!
AUGUST 16, 1846
REED'S GAP
THIS IS IMPOSSIBLE!
WHY CAN'T WE GO THROUGH WHERE HASTINGS DID?
THAT CANYON WAS TOO STEEP! IT WAS NOTHING BUT CLIFFS-- ASK PIKE AND STANTON!
IT'S TRUE.
HOW DID HASTINGS DO IT?
HASTINGS HAS MORE MEN AND MORE ANIMALS. HIS PARTY IS SIXTY WAGONS STRONG! WE ONLY HAVE NINETEEN WAGONS.
YOU HAVE TWENTY-TWO NOW.
WE'RE THE GRAVES FAMILY. CAN WE JOIN YOUR PARTY?

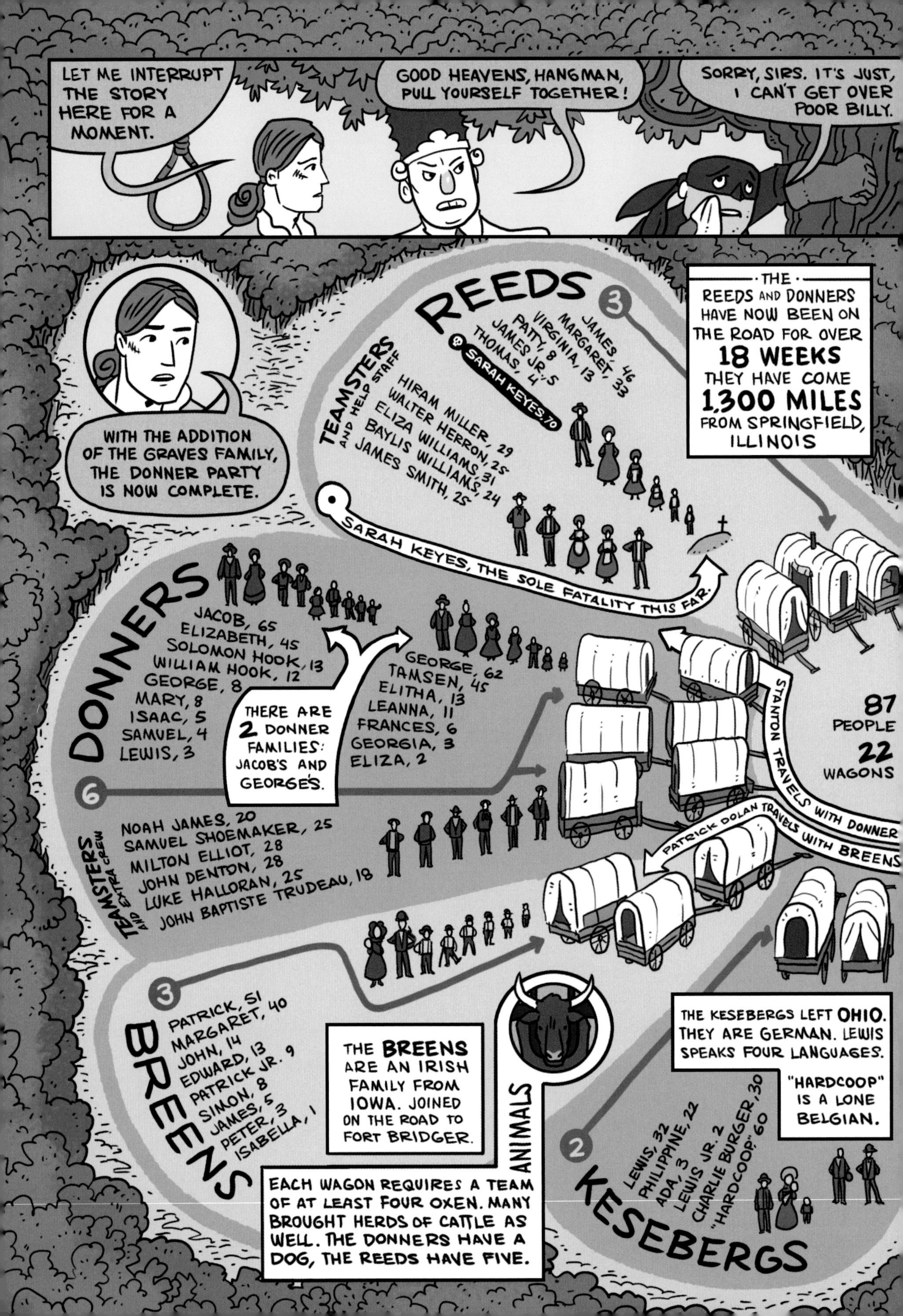

LET ME INTERRUPT THE STORY HERE FOR A MOMENT.
GOOD HEAVENS, HANGMAN, PULL YOURSELF TOGETHER!
SORRY, SIRS. IT'S JUST, I CAN'T GET OVER POOR BILLY.
WITH THE ADDITION OF THE GRAVES FAMILY, THE DONNER PARTY IS NOW COMPLETE.
THE REEDS AND DONNERS HAVE NOW BEEN ON THE ROAD FOR OVER 18 WEEKS THEY HAVE COME 1,300 MILES FROM SPRINGFIELD, ILLINOIS
REEDS
3
JAMES, 46
MARGARET, 33
VIRGINIA, 13
PATTY, 8
JAMES JR., 5
THOMAS, 4
SARAH KEYES, 70
TEAMSTERS AND HELP STAFF
HIRAM MILLER, 29
WALTER HERRON, 25
ELIZA WILLIAMS, 31
BAYLIS WILLIAMS, 24
JAMES SMITH, 25
SARAH KEYES, THE SOLE FATALITY THIS FAR.
DONNERS
6
JACOB, 65
ELIZABETH, 45
SOLOMON HOOK, 13
WILLIAM HOOK, 12
GEORGE, 8
MARY, 8
ISAAC, 5
SAMUEL, 4
LEWIS, 3
THERE ARE 2 DONNER FAMILIES: JACOB'S AND GEORGE'S.
GEORGE, 62
TAMSEN, 45
ELITHA, 13
LEANNA, 11
FRANCES, 6
GEORGIA, 3
ELIZA, 2
TEAMSTERS AND EXTRA CREW
NOAH JAMES, 20
SAMUEL SHOEMAKER, 25
MILTON ELLIOT, 28
JOHN DENTON, 28
LUKE HALLORAN, 25
JOHN BAPTISTE TRUDEAU, 18
STANTON TRAVELS WITH DONNER
PATRICK DOLAN TRAVELS WITH BREENS
87 PEOPLE
22 WAGONS
BREENS
3
PATRICK, 51
MARGARET, 40
JOHN, 14
EDWARD, 13
PATRICK JR. 9
SIMON, 8
JAMES, 5
PETER, 3
ISABELLA, 1
THE BREENS ARE AN IRISH FAMILY FROM IOWA. JOINED ON THE ROAD TO FORT BRIDGER.
ANIMALS
EACH WAGON REQUIRES A TEAM OF AT LEAST FOUR OXEN. MANY BROUGHT HERDS OF CATTLE AS WELL. THE DONNERS HAVE A DOG, THE REEDS HAVE FIVE.
THE KESEBERGS LEFT OHIO. THEY ARE GERMAN. LEWIS SPEAKS FOUR LANGUAGES.
"HARDCOOP" IS A LONE BELGIAN.
KESEBERGS
2
LEWIS, 32
PHILIPPINE, 22
ADA, 3
LEWIS JR. 2
CHARLIE BURGER, 30
"HARDCOOP," 60

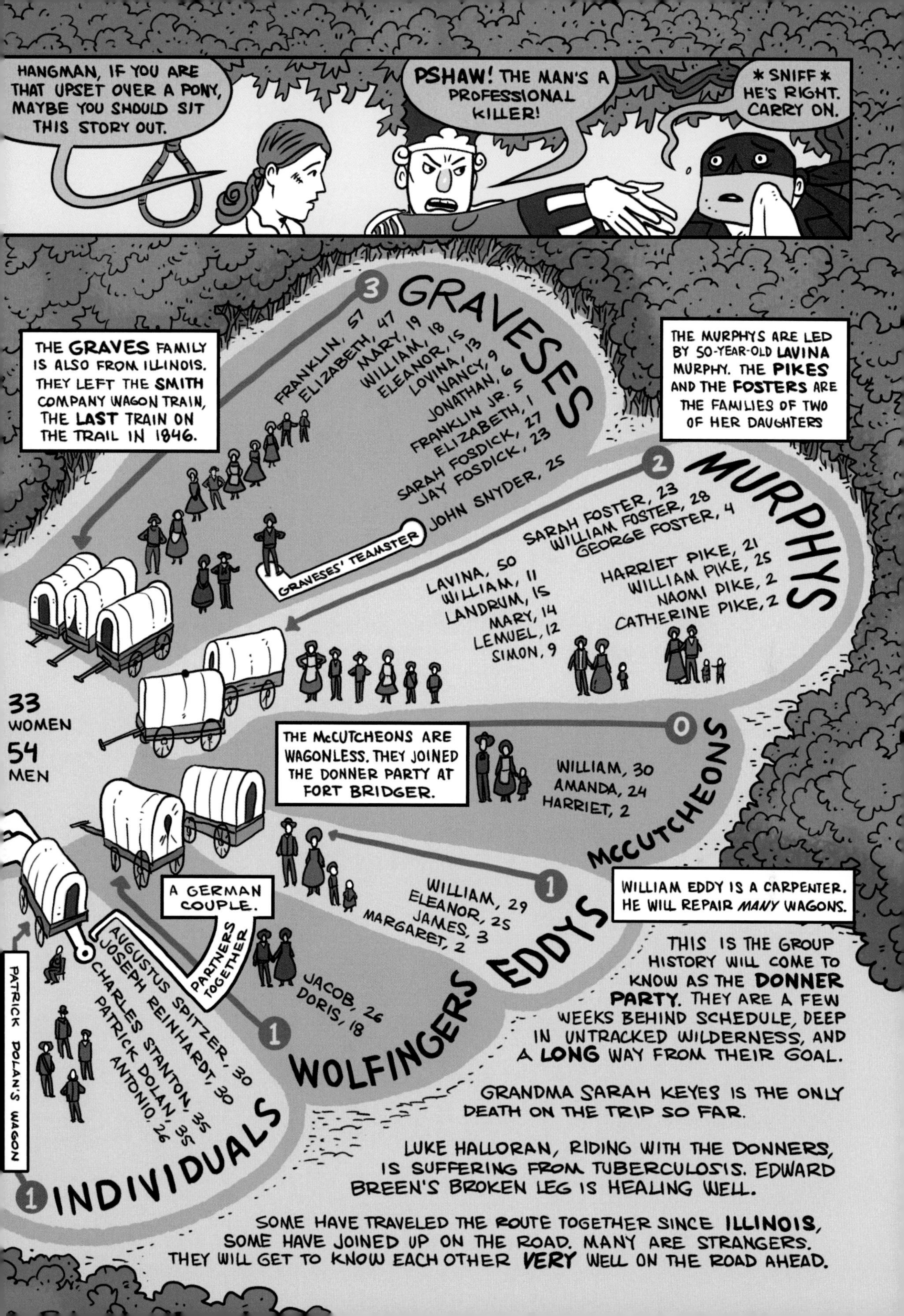

HANGMAN, IF YOU ARE THAT UPSET OVER A PONY, MAYBE YOU SHOULD SIT THIS STORY OUT.
PSHAW! THE MAN'S A PROFESSIONAL KILLER!
SNIFF HE'S RIGHT. CARRY ON.
THE GRAVES FAMILY IS ALSO FROM ILLINOIS. THEY LEFT THE SMITH COMPANY WAGON TRAIN, THE LAST TRAIN ON THE TRAIL IN 1846.
3 GRAVESES
FRANKLIN, 57
ELIZABETH, 47
MARY, 19
WILLIAM, 18
ELEANOR, 15
LOVINA, 13
NANCY, 9
JONATHAN, 6
FRANKLIN JR. 5
ELIZABETH, 1
SARAH FOSDICK, 27
JAY FOSDICK, 23
JOHN SNYDER, 25
GRAVESES' TEAMSTER
THE MURPHYS ARE LED BY 50-YEAR-OLD LAVINA MURPHY. THE PIKES AND THE FOSTERS ARE THE FAMILIES OF TWO OF HER DAUGHTERS
2 MURPHYS
SARAH FOSTER, 23
WILLIAM FOSTER, 28
GEORGE FOSTER, 4
LAVINA, 50
WILLIAM, 11
LANDRUM, 15
MARY, 14
LEMUEL, 12
SIMON, 9
HARRIET PIKE, 21
WILLIAM PIKE, 25
NAOMI PIKE, 2
CATHERINE PIKE, 2
33 WOMEN
54 MEN
THE McCUTCHEONS ARE WAGONLESS. THEY JOINED THE DONNER PARTY AT FORT BRIDGER.
0 McCUTCHEONS
WILLIAM, 30
AMANDA, 24
HARRIET, 2
WILLIAM EDDY IS A CARPENTER. HE WILL REPAIR MANY WAGONS.
1 EDDYS
WILLIAM, 29
ELEANOR, 25
JAMES, 3
MARGARET, 2
A GERMAN COUPLE.
1 WOLFINGERS
JACOB, 26
DORIS, 18
PARTNERS TOGETHER
AUGUSTUS SPITZER, 30
JOSEPH REINHARDT, 30
CHARLES STANTON, 35
PATRICK DOLAN, 35
ANTONIO, 26
PATRICK DOLAN'S WAGON
1 INDIVIDUALS
THIS IS THE GROUP HISTORY WILL COME TO KNOW AS THE DONNER PARTY. THEY ARE A FEW WEEKS BEHIND SCHEDULE, DEEP IN UNTRACKED WILDERNESS, AND A LONG WAY FROM THEIR GOAL.
GRANDMA SARAH KEYES IS THE ONLY DEATH ON THE TRIP SO FAR.
LUKE HALLORAN, RIDING WITH THE DONNERS, IS SUFFERING FROM TUBERCULOSIS. EDWARD BREEN'S BROKEN LEG IS HEALING WELL.
SOME HAVE TRAVELED THE ROUTE TOGETHER SINCE ILLINOIS, SOME HAVE JOINED UP ON THE ROAD. MANY ARE STRANGERS. THEY WILL GET TO KNOW EACH OTHER VERY WELL ON THE ROAD AHEAD.

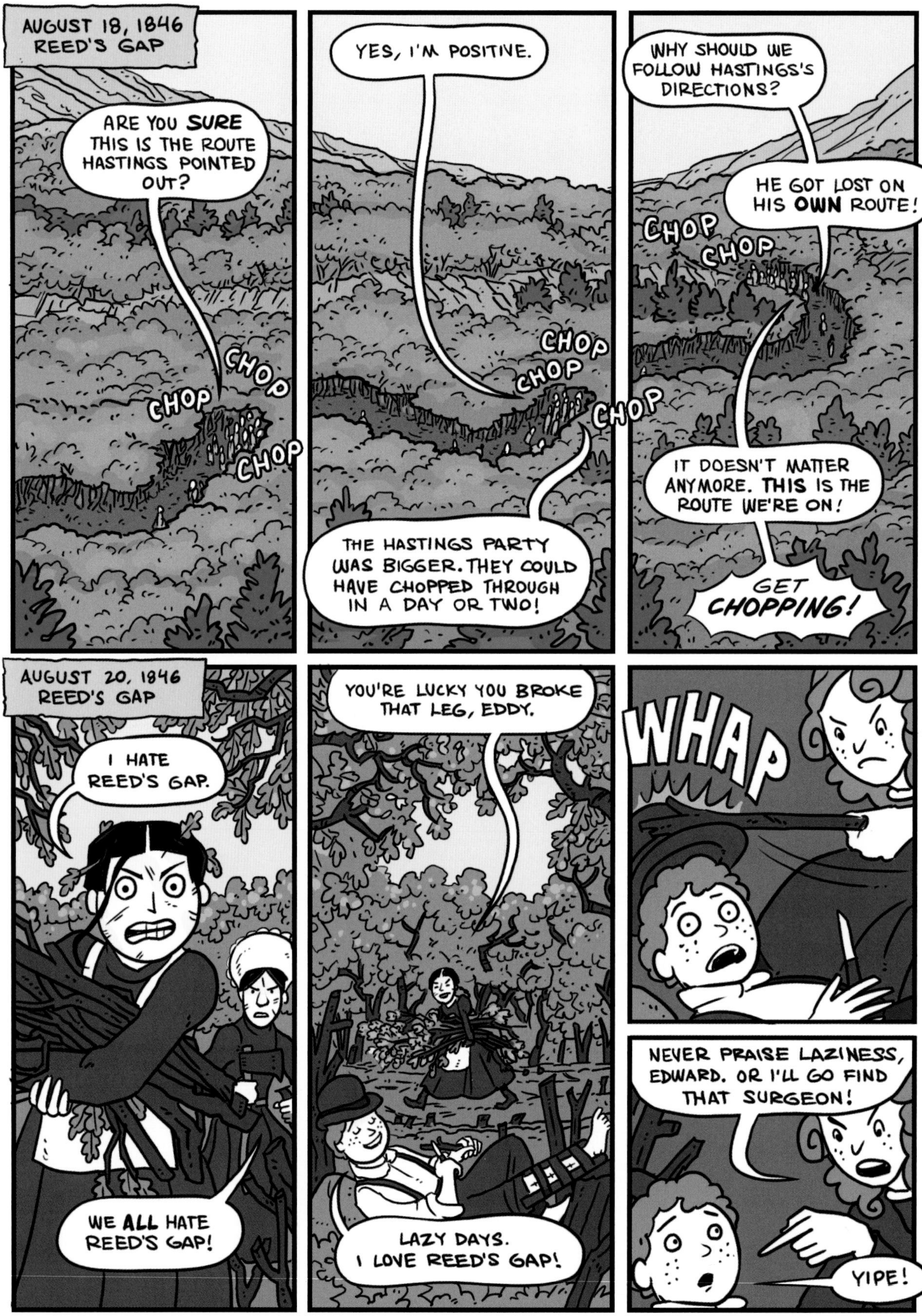

AUGUST 18, 1846
REED'S GAP
ARE YOU **SURE** THIS IS THE ROUTE HASTINGS POINTED OUT?
CHOP
CHOP
CHOP
YES, I'M POSITIVE.
CHOP
CHOP
CHOP
THE HASTINGS PARTY WAS BIGGER. THEY COULD HAVE CHOPPED THROUGH IN A DAY OR TWO!
WHY SHOULD WE FOLLOW HASTINGS'S DIRECTIONS?
HE GOT LOST ON HIS **OWN** ROUTE!
CHOP
CHOP
IT DOESN'T MATTER ANYMORE. **THIS** IS THE ROUTE WE'RE ON!
GET **CHOPPING!**
AUGUST 20, 1846
REED'S GAP
I HATE REED'S GAP.
WE **ALL** HATE REED'S GAP!
YOU'RE LUCKY YOU BROKE THAT LEG, EDDY.
LAZY DAYS. I LOVE REED'S GAP!
WHAP
NEVER PRAISE LAZINESS, EDWARD. OR I'LL GO FIND THAT SURGEON!
YIPE!

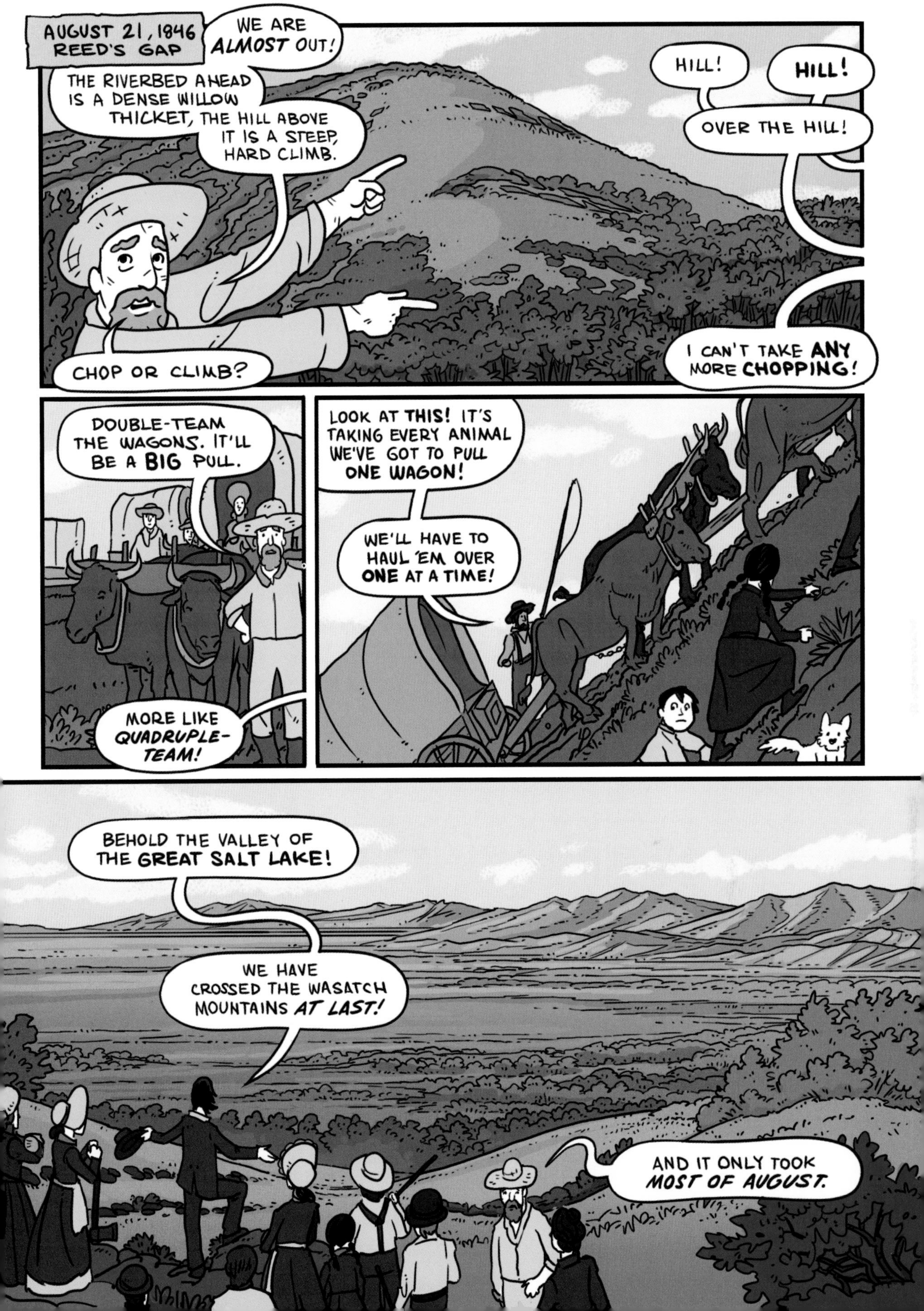
AUGUST 21, 1846
REED'S GAP
WE ARE *ALMOST* OUT!
THE RIVERBED AHEAD IS A DENSE WILLOW THICKET, THE HILL ABOVE IT IS A STEEP, HARD CLIMB.
CHOP OR CLIMB?
HILL!
HILL!
OVER THE HILL!
I CAN'T TAKE **ANY** MORE **CHOPPING**!
DOUBLE-TEAM THE WAGONS. IT'LL BE A **BIG** PULL.
MORE LIKE *QUADRUPLE-TEAM!*
LOOK AT **THIS!** IT'S TAKING EVERY ANIMAL WE'VE GOT TO PULL **ONE WAGON!**
WE'LL HAVE TO HAUL 'EM OVER **ONE** AT A TIME!
BEHOLD THE VALLEY OF THE **GREAT SALT LAKE!**
WE HAVE CROSSED THE WASATCH MOUNTAINS *AT LAST!*
AND IT ONLY TOOK *MOST OF AUGUST.*

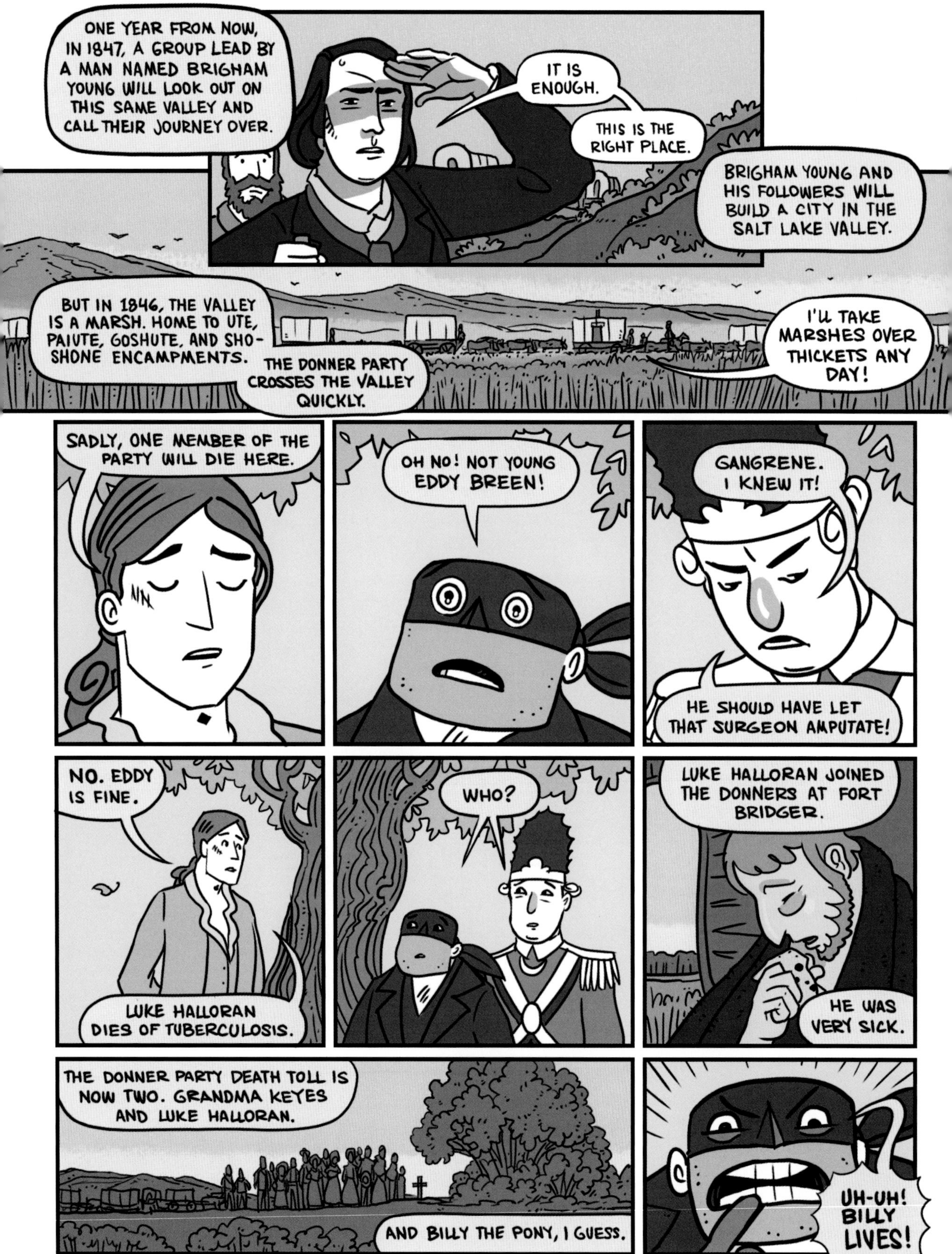
ONE YEAR FROM NOW, IN 1847, A GROUP LEAD BY A MAN NAMED BRIGHAM YOUNG WILL LOOK OUT ON THIS SAME VALLEY AND CALL THEIR JOURNEY OVER.
IT IS ENOUGH.
THIS IS THE RIGHT PLACE.
BRIGHAM YOUNG AND HIS FOLLOWERS WILL BUILD A CITY IN THE SALT LAKE VALLEY.
BUT IN 1846, THE VALLEY IS A MARSH. HOME TO UTE, PAIUTE, GOSHUTE, AND SHOSHONE ENCAMPMENTS.
THE DONNER PARTY CROSSES THE VALLEY QUICKLY.
I'LL TAKE MARSHES OVER THICKETS ANY DAY!
SADLY, ONE MEMBER OF THE PARTY WILL DIE HERE.
OH NO! NOT YOUNG EDDY BREEN!
GANGRENE. I KNEW IT!
HE SHOULD HAVE LET THAT SURGEON AMPUTATE!
NO. EDDY IS FINE.
LUKE HALLORAN DIES OF TUBERCULOSIS.
WHO?
LUKE HALLORAN JOINED THE DONNERS AT FORT BRIDGER.
HE WAS VERY SICK.
THE DONNER PARTY DEATH TOLL IS NOW TWO. GRANDMA KEYES AND LUKE HALLORAN.
AND BILLY THE PONY, I GUESS.
UH-UH! BILLY LIVES!

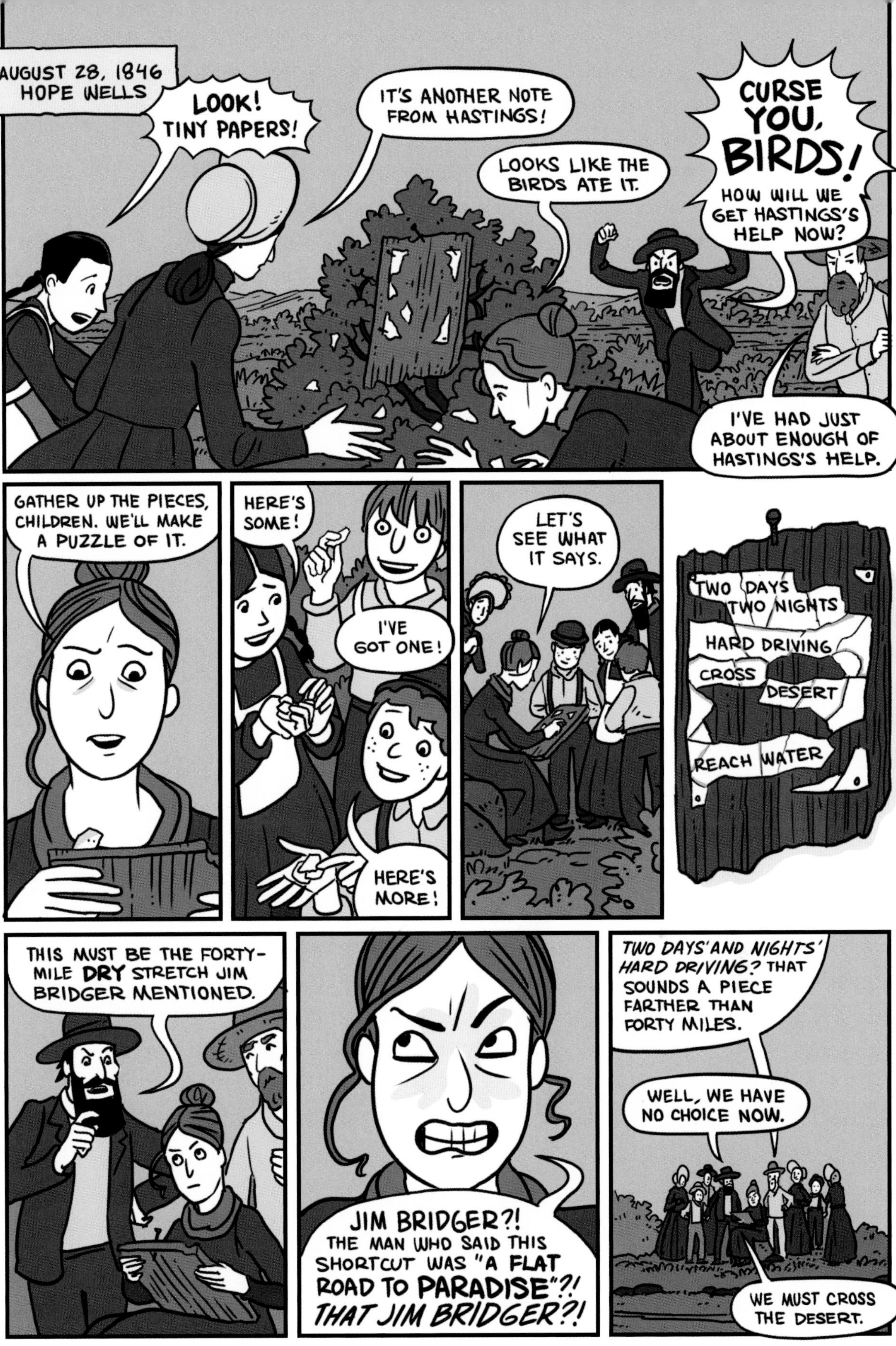

AUGUST 28, 1846
HOPE WELLS
LOOK! TINY PAPERS!
IT'S ANOTHER NOTE FROM HASTINGS!
LOOKS LIKE THE BIRDS ATE IT.
CURSE YOU, BIRDS!
HOW WILL WE GET HASTINGS'S HELP NOW?
I'VE HAD JUST ABOUT ENOUGH OF HASTINGS'S HELP.
GATHER UP THE PIECES, CHILDREN. WE'LL MAKE A PUZZLE OF IT.
HERE'S SOME!
I'VE GOT ONE!
HERE'S MORE!
LET'S SEE WHAT IT SAYS.
TWO DAYS TWO NIGHTS
HARD DRIVING
CROSS DESERT
REACH WATER
THIS MUST BE THE FORTY-MILE DRY STRETCH JIM BRIDGER MENTIONED.
JIM BRIDGER?! THE MAN WHO SAID THIS SHORTCUT WAS "A FLAT ROAD TO PARADISE"?! THAT JIM BRIDGER?!
TWO DAYS' AND NIGHTS' HARD DRIVING? THAT SOUNDS A PIECE FARTHER THAN FORTY MILES.
WELL, WE HAVE NO CHOICE NOW.
WE MUST CROSS THE DESERT.

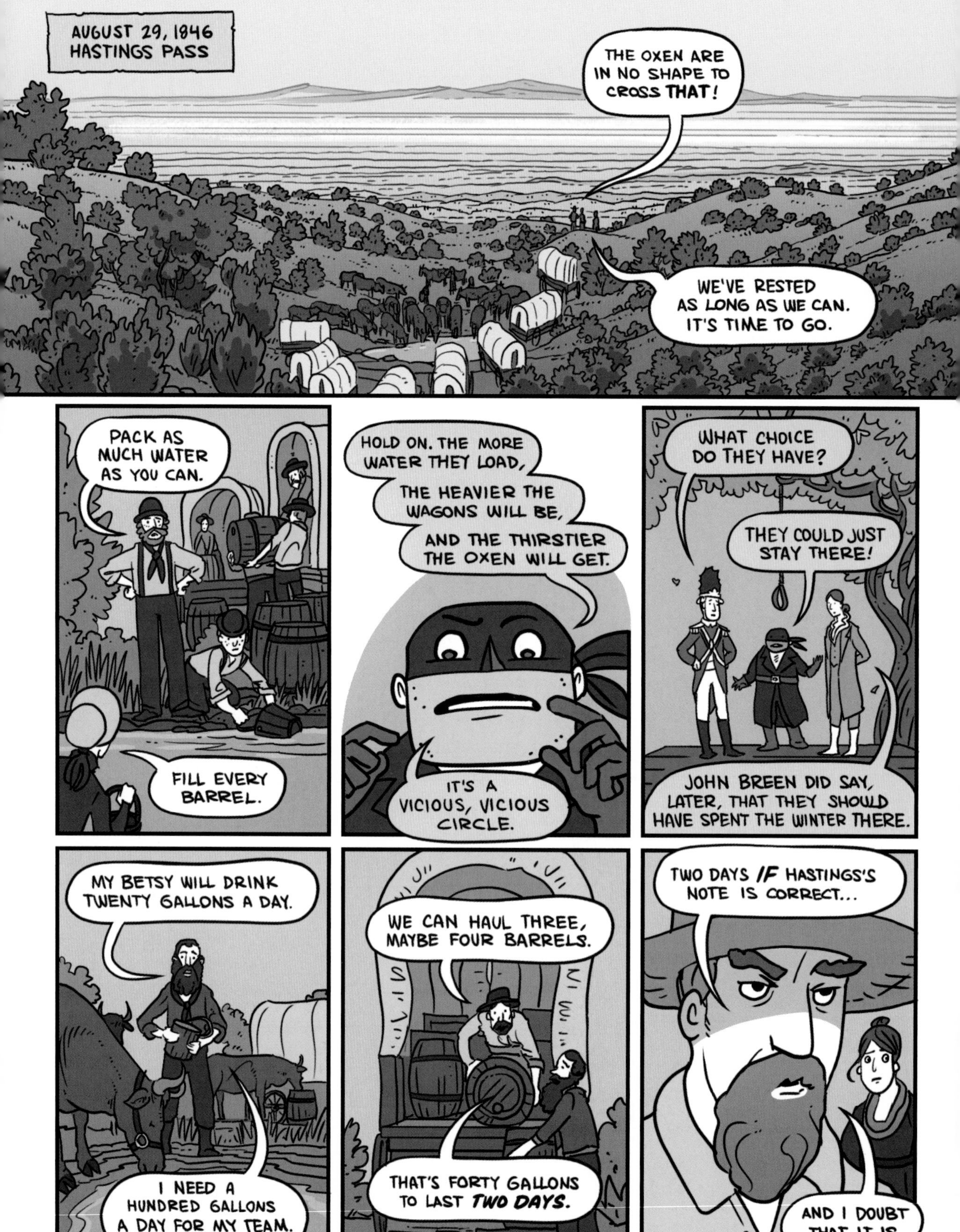
AUGUST 29, 1846
HASTINGS PASS
THE OXEN ARE IN NO SHAPE TO CROSS THAT!
WE'VE RESTED AS LONG AS WE CAN. IT'S TIME TO GO.
PACK AS MUCH WATER AS YOU CAN.
FILL EVERY BARREL.
HOLD ON. THE MORE WATER THEY LOAD,
THE HEAVIER THE WAGONS WILL BE,
AND THE THIRSTIER THE OXEN WILL GET.
IT'S A VICIOUS, VICIOUS CIRCLE.
WHAT CHOICE DO THEY HAVE?
THEY COULD JUST STAY THERE!
JOHN BREEN DID SAY, LATER, THAT THEY SHOULD HAVE SPENT THE WINTER THERE.
MY BETSY WILL DRINK TWENTY GALLONS A DAY.
I NEED A HUNDRED GALLONS A DAY FOR MY TEAM.
WE CAN HAUL THREE, MAYBE FOUR BARRELS.
THAT'S FORTY GALLONS TO LAST TWO DAYS.
TWO DAYS IF HASTINGS'S NOTE IS CORRECT...
AND I DOUBT THAT IT IS.

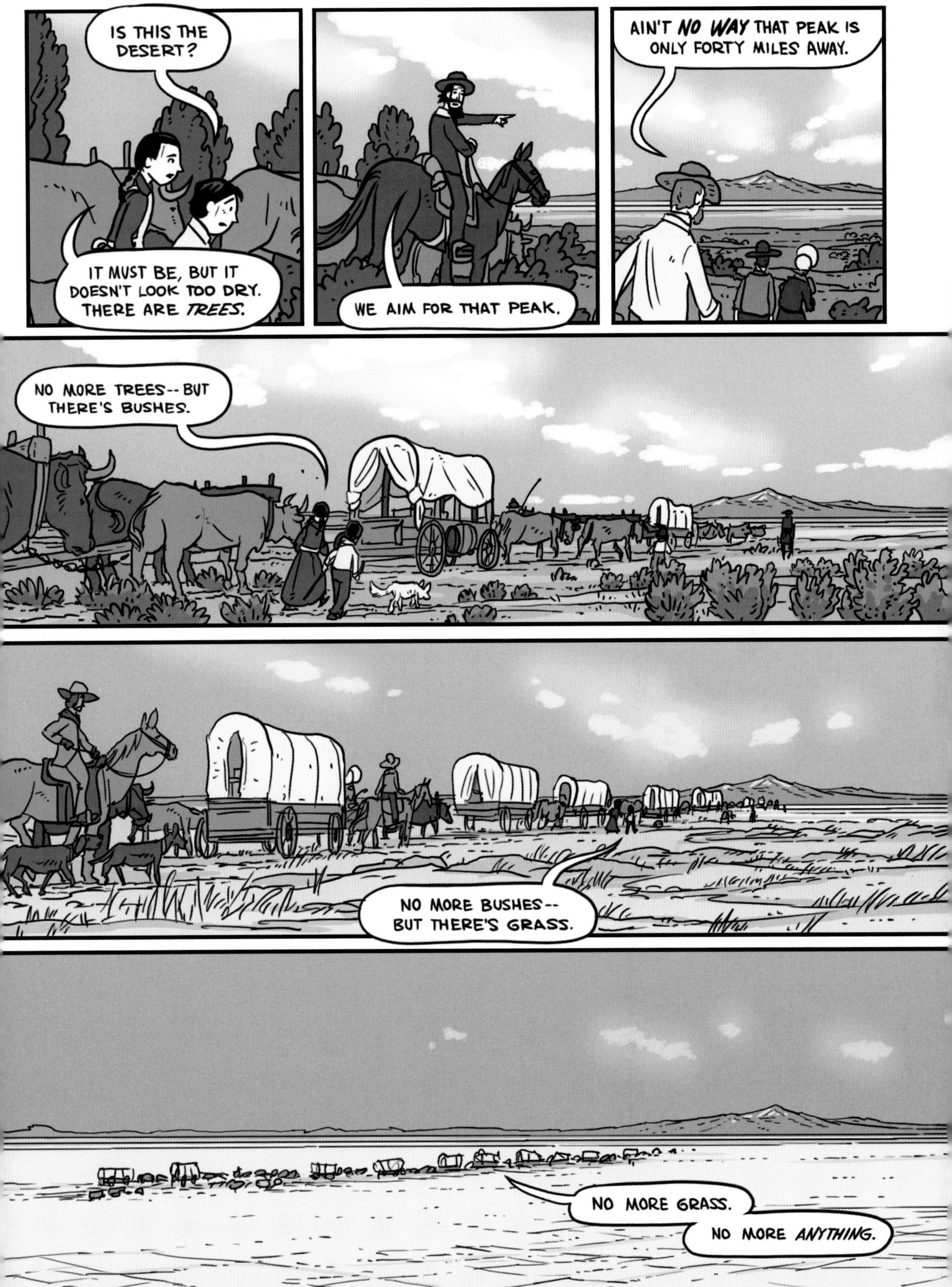
IS THIS THE DESERT?
IT MUST BE, BUT IT DOESN'T LOOK TOO DRY. THERE ARE *TREES*.
WE AIM FOR THAT PEAK.
AIN'T ***NO WAY*** THAT PEAK IS ONLY FORTY MILES AWAY.
NO MORE TREES-- BUT THERE'S BUSHES.
NO MORE BUSHES-- BUT THERE'S GRASS.
NO MORE GRASS.
NO MORE *ANYTHING*.

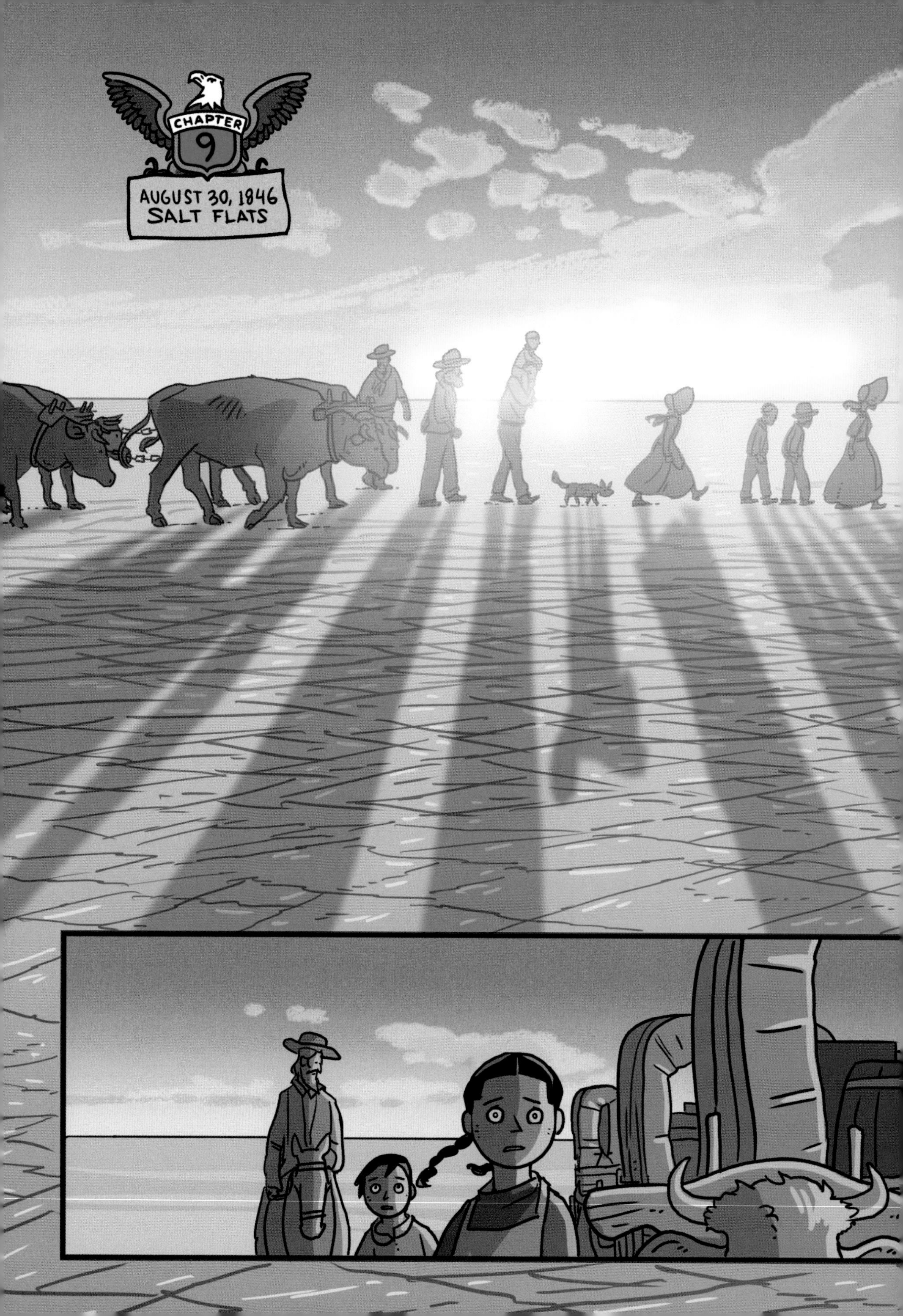
CHAPTER
9
AUGUST 30, 1846
SALT FLATS

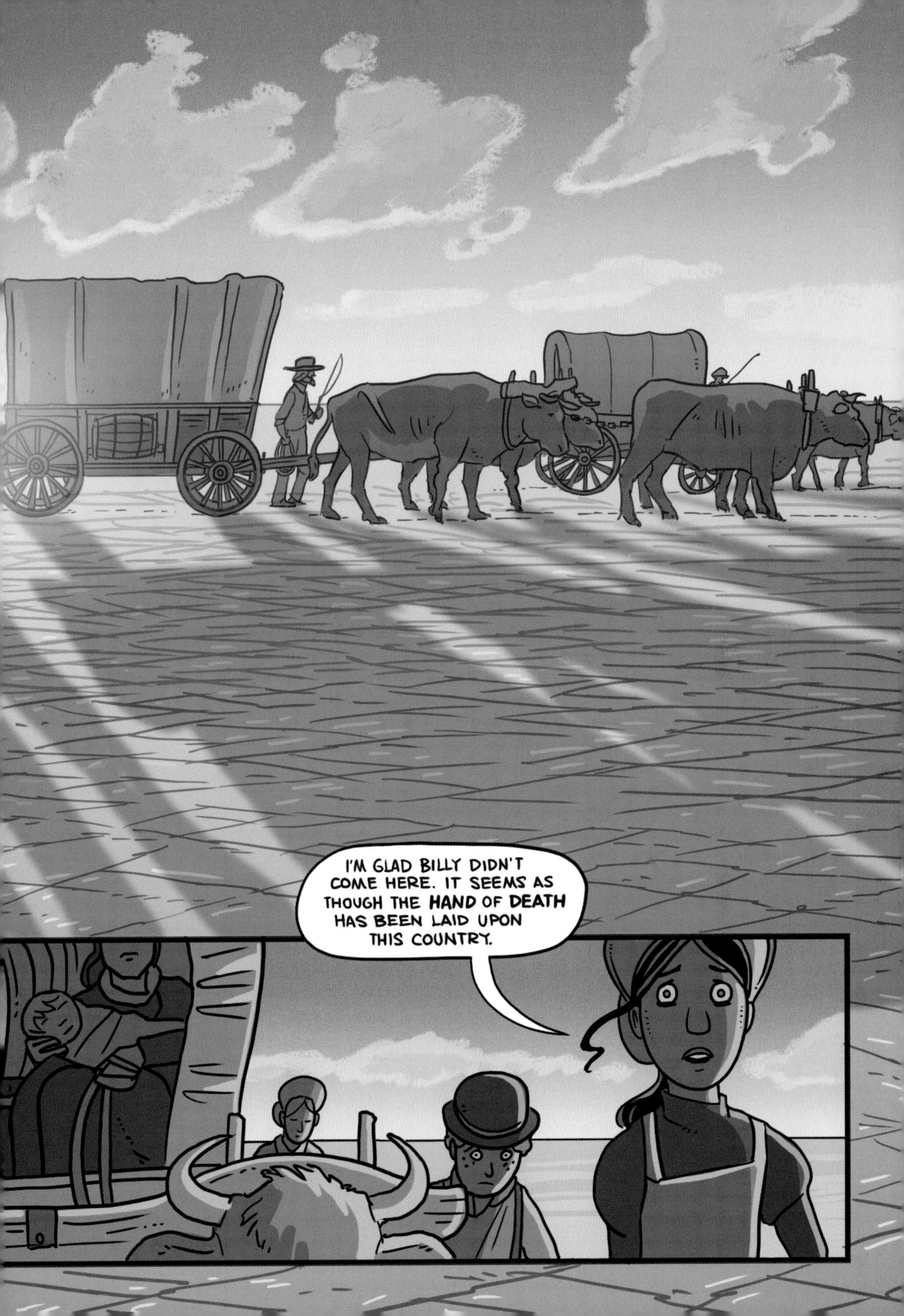
I'M GLAD BILLY DIDN'T COME HERE. IT SEEMS AS THOUGH THE HAND OF DEATH HAS BEEN LAID UPON THIS COUNTRY.

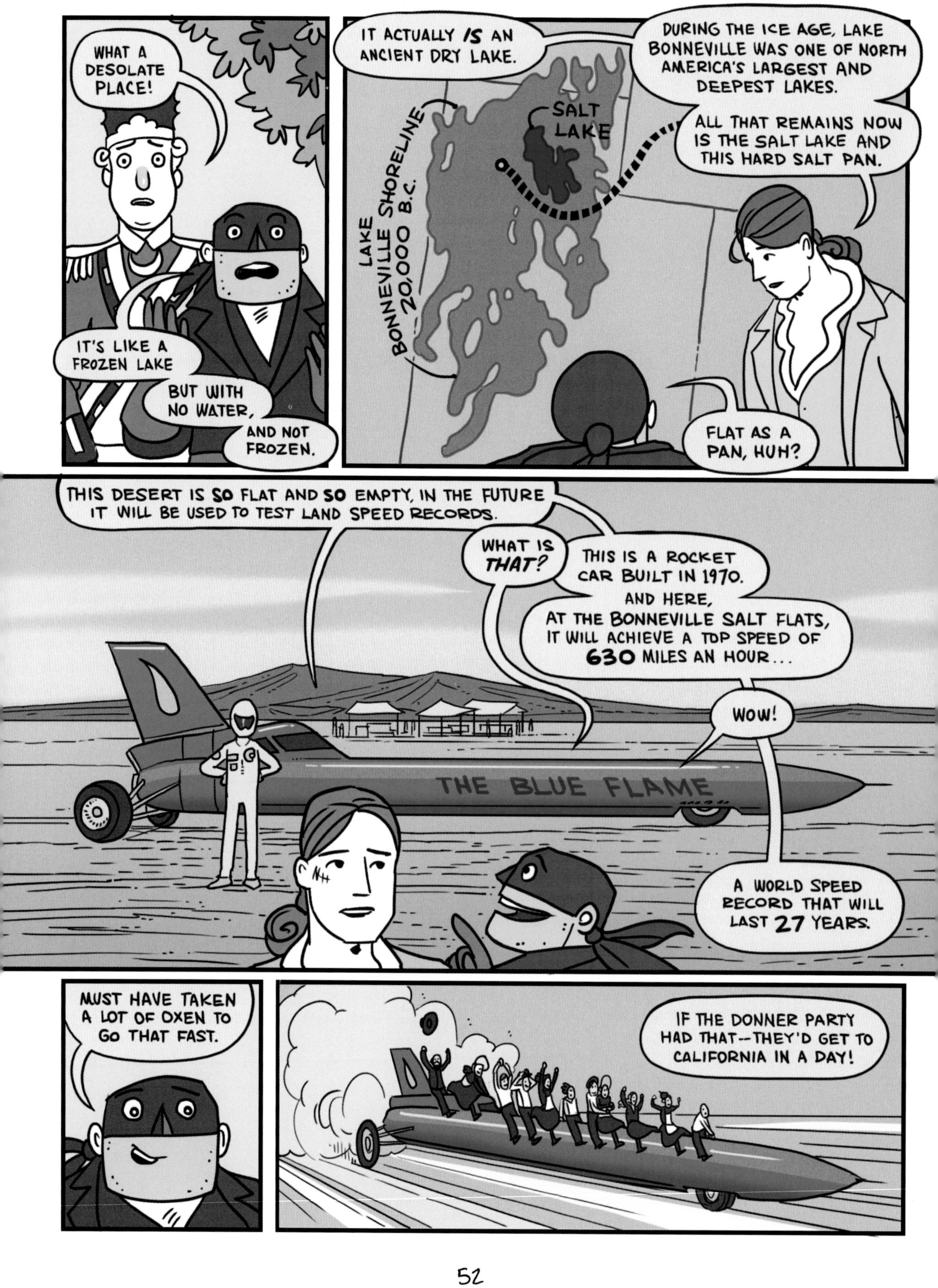
WHAT A DESOLATE PLACE!
IT'S LIKE A FROZEN LAKE
BUT WITH NO WATER,
AND NOT FROZEN.
IT ACTUALLY IS AN ANCIENT DRY LAKE.
DURING THE ICE AGE, LAKE BONNEVILLE WAS ONE OF NORTH AMERICA'S LARGEST AND DEEPEST LAKES.
SALT LAKE
LAKE BONNEVILLE SHORELINE 20,000 B.C.
ALL THAT REMAINS NOW IS THE SALT LAKE AND THIS HARD SALT PAN.
FLAT AS A PAN, HUH?
THIS DESERT IS SO FLAT AND SO EMPTY, IN THE FUTURE IT WILL BE USED TO TEST LAND SPEED RECORDS.
WHAT IS THAT?
THIS IS A ROCKET CAR BUILT IN 1970.
AND HERE, AT THE BONNEVILLE SALT FLATS, IT WILL ACHIEVE A TOP SPEED OF 630 MILES AN HOUR...
WOW!
THE BLUE FLAME
A WORLD SPEED RECORD THAT WILL LAST 27 YEARS.
MUST HAVE TAKEN A LOT OF OXEN TO GO THAT FAST.
IF THE DONNER PARTY HAD THAT--THEY'D GET TO CALIFORNIA IN A DAY!

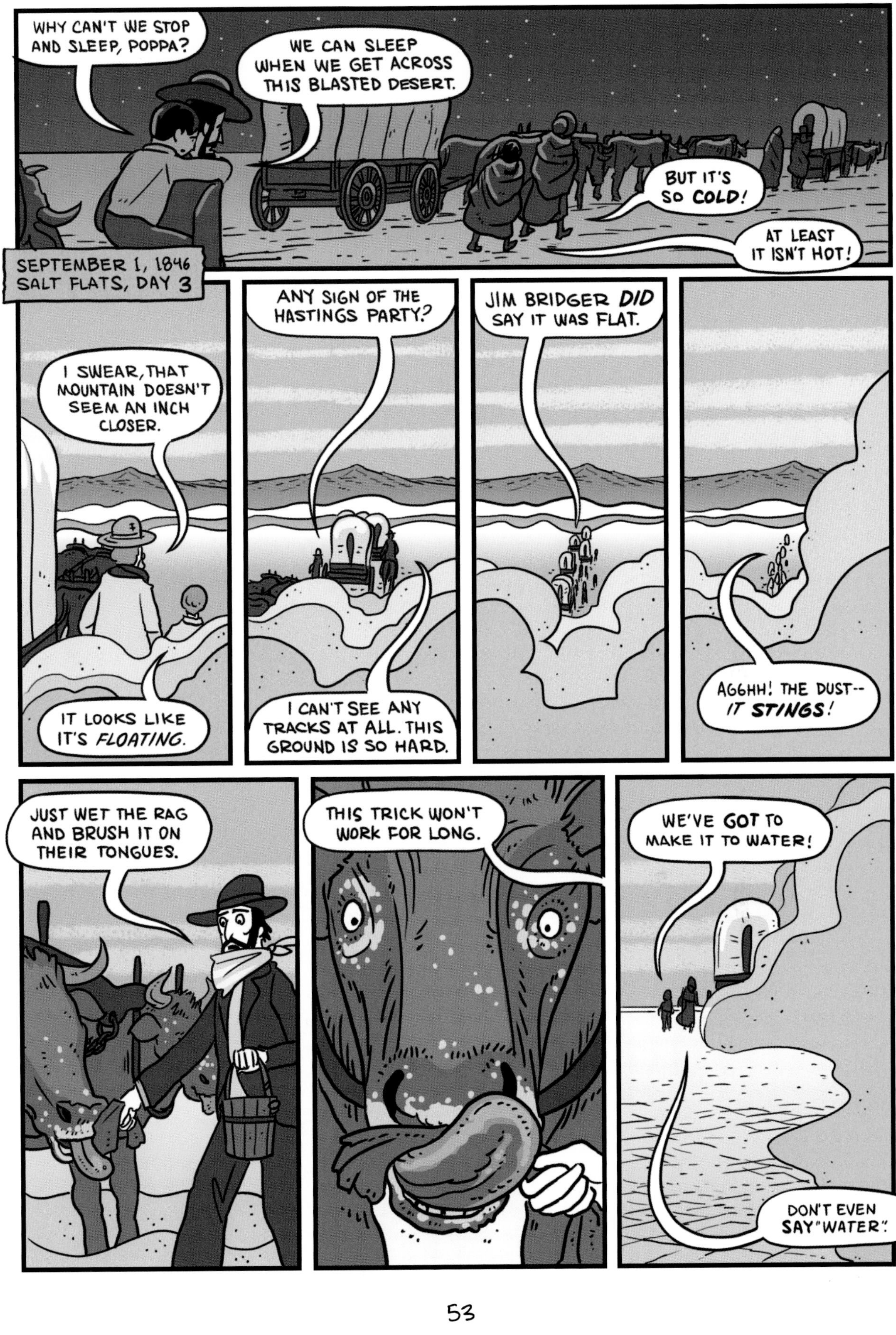
WHY CAN'T WE STOP AND SLEEP, POPPA?
WE CAN SLEEP WHEN WE GET ACROSS THIS BLASTED DESERT.
BUT IT'S SO **COLD**!
AT LEAST IT ISN'T HOT!
SEPTEMBER 1, 1846 SALT FLATS, DAY 3
I SWEAR, THAT MOUNTAIN DOESN'T SEEM AN INCH CLOSER.
IT LOOKS LIKE IT'S *FLOATING*.
ANY SIGN OF THE HASTINGS PARTY?
I CAN'T SEE ANY TRACKS AT ALL. THIS GROUND IS SO HARD.
JIM BRIDGER ***DID*** SAY IT WAS FLAT.
AGGHH! THE DUST-- *IT* ***STINGS***!
JUST WET THE RAG AND BRUSH IT ON THEIR TONGUES.
THIS TRICK WON'T WORK FOR LONG.
WE'VE **GOT** TO MAKE IT TO WATER!
DON'T EVEN **SAY** "WATER".

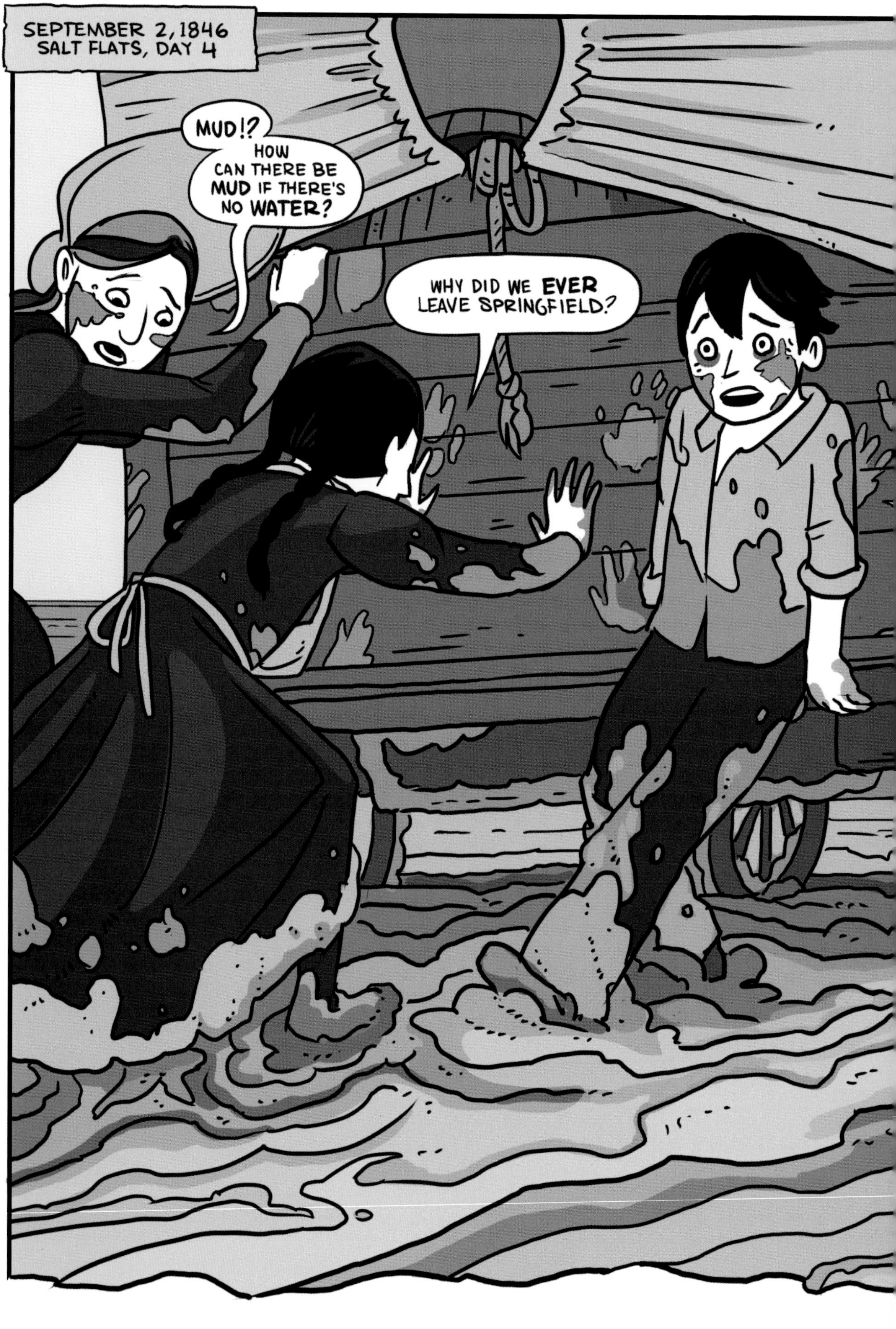
SEPTEMBER 2, 1846
SALT FLATS, DAY 4
MUD!? HOW CAN THERE BE MUD IF THERE'S NO WATER?
WHY DID WE EVER LEAVE SPRINGFIELD?

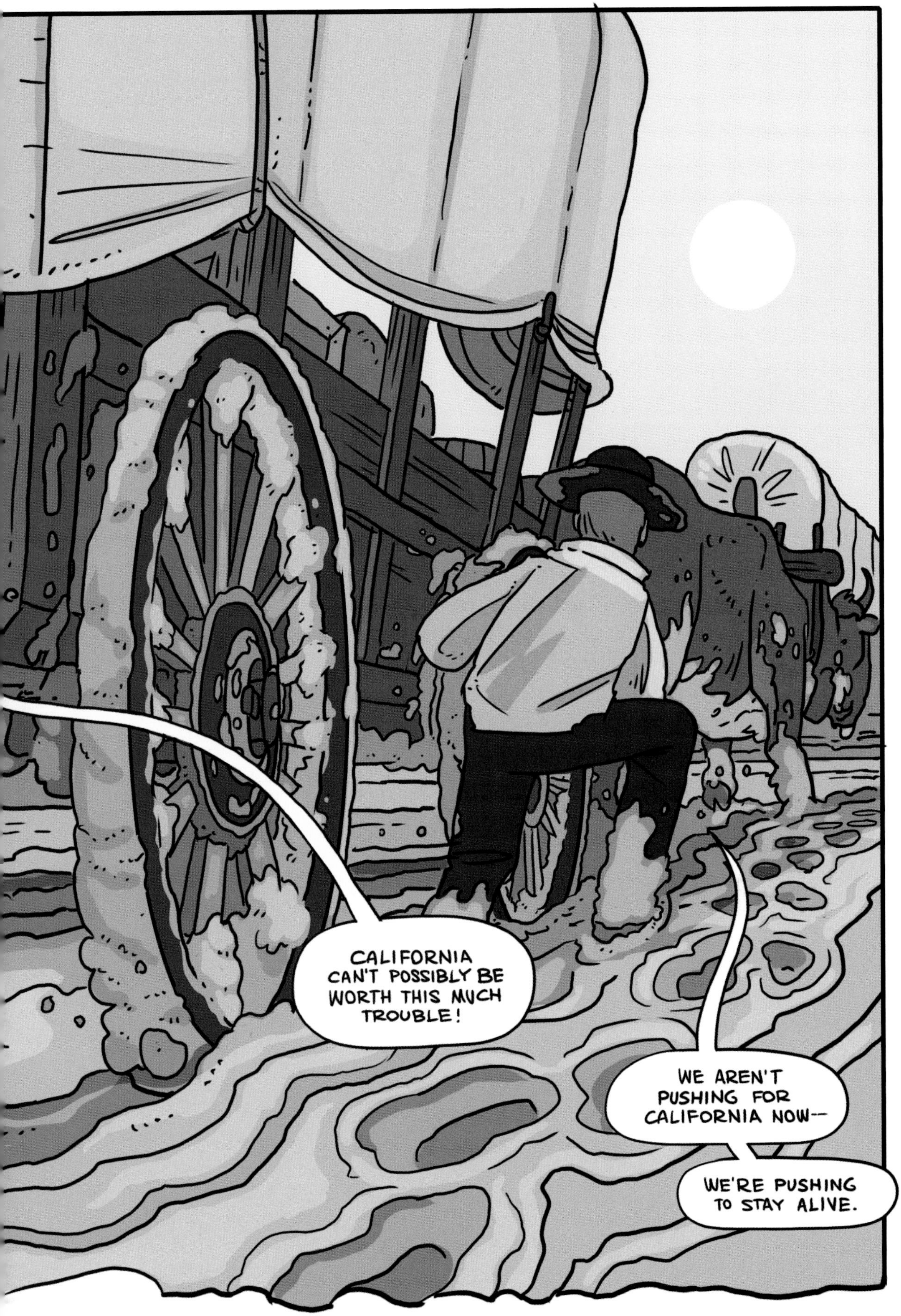
CALIFORNIA CAN'T POSSIBLY BE WORTH THIS MUCH TROUBLE!
WE AREN'T PUSHING FOR CALIFORNIA NOW--
WE'RE PUSHING TO STAY ALIVE.

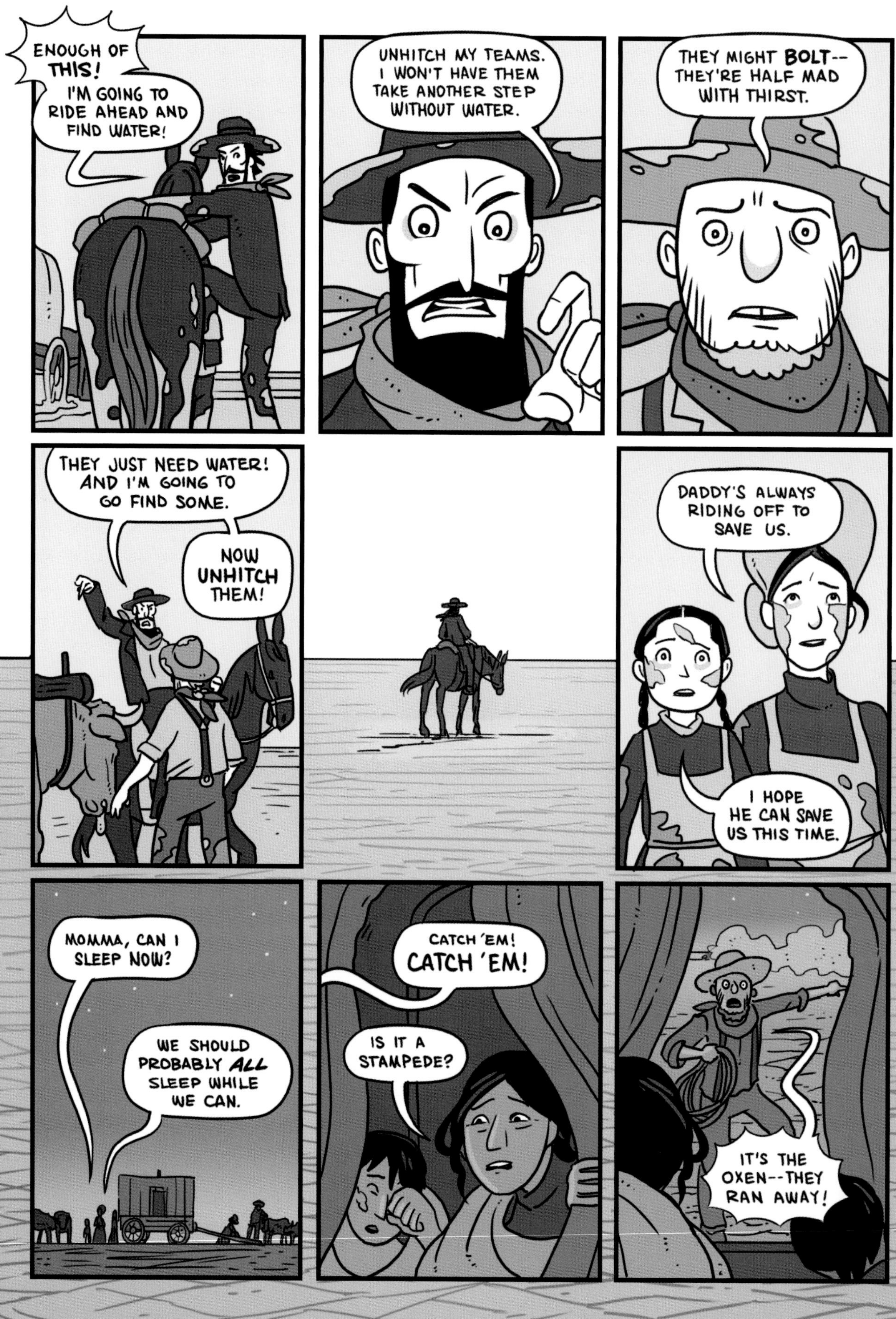
ENOUGH OF THIS!
I'M GOING TO RIDE AHEAD AND FIND WATER!
UNHITCH MY TEAMS. I WON'T HAVE THEM TAKE ANOTHER STEP WITHOUT WATER.
THEY MIGHT BOLT-- THEY'RE HALF MAD WITH THIRST.
THEY JUST NEED WATER! AND I'M GOING TO GO FIND SOME.
NOW UNHITCH THEM!
DADDY'S ALWAYS RIDING OFF TO SAVE US.
I HOPE HE CAN SAVE US THIS TIME.
MOMMA, CAN I SLEEP NOW?
WE SHOULD PROBABLY ALL SLEEP WHILE WE CAN.
CATCH 'EM! CATCH 'EM!
IS IT A STAMPEDE?
IT'S THE OXEN--THEY RAN AWAY!

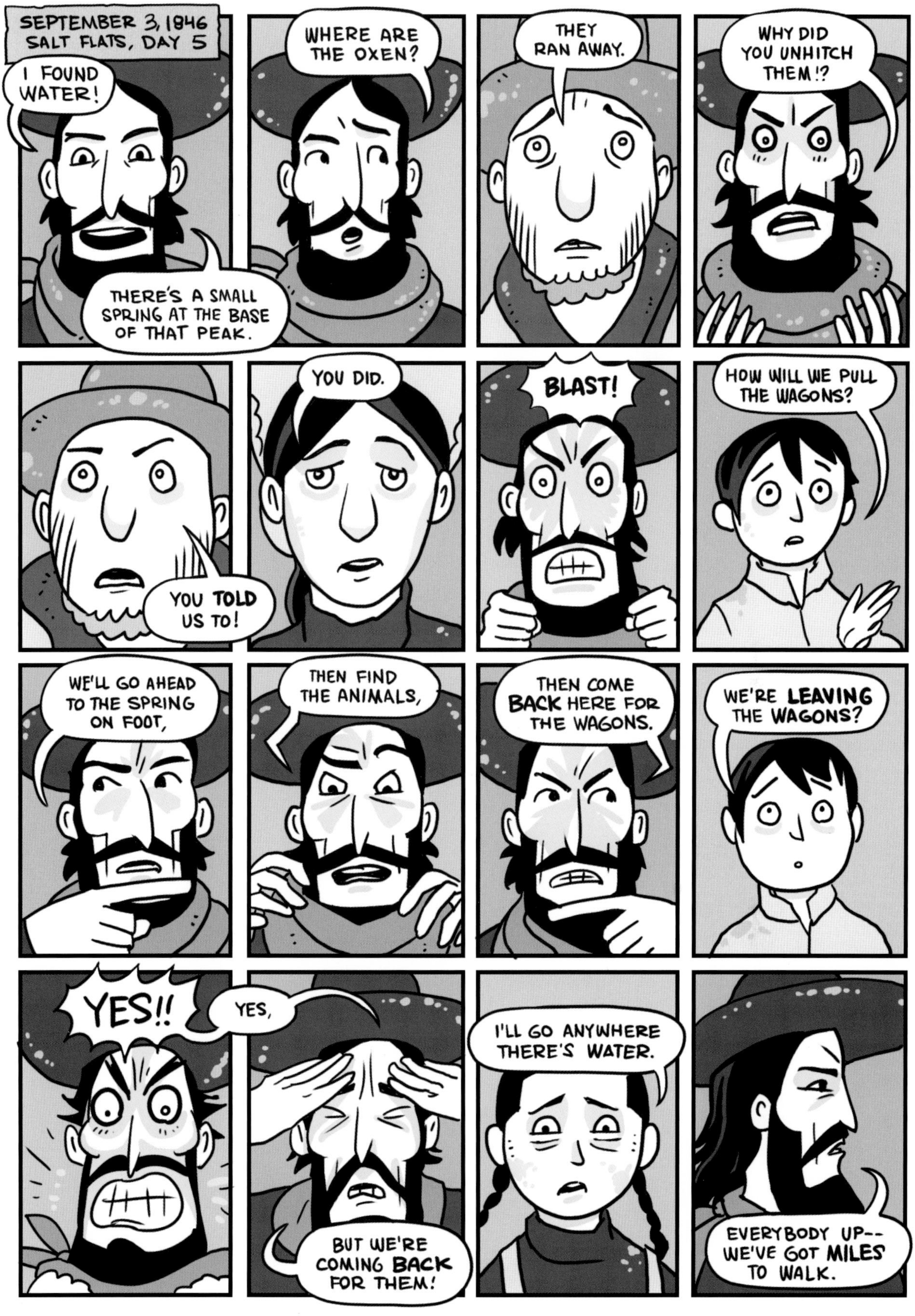
SEPTEMBER 3, 1846
SALT FLATS, DAY 5
I FOUND WATER!
THERE'S A SMALL SPRING AT THE BASE OF THAT PEAK.
WHERE ARE THE OXEN?
THEY RAN AWAY.
WHY DID YOU UNHITCH THEM!?
YOU TOLD US TO!
YOU DID.
BLAST!
HOW WILL WE PULL THE WAGONS?
WE'LL GO AHEAD TO THE SPRING ON FOOT,
THEN FIND THE ANIMALS,
THEN COME BACK HERE FOR THE WAGONS.
WE'RE LEAVING THE WAGONS?
YES!!
YES,
BUT WE'RE COMING BACK FOR THEM!
I'LL GO ANYWHERE THERE'S WATER.
EVERYBODY UP-- WE'VE GOT MILES TO WALK.

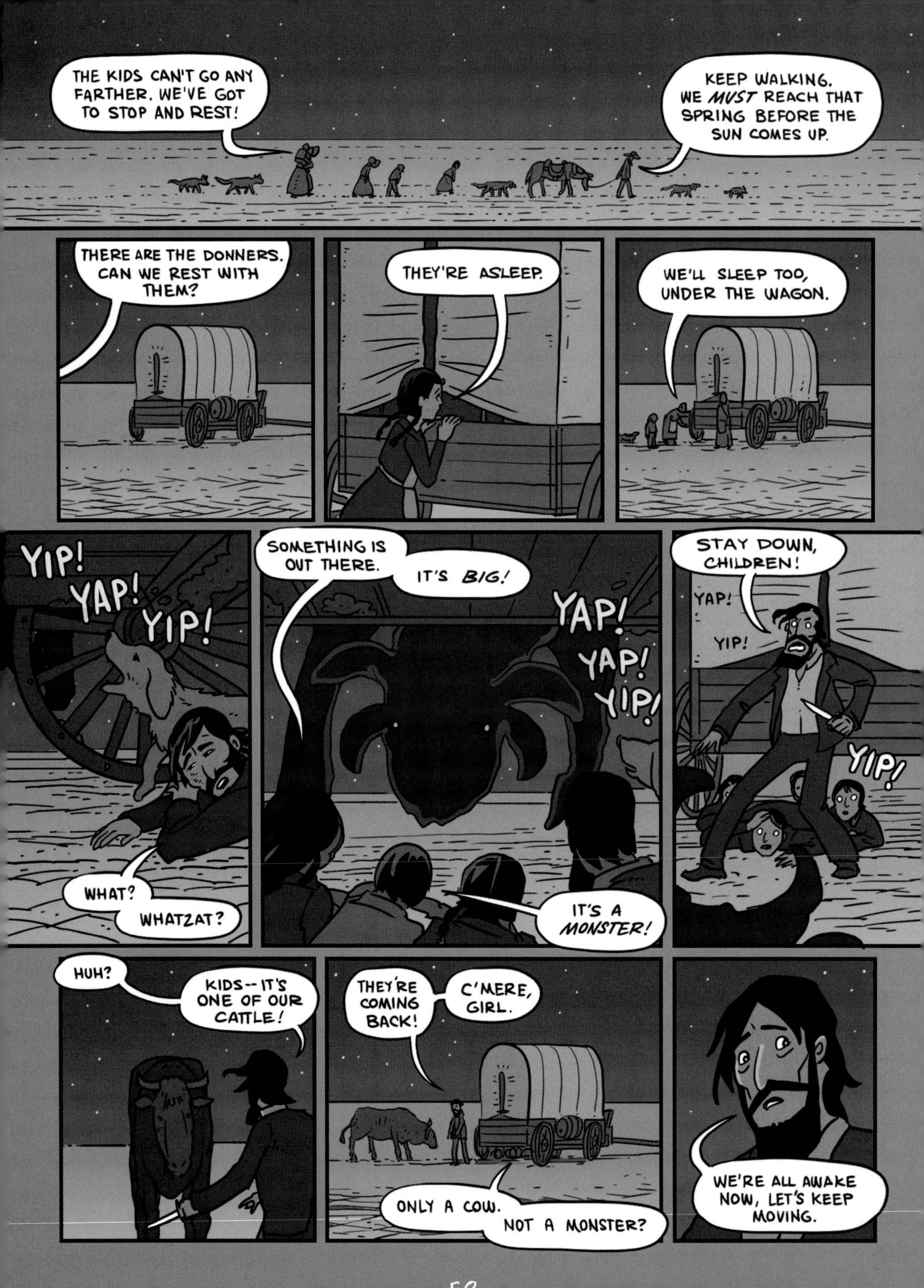
THE KIDS CAN'T GO ANY FARTHER. WE'VE GOT TO STOP AND REST!
KEEP WALKING. WE *MUST* REACH THAT SPRING BEFORE THE SUN COMES UP.
THERE ARE THE DONNERS. CAN WE REST WITH THEM?
THEY'RE ASLEEP.
WE'LL SLEEP TOO, UNDER THE WAGON.
YIP!
YAP!
YIP!
WHAT?
WHATZAT?
SOMETHING IS OUT THERE.
IT'S *BIG*!
YAP!
YAP!
YIP!
IT'S A *MONSTER*!
STAY DOWN, CHILDREN!
YAP!
YIP!
YIP!
HUH?
KIDS-- IT'S ONE OF OUR CATTLE!
THEY'RE COMING BACK!
C'MERE, GIRL.
ONLY A COW.
NOT A MONSTER?
WE'RE ALL AWAKE NOW, LET'S KEEP MOVING.

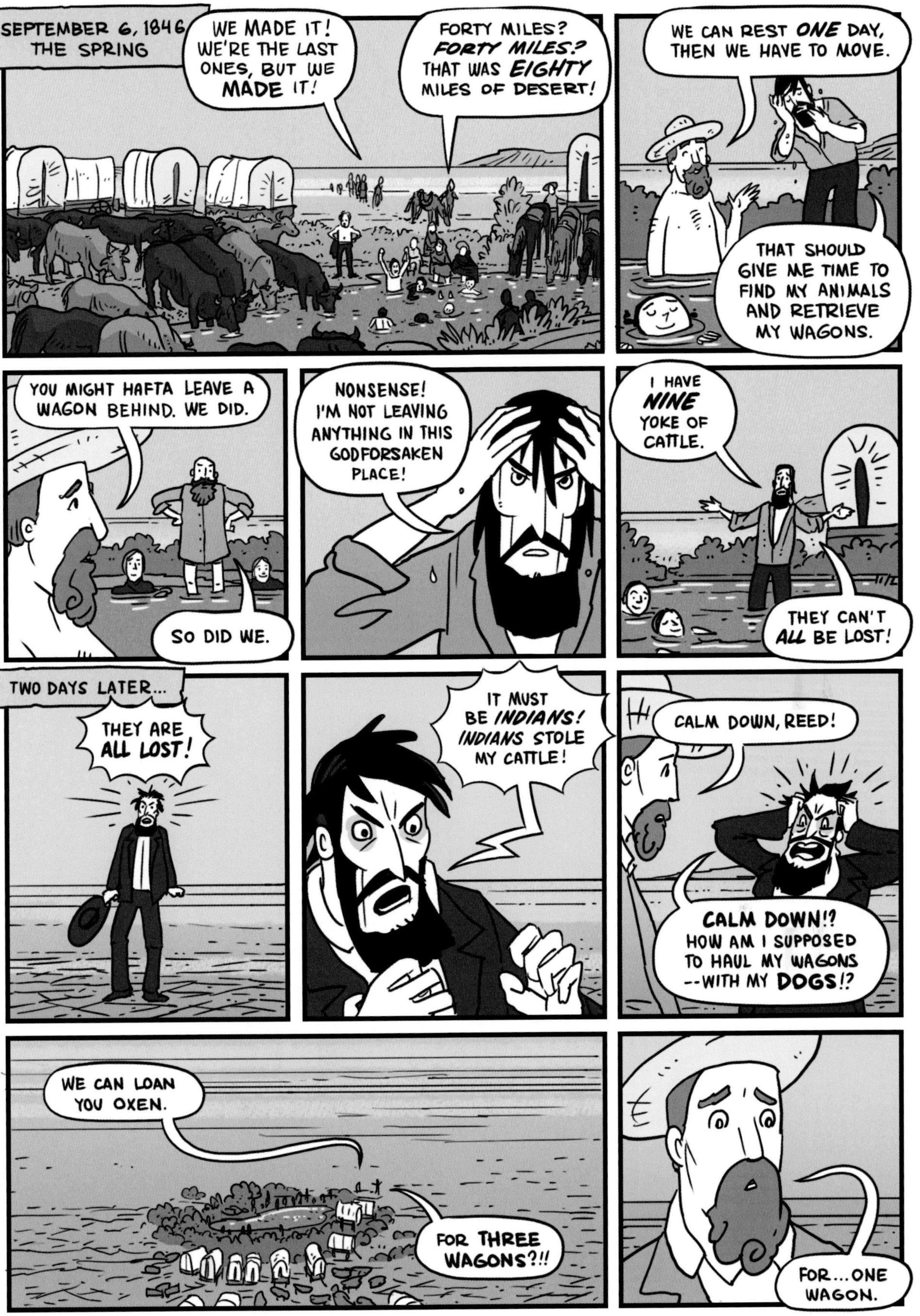
SEPTEMBER 6, 1846
THE SPRING
WE MADE IT! WE'RE THE LAST ONES, BUT WE MADE IT!
FORTY MILES? FORTY MILES? THAT WAS EIGHTY MILES OF DESERT!
WE CAN REST ONE DAY, THEN WE HAVE TO MOVE.
THAT SHOULD GIVE ME TIME TO FIND MY ANIMALS AND RETRIEVE MY WAGONS.
YOU MIGHT HAFTA LEAVE A WAGON BEHIND. WE DID.
SO DID WE.
NONSENSE! I'M NOT LEAVING ANYTHING IN THIS GODFORSAKEN PLACE!
I HAVE NINE YOKE OF CATTLE.
THEY CAN'T ALL BE LOST!
TWO DAYS LATER...
THEY ARE ALL LOST!
IT MUST BE INDIANS! INDIANS STOLE MY CATTLE!
CALM DOWN, REED!
CALM DOWN!? HOW AM I SUPPOSED TO HAUL MY WAGONS --WITH MY DOGS!?
WE CAN LOAN YOU OXEN.
FOR THREE WAGONS?!!
FOR...ONE WAGON.

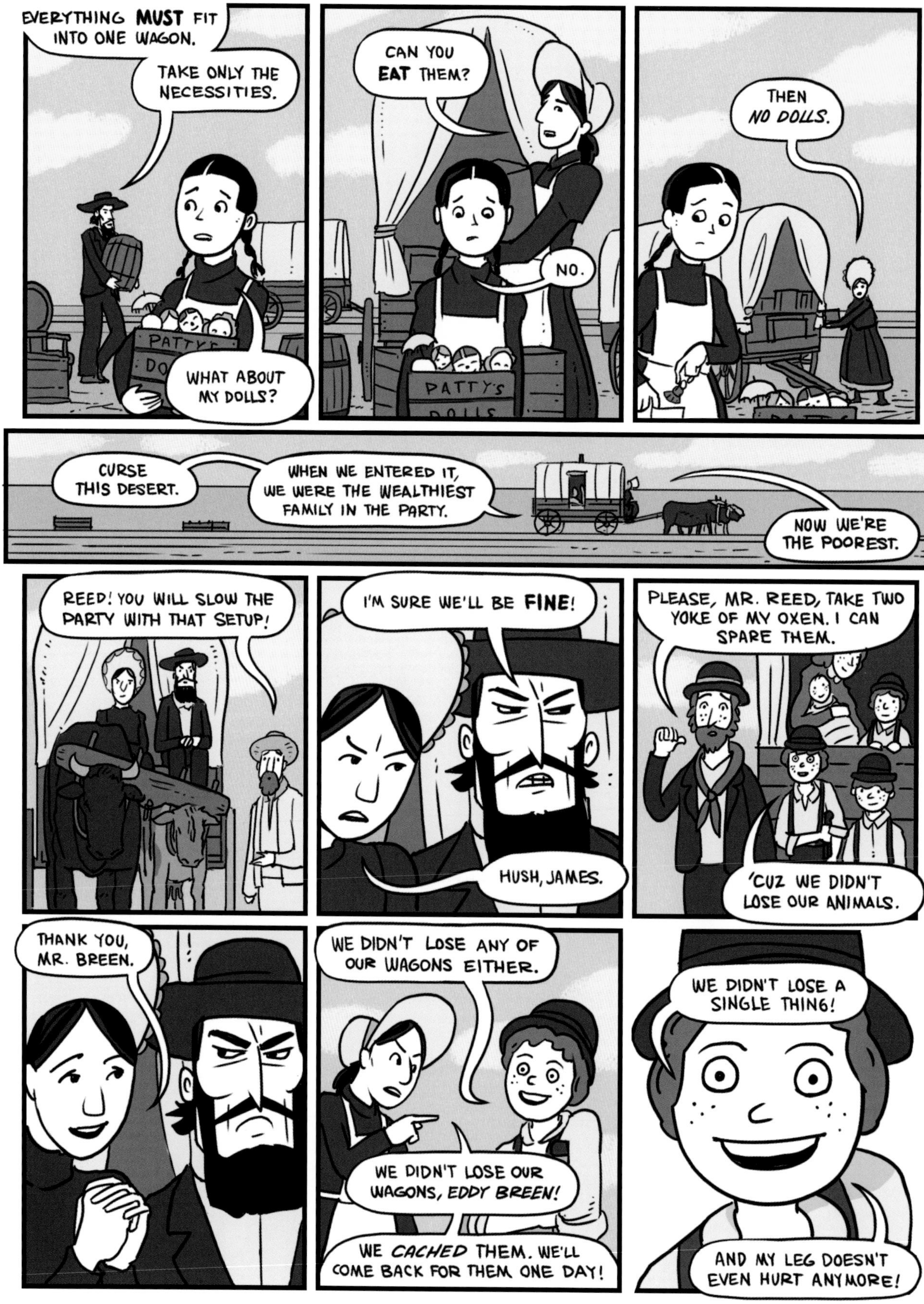
EVERYTHING MUST FIT INTO ONE WAGON.
TAKE ONLY THE NECESSITIES.
PATTY'S DOLLS
WHAT ABOUT MY DOLLS?
CAN YOU EAT THEM?
NO.
PATTY'S DOLLS
THEN NO DOLLS.
CURSE THIS DESERT.
WHEN WE ENTERED IT, WE WERE THE WEALTHIEST FAMILY IN THE PARTY.
NOW WE'RE THE POOREST.
REED! YOU WILL SLOW THE PARTY WITH THAT SETUP!
I'M SURE WE'LL BE FINE!
HUSH, JAMES.
PLEASE, MR. REED, TAKE TWO YOKE OF MY OXEN. I CAN SPARE THEM.
'CUZ WE DIDN'T LOSE OUR ANIMALS.
THANK YOU, MR. BREEN.
!
WE DIDN'T LOSE ANY OF OUR WAGONS EITHER.
WE DIDN'T LOSE OUR WAGONS, EDDY BREEN!
WE CACHED THEM. WE'LL COME BACK FOR THEM ONE DAY!
WE DIDN'T LOSE A SINGLE THING!
AND MY LEG DOESN'T EVEN HURT ANYMORE!

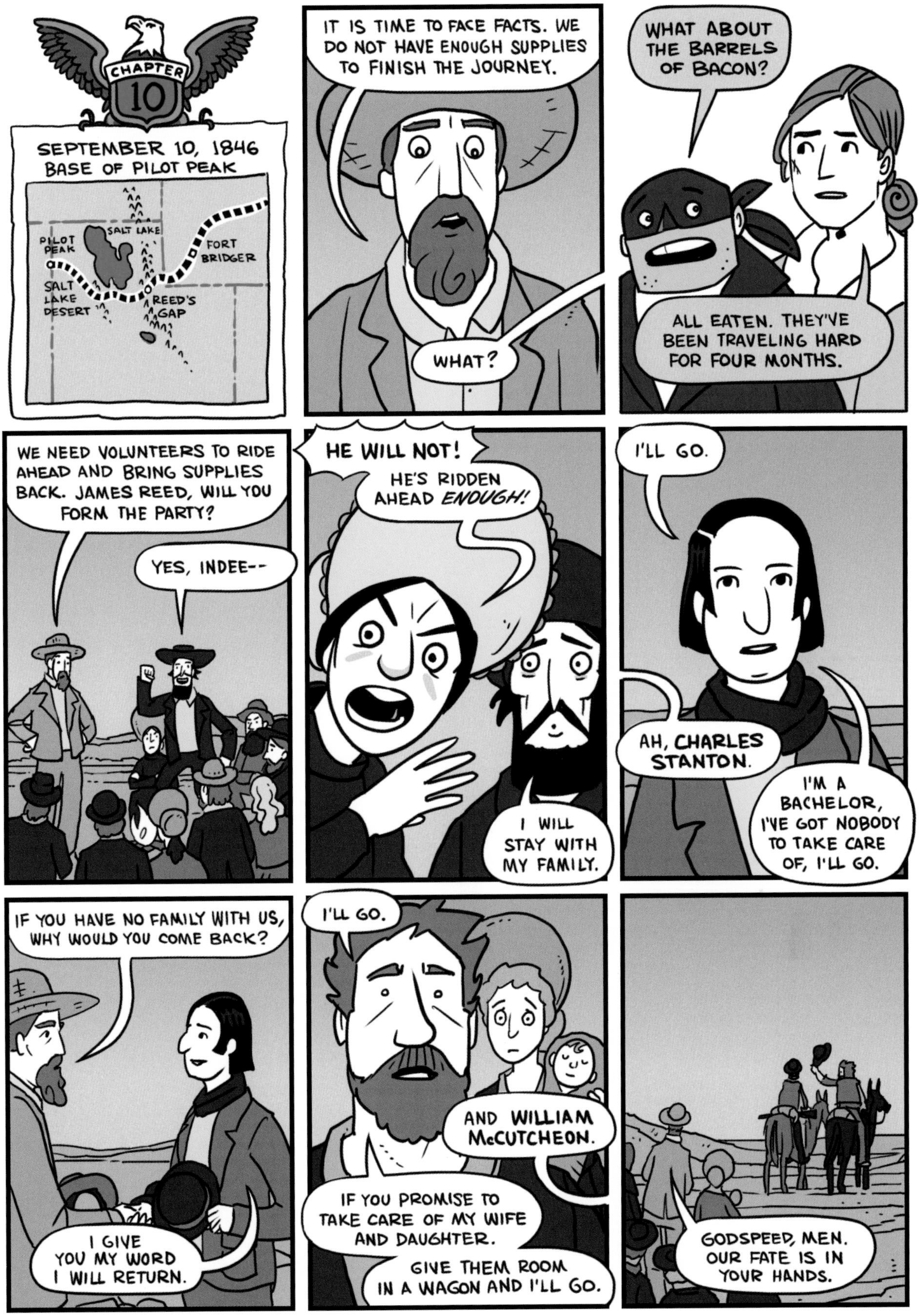
CHAPTER
10
SEPTEMBER 10, 1846
BASE OF PILOT PEAK
PILOT PEAK
SALT LAKE
FORT BRIDGER
SALT LAKE DESERT
REED'S GAP
IT IS TIME TO FACE FACTS. WE DO NOT HAVE ENOUGH SUPPLIES TO FINISH THE JOURNEY.
WHAT?
WHAT ABOUT THE BARRELS OF BACON?
ALL EATEN. THEY'VE BEEN TRAVELING HARD FOR FOUR MONTHS.
WE NEED VOLUNTEERS TO RIDE AHEAD AND BRING SUPPLIES BACK. JAMES REED, WILL YOU FORM THE PARTY?
YES, INDEE--
HE WILL NOT!
HE'S RIDDEN AHEAD ENOUGH!
I WILL STAY WITH MY FAMILY.
I'LL GO.
AH, CHARLES STANTON.
I'M A BACHELOR, I'VE GOT NOBODY TO TAKE CARE OF, I'LL GO.
IF YOU HAVE NO FAMILY WITH US, WHY WOULD YOU COME BACK?
I GIVE YOU MY WORD I WILL RETURN.
I'LL GO.
AND WILLIAM McCUTCHEON.
IF YOU PROMISE TO TAKE CARE OF MY WIFE AND DAUGHTER.
GIVE THEM ROOM IN A WAGON AND I'LL GO.
GODSPEED, MEN. OUR FATE IS IN YOUR HANDS.

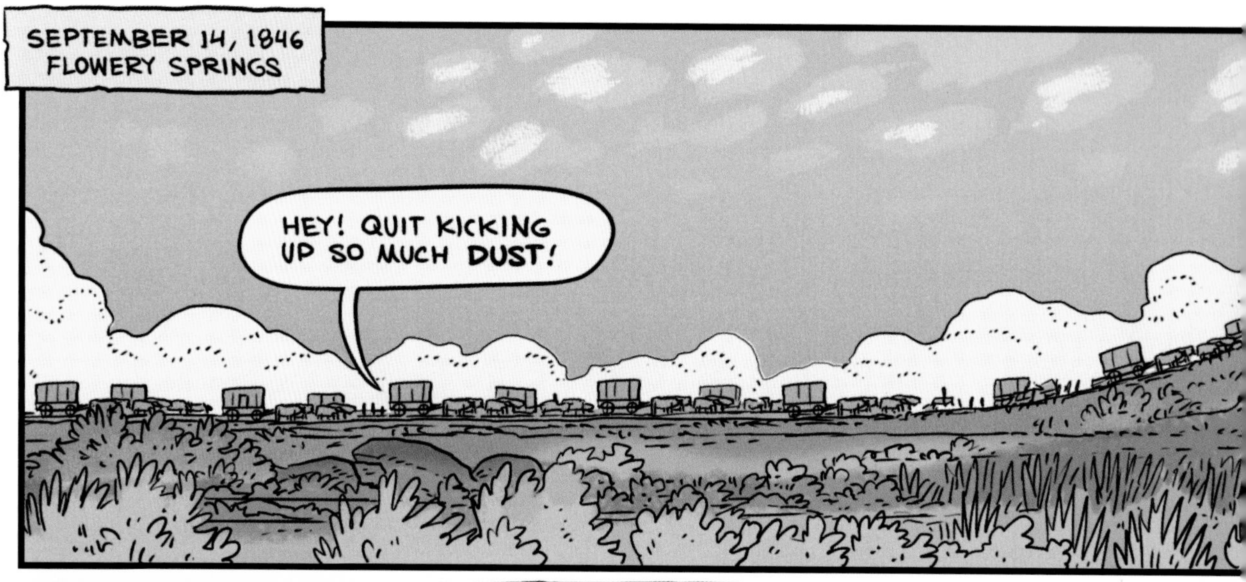
SEPTEMBER 14, 1846
FLOWERY SPRINGS
HEY! QUIT KICKING UP SO MUCH DUST!

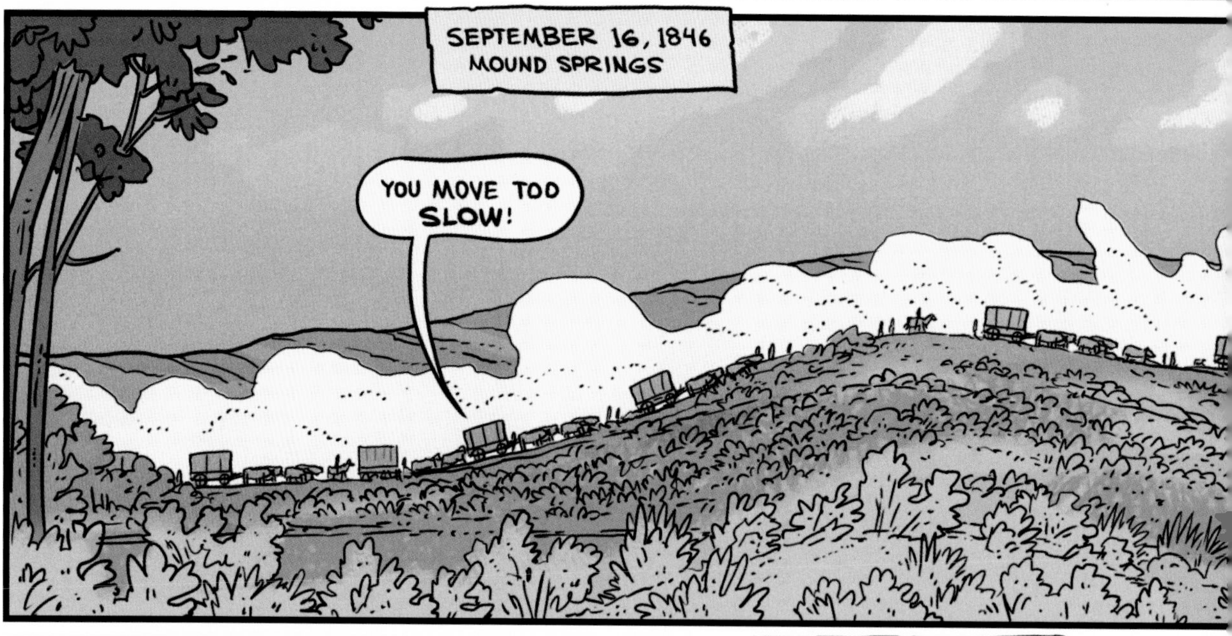
SEPTEMBER 16, 1846
MOUND SPRINGS
YOU MOVE TOO SLOW!

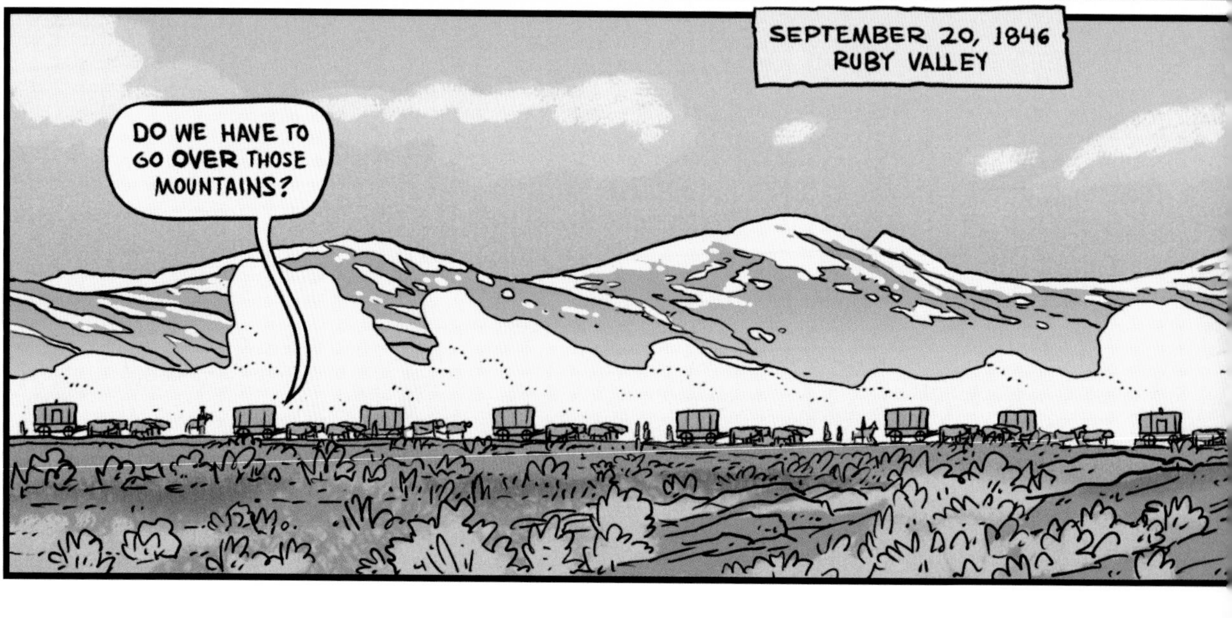
SEPTEMBER 20, 1846
RUBY VALLEY
DO WE HAVE TO GO OVER THOSE MOUNTAINS?

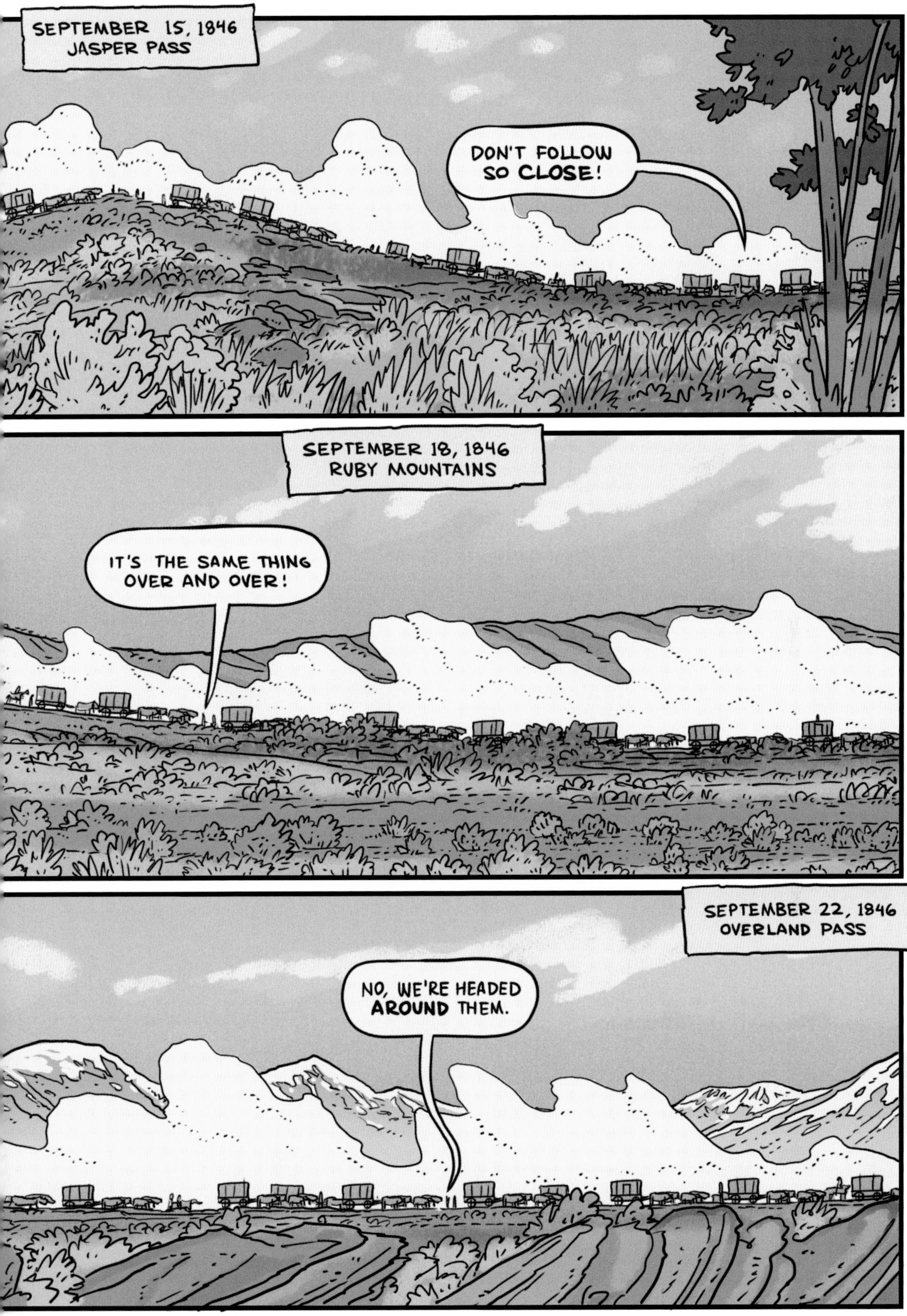
SEPTEMBER 15, 1846
JASPER PASS
DON'T FOLLOW SO CLOSE!
SEPTEMBER 18, 1846
RUBY MOUNTAINS
IT'S THE SAME THING OVER AND OVER!
SEPTEMBER 22, 1846
OVERLAND PASS
NO, WE'RE HEADED AROUND THEM.

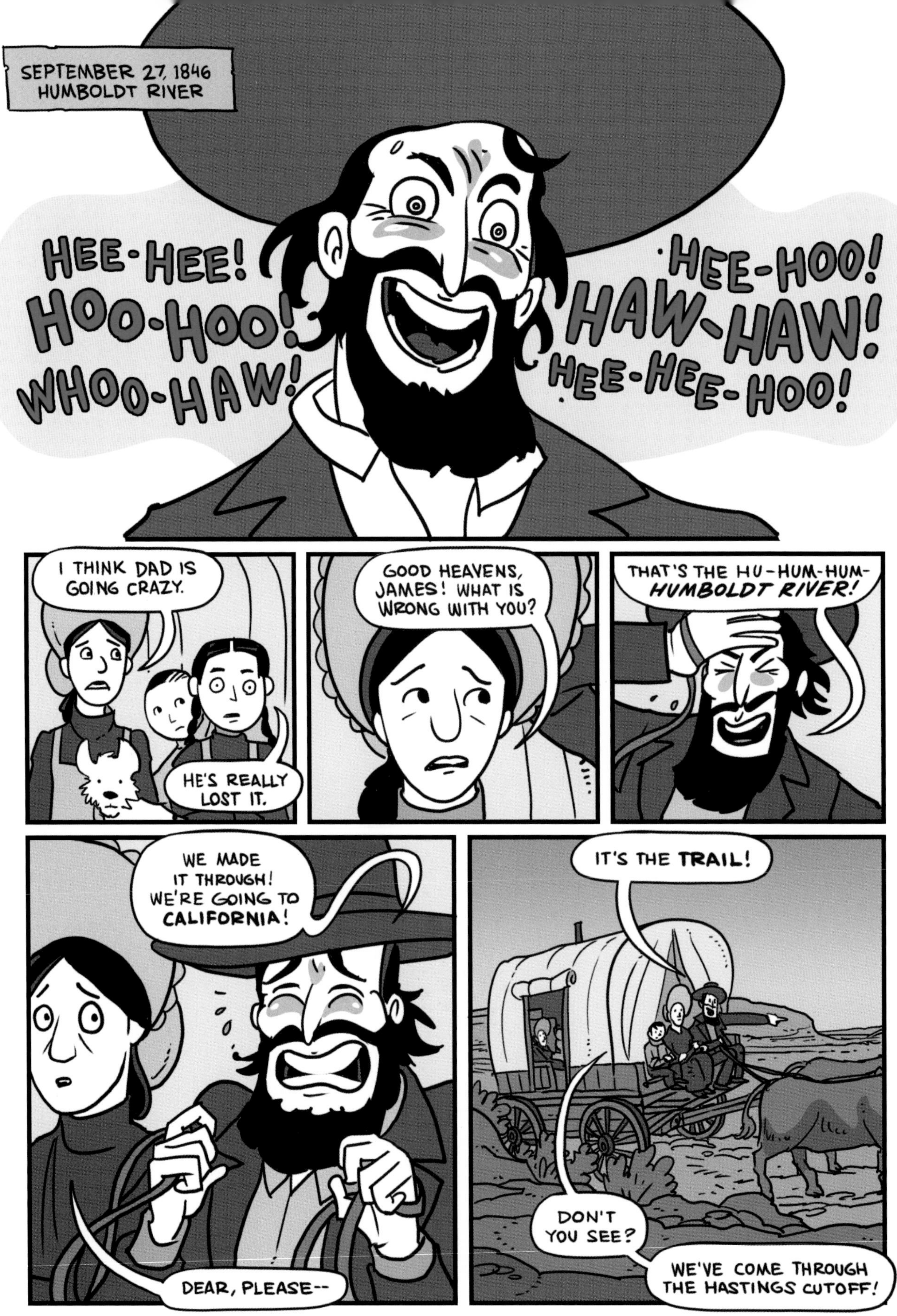
SEPTEMBER 27, 1846
HUMBOLDT RIVER
HEE-HEE!
HOO-HOO!
WHOO-HAW!
HEE-HOO!
HAW-HAW!
HEE-HEE-HOO!
I THINK DAD IS GOING CRAZY.
HE'S REALLY LOST IT.
GOOD HEAVENS, JAMES! WHAT IS WRONG WITH YOU?
THAT'S THE HU-HUM-HUM-*HUMBOLDT RIVER!*
WE MADE IT THROUGH! WE'RE GOING TO **CALIFORNIA**!
DEAR, PLEASE--
IT'S THE **TRAIL**!
DON'T YOU SEE?
WE'VE COME THROUGH THE HASTINGS CUTOFF!

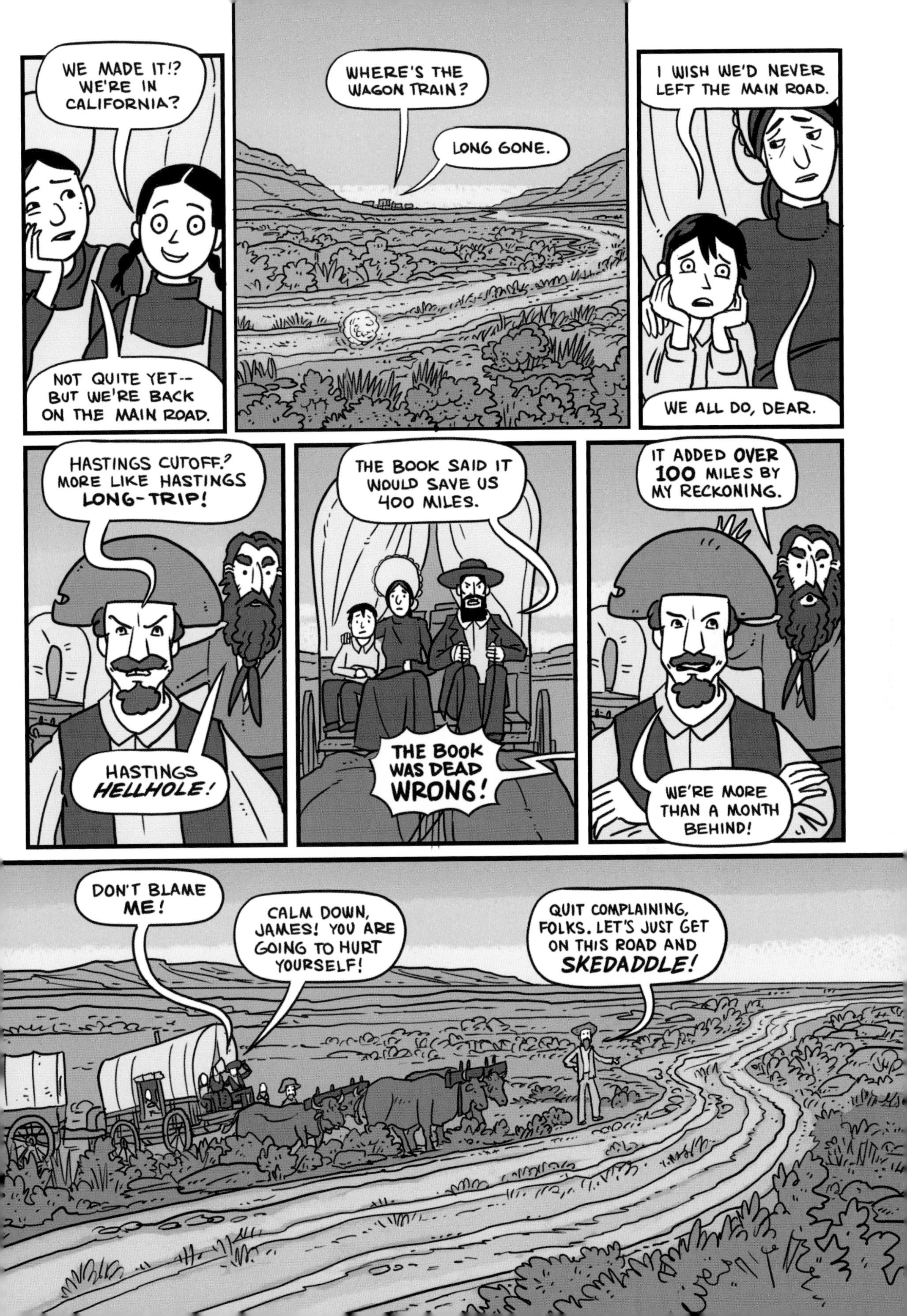
WE MADE IT!? WE'RE IN CALIFORNIA?
NOT QUITE YET-- BUT WE'RE BACK ON THE MAIN ROAD.
WHERE'S THE WAGON TRAIN?
LONG GONE.
I WISH WE'D NEVER LEFT THE MAIN ROAD.
WE ALL DO, DEAR.
HASTINGS CUTOFF? MORE LIKE HASTINGS LONG-TRIP!
HASTINGS HELLHOLE!
THE BOOK SAID IT WOULD SAVE US 400 MILES.
THE BOOK WAS DEAD WRONG!
IT ADDED OVER 100 MILES BY MY RECKONING.
WE'RE MORE THAN A MONTH BEHIND!
DON'T BLAME ME!
CALM DOWN, JAMES! YOU ARE GOING TO HURT YOURSELF!
QUIT COMPLAINING, FOLKS. LET'S JUST GET ON THIS ROAD AND SKEDADDLE!

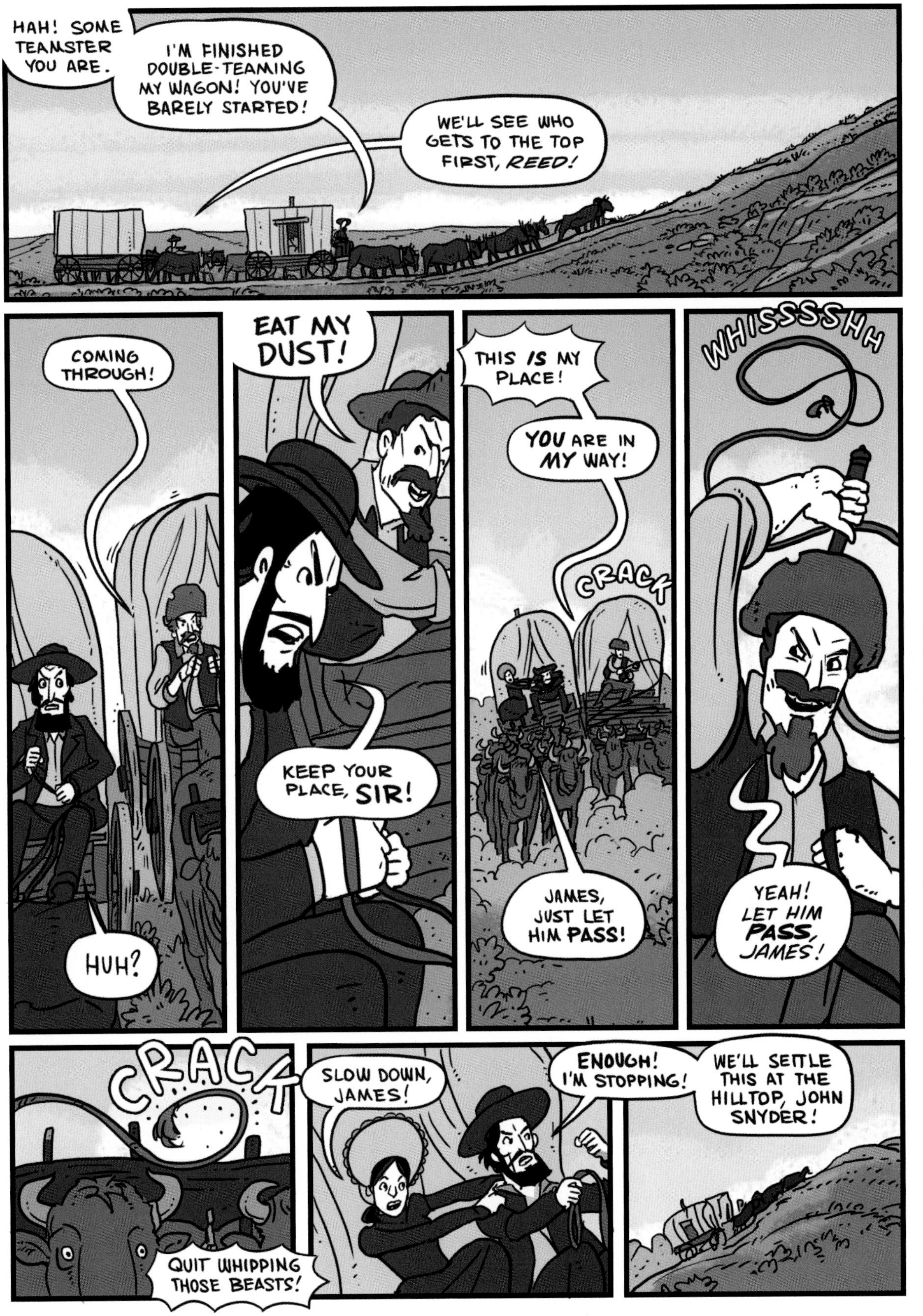

HAH! SOME TEAMSTER YOU ARE.
I'M FINISHED DOUBLE-TEAMING MY WAGON! YOU'VE BARELY STARTED!
WE'LL SEE WHO GETS TO THE TOP FIRST, REED!
COMING THROUGH!
HUH?
EAT MY DUST!
KEEP YOUR PLACE, SIR!
THIS IS MY PLACE!
YOU ARE IN MY WAY!
CRACK
JAMES, JUST LET HIM PASS!
WHISSSSHH
YEAH! LET HIM PASS, JAMES!
CRACK
QUIT WHIPPING THOSE BEASTS!
SLOW DOWN, JAMES!
ENOUGH! I'M STOPPING!
WE'LL SETTLE THIS AT THE HILLTOP, JOHN SNYDER!

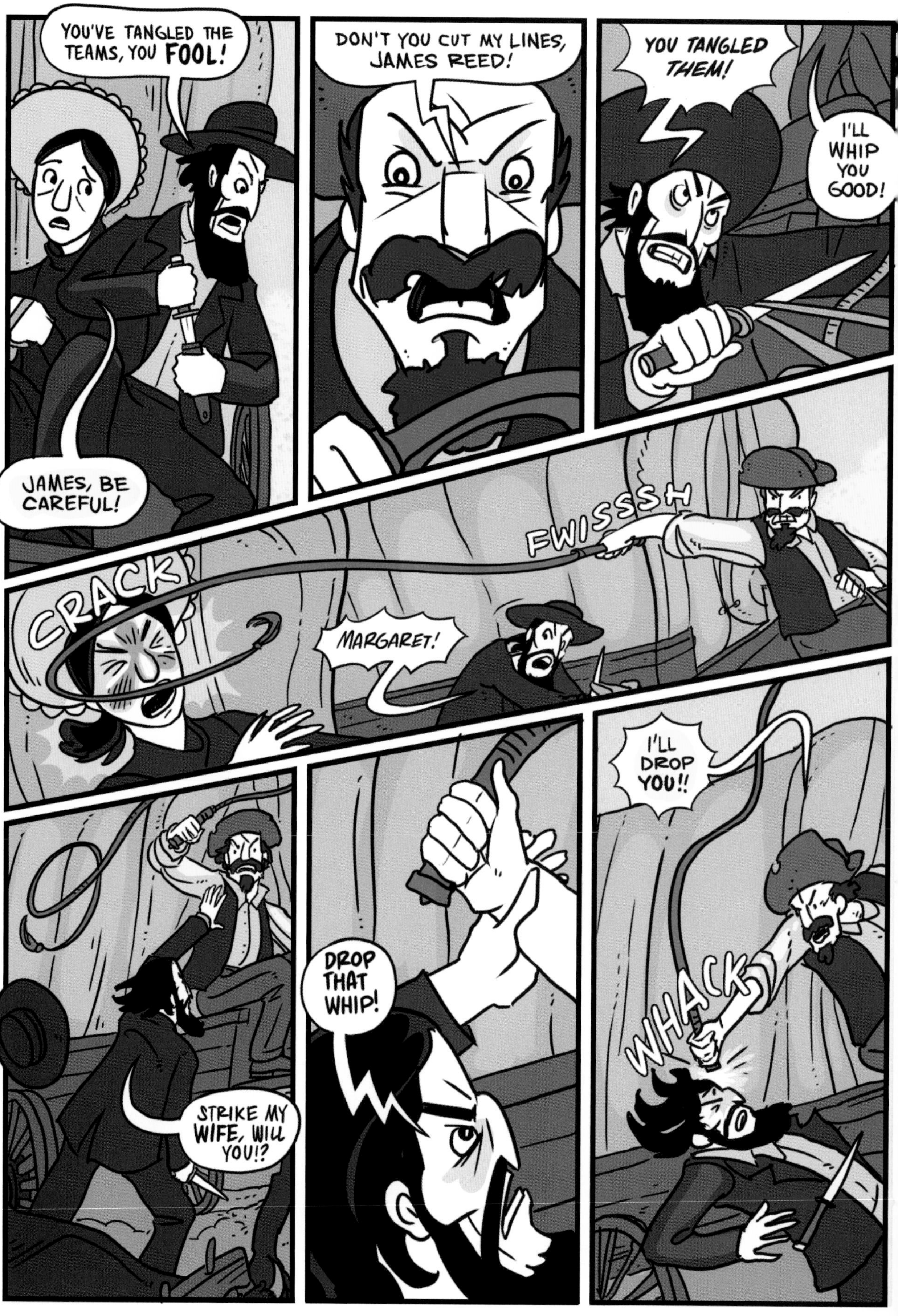

YOU'VE TANGLED THE TEAMS, YOU FOOL!
JAMES, BE CAREFUL!
DON'T YOU CUT MY LINES, JAMES REED!
YOU TANGLED THEM!
I'LL WHIP YOU GOOD!
FWISSSH
CRACK
MARGARET!
STRIKE MY WIFE, WILL YOU!?
DROP THAT WHIP!
I'LL DROP YOU!!
WHACK

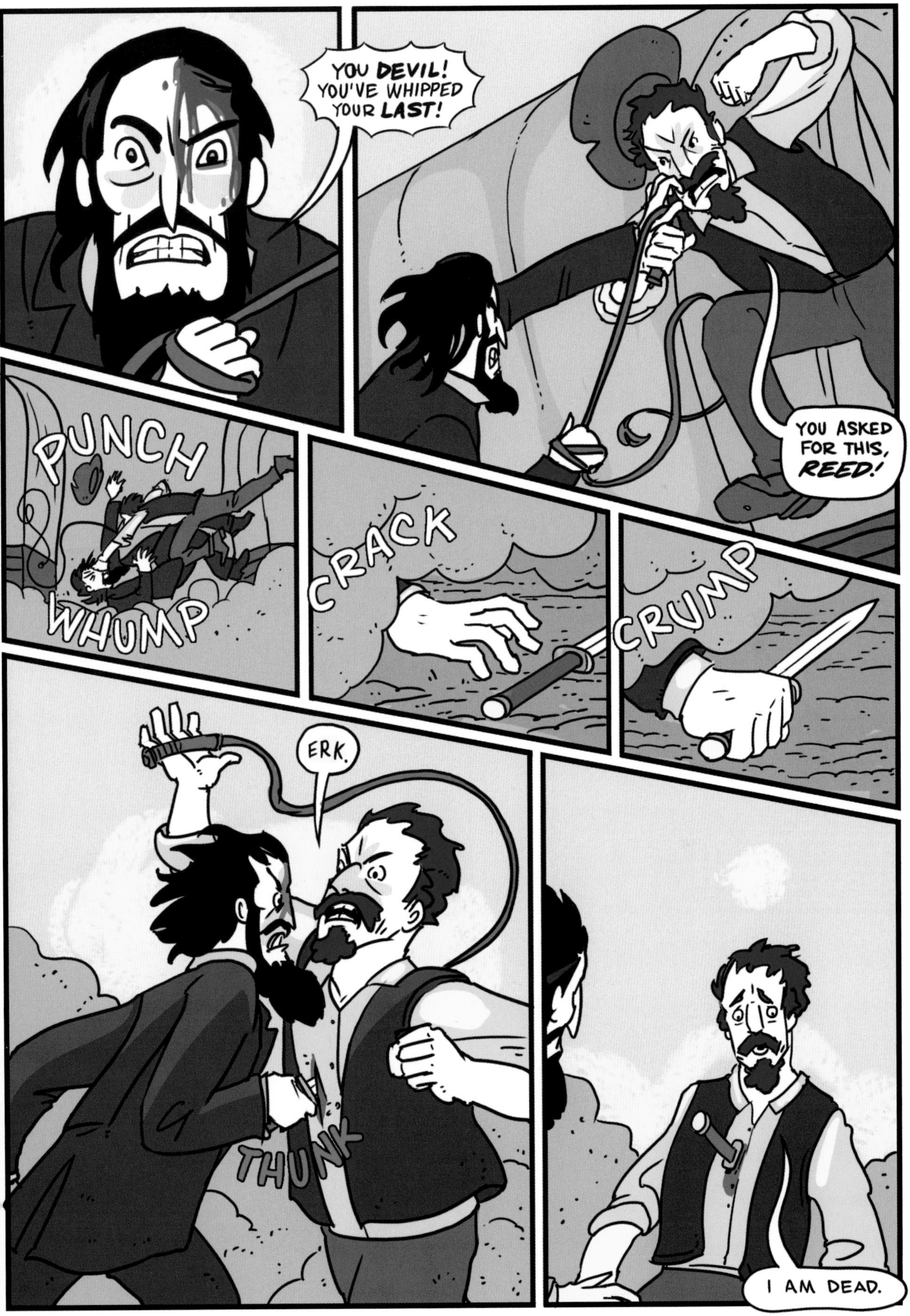

YOU DEVIL! YOU'VE WHIPPED YOUR LAST!
YOU ASKED FOR THIS, REED!
PUNCH
WHUMP
CRACK
CRUMP
ERK.
THUNK
I AM DEAD.

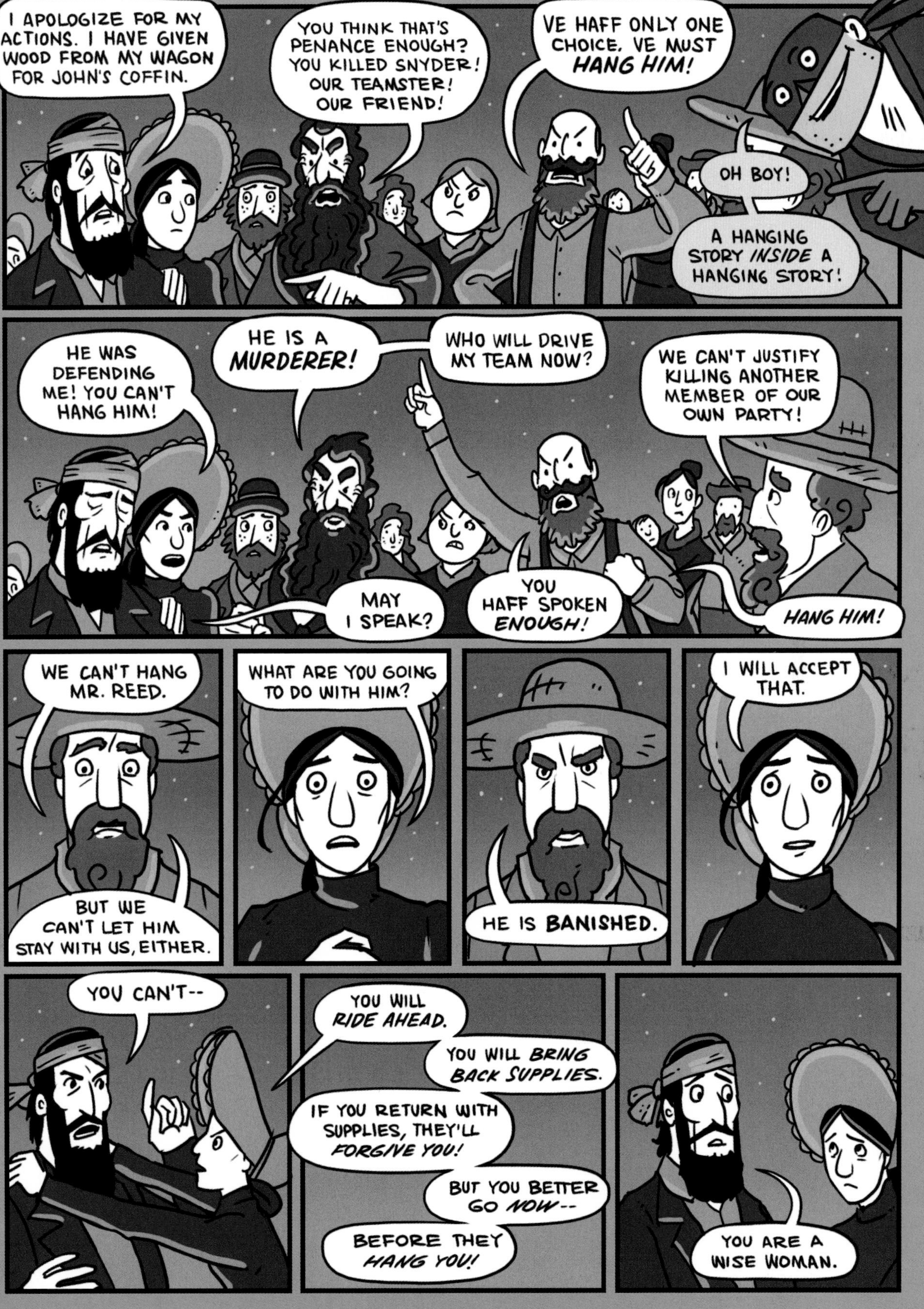
I APOLOGIZE FOR MY ACTIONS. I HAVE GIVEN WOOD FROM MY WAGON FOR JOHN'S COFFIN.
YOU THINK THAT'S PENANCE ENOUGH? YOU KILLED SNYDER! OUR TEAMSTER! OUR FRIEND!
VE HAFF ONLY ONE CHOICE. VE MUST *HANG HIM!*
OH BOY!
A HANGING STORY *INSIDE* A HANGING STORY!
HE WAS DEFENDING ME! YOU CAN'T HANG HIM!
HE IS A *MURDERER!*
WHO WILL DRIVE MY TEAM NOW?
WE CAN'T JUSTIFY KILLING ANOTHER MEMBER OF OUR OWN PARTY!
MAY I SPEAK?
YOU HAFF SPOKEN *ENOUGH!*
HANG HIM!
WE CAN'T HANG MR. REED.
BUT WE CAN'T LET HIM STAY WITH US, EITHER.
WHAT ARE YOU GOING TO DO WITH HIM?
HE IS **BANISHED.**
I WILL ACCEPT THAT.
YOU CAN'T--
YOU WILL *RIDE AHEAD.*
YOU WILL *BRING BACK SUPPLIES.*
IF YOU RETURN WITH SUPPLIES, THEY'LL *FORGIVE YOU!*
BUT YOU BETTER GO *NOW*--
BEFORE THEY *HANG YOU!*
YOU ARE A WISE WOMAN.

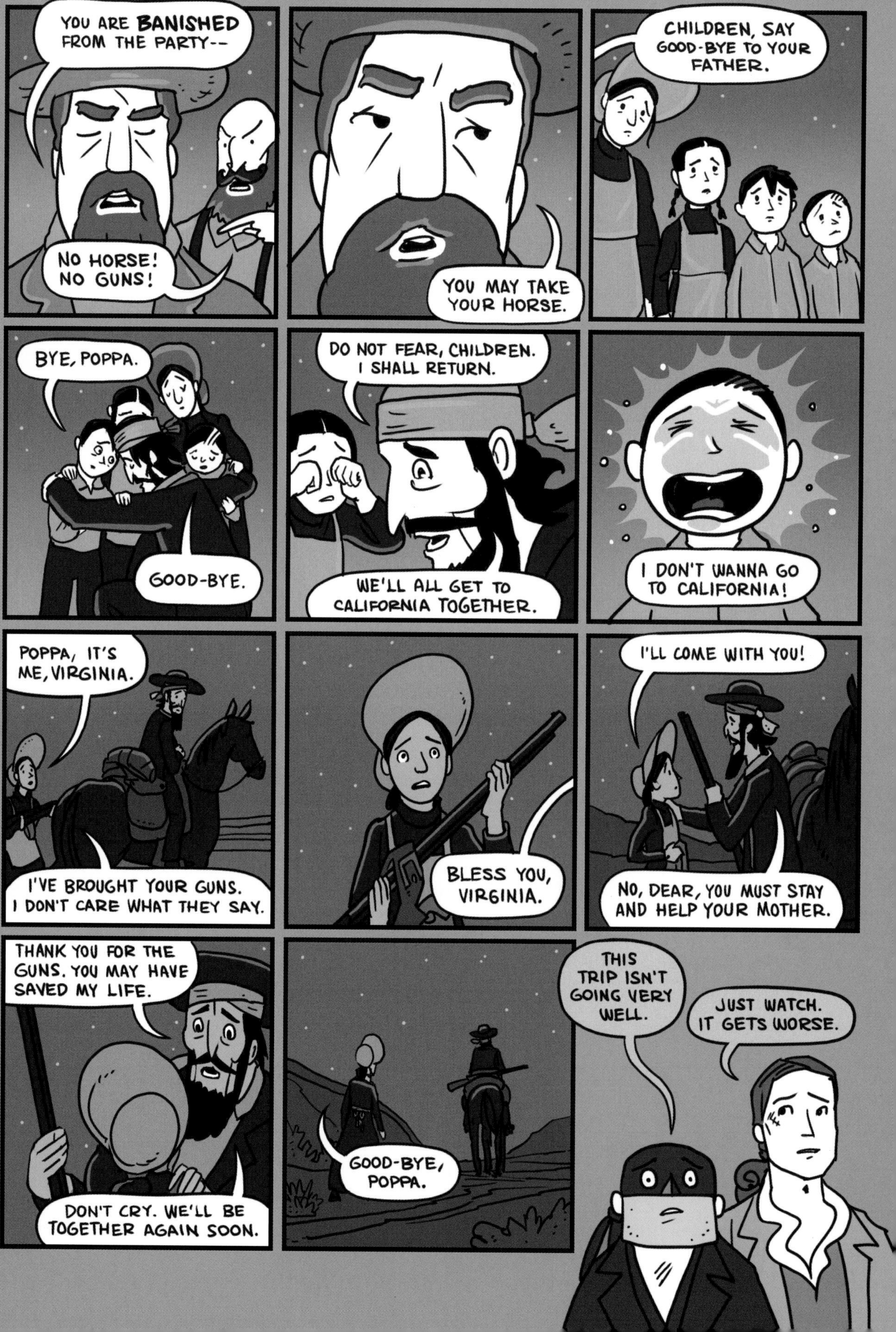
YOU ARE BANISHED FROM THE PARTY--
NO HORSE! NO GUNS!
YOU MAY TAKE YOUR HORSE.
CHILDREN, SAY GOOD-BYE TO YOUR FATHER.
BYE, POPPA.
GOOD-BYE.
DO NOT FEAR, CHILDREN. I SHALL RETURN.
WE'LL ALL GET TO CALIFORNIA TOGETHER.
I DON'T WANNA GO TO CALIFORNIA!
POPPA, IT'S ME, VIRGINIA.
I'VE BROUGHT YOUR GUNS. I DON'T CARE WHAT THEY SAY.
BLESS YOU, VIRGINIA.
I'LL COME WITH YOU!
NO, DEAR, YOU MUST STAY AND HELP YOUR MOTHER.
THANK YOU FOR THE GUNS. YOU MAY HAVE SAVED MY LIFE.
DON'T CRY. WE'LL BE TOGETHER AGAIN SOON.
GOOD-BYE, POPPA.
THIS TRIP ISN'T GOING VERY WELL.
JUST WATCH. IT GETS WORSE.

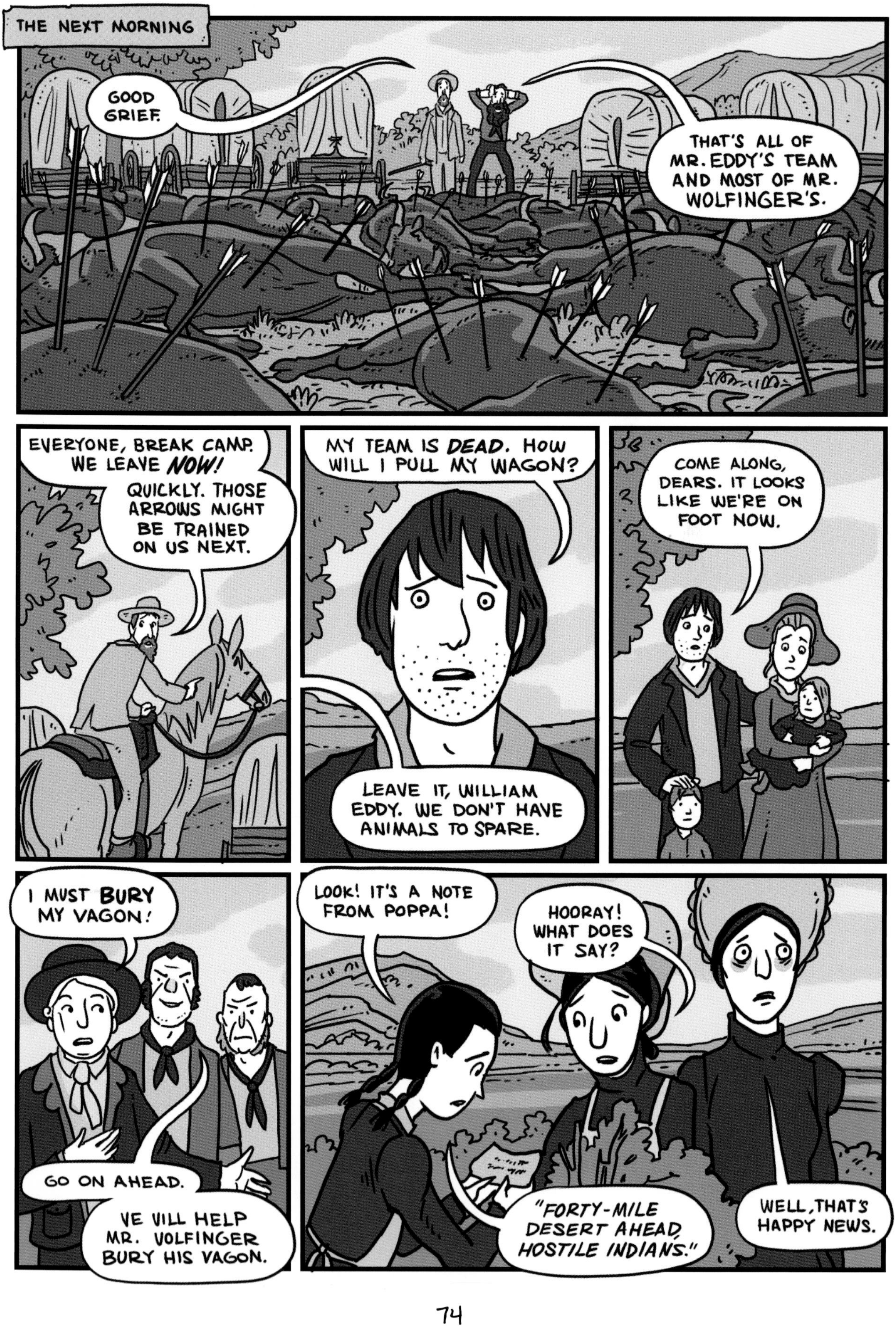
THE NEXT MORNING
GOOD GRIEF.
THAT'S ALL OF MR. EDDY'S TEAM AND MOST OF MR. WOLFINGER'S.
EVERYONE, BREAK CAMP. WE LEAVE NOW!
QUICKLY. THOSE ARROWS MIGHT BE TRAINED ON US NEXT.
MY TEAM IS DEAD. HOW WILL I PULL MY WAGON?
LEAVE IT, WILLIAM EDDY. WE DON'T HAVE ANIMALS TO SPARE.
COME ALONG, DEARS. IT LOOKS LIKE WE'RE ON FOOT NOW.
I MUST BURY MY VAGON!
GO ON AHEAD.
VE VILL HELP MR. VOLFINGER BURY HIS VAGON.
LOOK! IT'S A NOTE FROM POPPA!
HOORAY! WHAT DOES IT SAY?
"FORTY-MILE DESERT AHEAD, HOSTILE INDIANS."
WELL, THAT'S HAPPY NEWS.

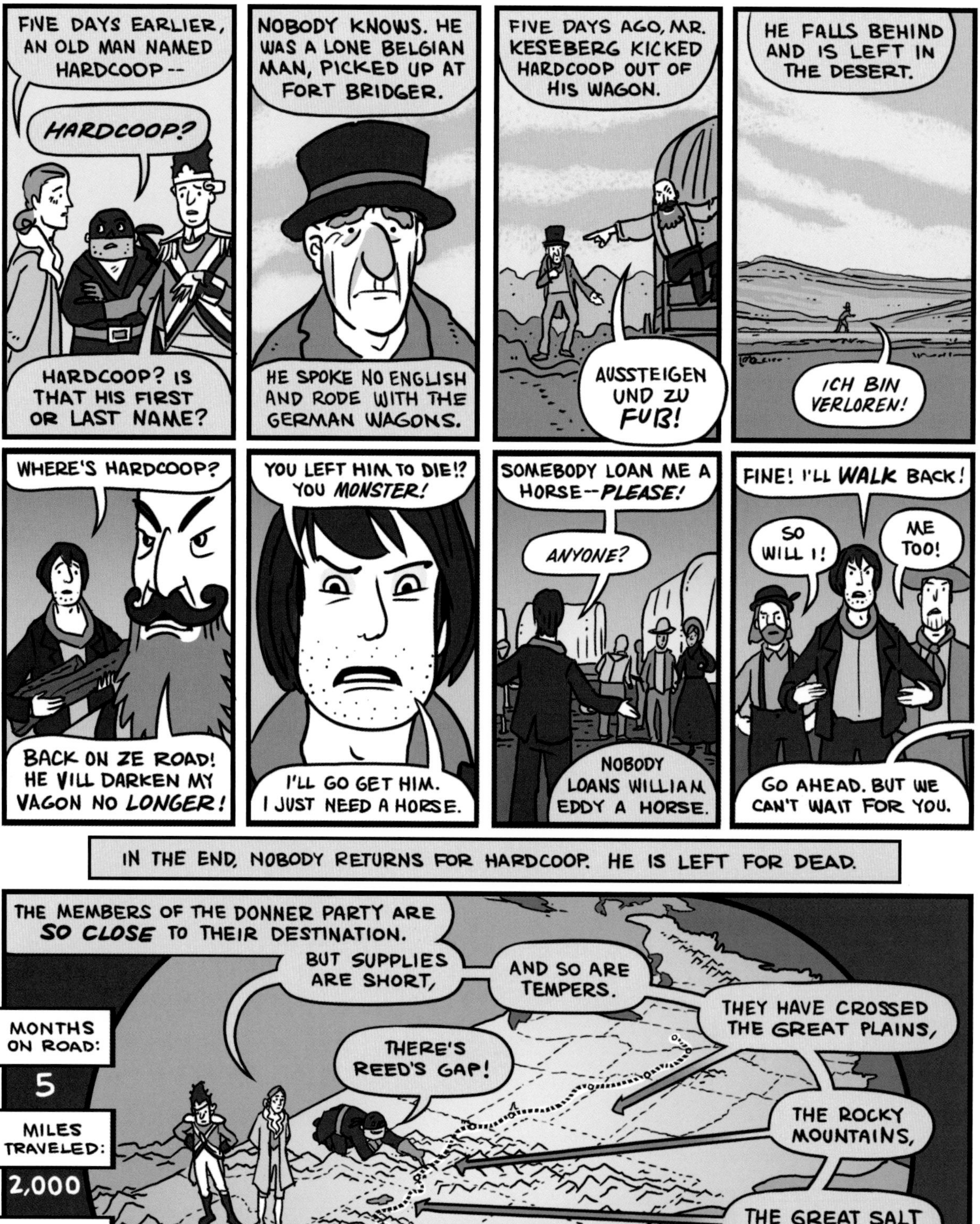
FIVE DAYS EARLIER, AN OLD MAN NAMED HARDCOOP--
HARDCOOP?
HARDCOOP? IS THAT HIS FIRST OR LAST NAME?
NOBODY KNOWS. HE WAS A LONE BELGIAN MAN, PICKED UP AT FORT BRIDGER.
HE SPOKE NO ENGLISH AND RODE WITH THE GERMAN WAGONS.
FIVE DAYS AGO, MR. KESEBERG KICKED HARDCOOP OUT OF HIS WAGON.
AUSSTEIGEN UND ZU FUß!
HE FALLS BEHIND AND IS LEFT IN THE DESERT.
ICH BIN VERLOREN!
WHERE'S HARDCOOP?
BACK ON ZE ROAD! HE VILL DARKEN MY VAGON NO LONGER!
YOU LEFT HIM TO DIE!? YOU MONSTER!
I'LL GO GET HIM. I JUST NEED A HORSE.
SOMEBODY LOAN ME A HORSE--PLEASE!
ANYONE?
NOBODY LOANS WILLIAM EDDY A HORSE.
FINE! I'LL WALK BACK!
SO WILL I!
ME TOO!
GO AHEAD. BUT WE CAN'T WAIT FOR YOU.
IN THE END, NOBODY RETURNS FOR HARDCOOP. HE IS LEFT FOR DEAD.
THE MEMBERS OF THE DONNER PARTY ARE SO CLOSE TO THEIR DESTINATION.
BUT SUPPLIES ARE SHORT,
AND SO ARE TEMPERS.
MONTHS ON ROAD:
5
MILES TRAVELED:
2,000
MILES TO GO:
70
THERE'S REED'S GAP!
THEY HAVE CROSSED THE GREAT PLAINS,
THE ROCKY MOUNTAINS,
THE GREAT SALT LAKE DESERT,
AND THE RUBY MOUNTAINS.
BUT THERE IS ONE FINAL RANGE BETWEEN THEM AND SAFETY,
THE SIERRA NEVADA.

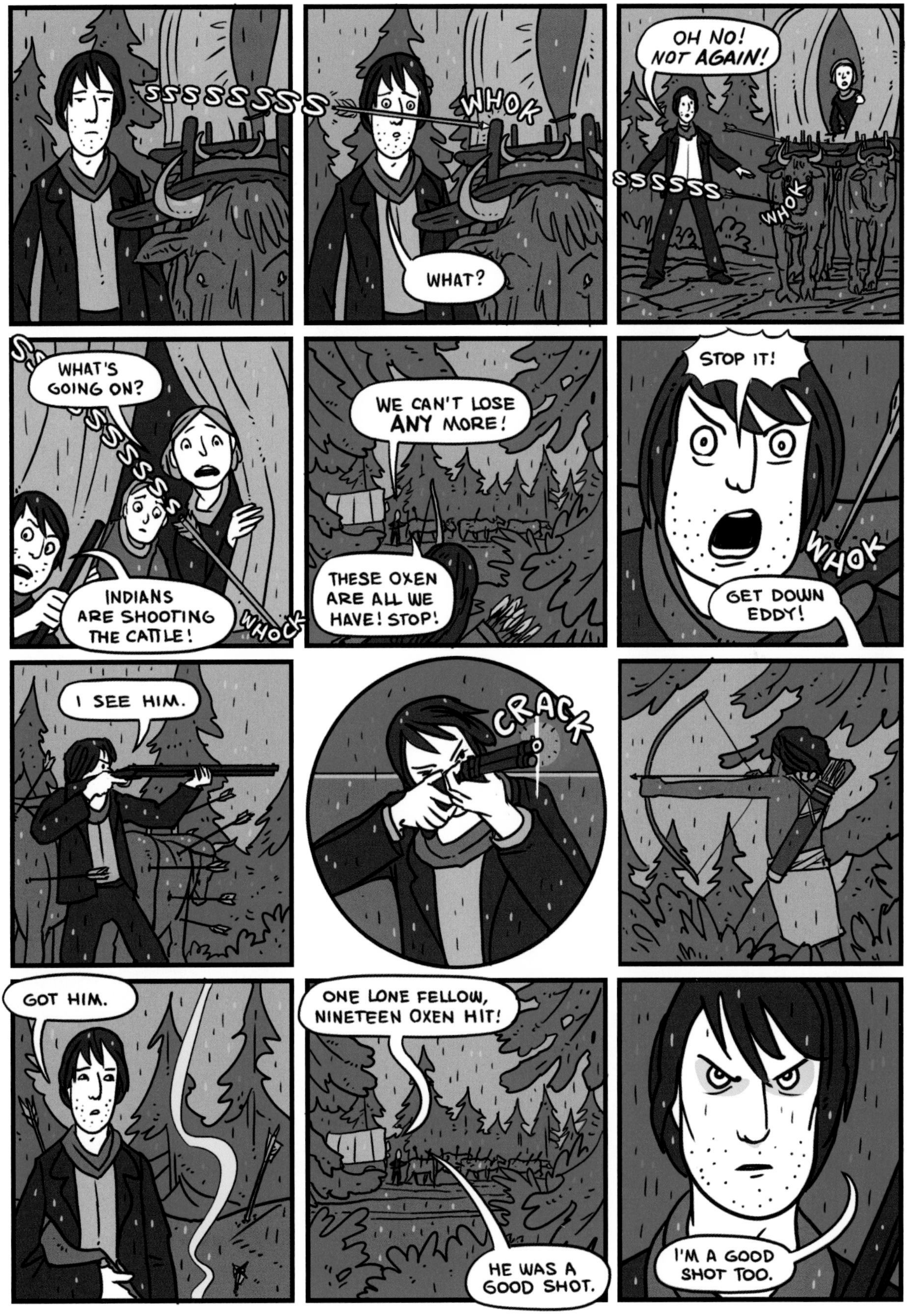
SSSSSSSS
WHOK
WHAT?
OH NO! NOT AGAIN!
SSSSSS
WHOK
WHAT'S GOING ON?
INDIANS ARE SHOOTING THE CATTLE!
WHOCK
WE CAN'T LOSE ANY MORE!
THESE OXEN ARE ALL WE HAVE! STOP!
STOP IT!
WHOK
GET DOWN EDDY!
I SEE HIM.
CRACK
GOT HIM.
ONE LONE FELLOW, NINETEEN OXEN HIT!
HE WAS A GOOD SHOT.
I'M A GOOD SHOT TOO.

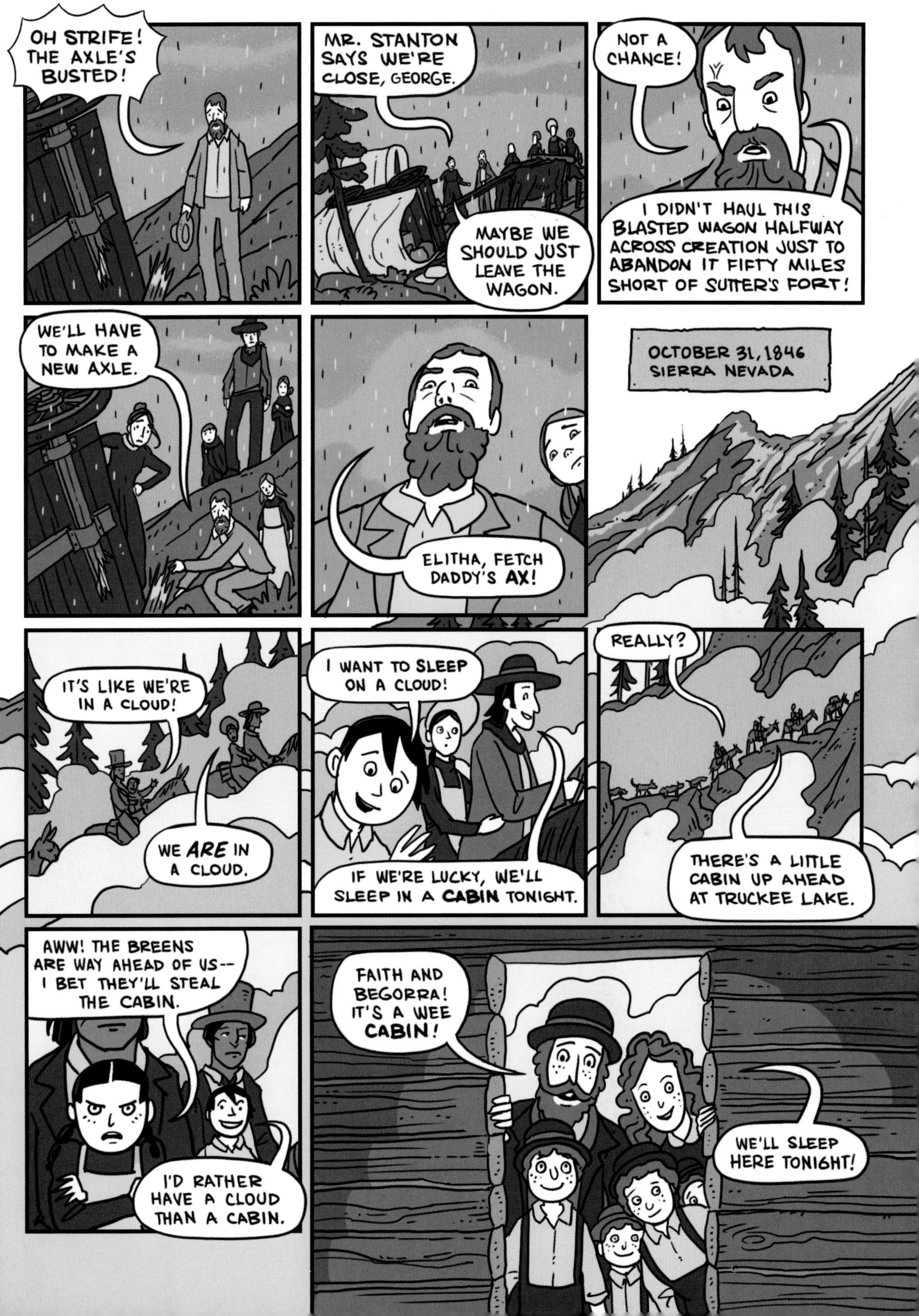
OH STRIFE! THE AXLE'S BUSTED!
MR. STANTON SAYS WE'RE CLOSE, GEORGE.
MAYBE WE SHOULD JUST LEAVE THE WAGON.
NOT A CHANCE!
I DIDN'T HAUL THIS BLASTED WAGON HALFWAY ACROSS CREATION JUST TO ABANDON IT FIFTY MILES SHORT OF SUTTER'S FORT!
WE'LL HAVE TO MAKE A NEW AXLE.
ELITHA, FETCH DADDY'S AX!
OCTOBER 31, 1846
SIERRA NEVADA
IT'S LIKE WE'RE IN A CLOUD!
WE ARE IN A CLOUD.
I WANT TO SLEEP ON A CLOUD!
IF WE'RE LUCKY, WE'LL SLEEP IN A CABIN TONIGHT.
REALLY?
THERE'S A LITTLE CABIN UP AHEAD AT TRUCKEE LAKE.
AWW! THE BREENS ARE WAY AHEAD OF US-- I BET THEY'LL STEAL THE CABIN.
I'D RATHER HAVE A CLOUD THAN A CABIN.
FAITH AND BEGORRA! IT'S A WEE CABIN!
WE'LL SLEEP HERE TONIGHT!

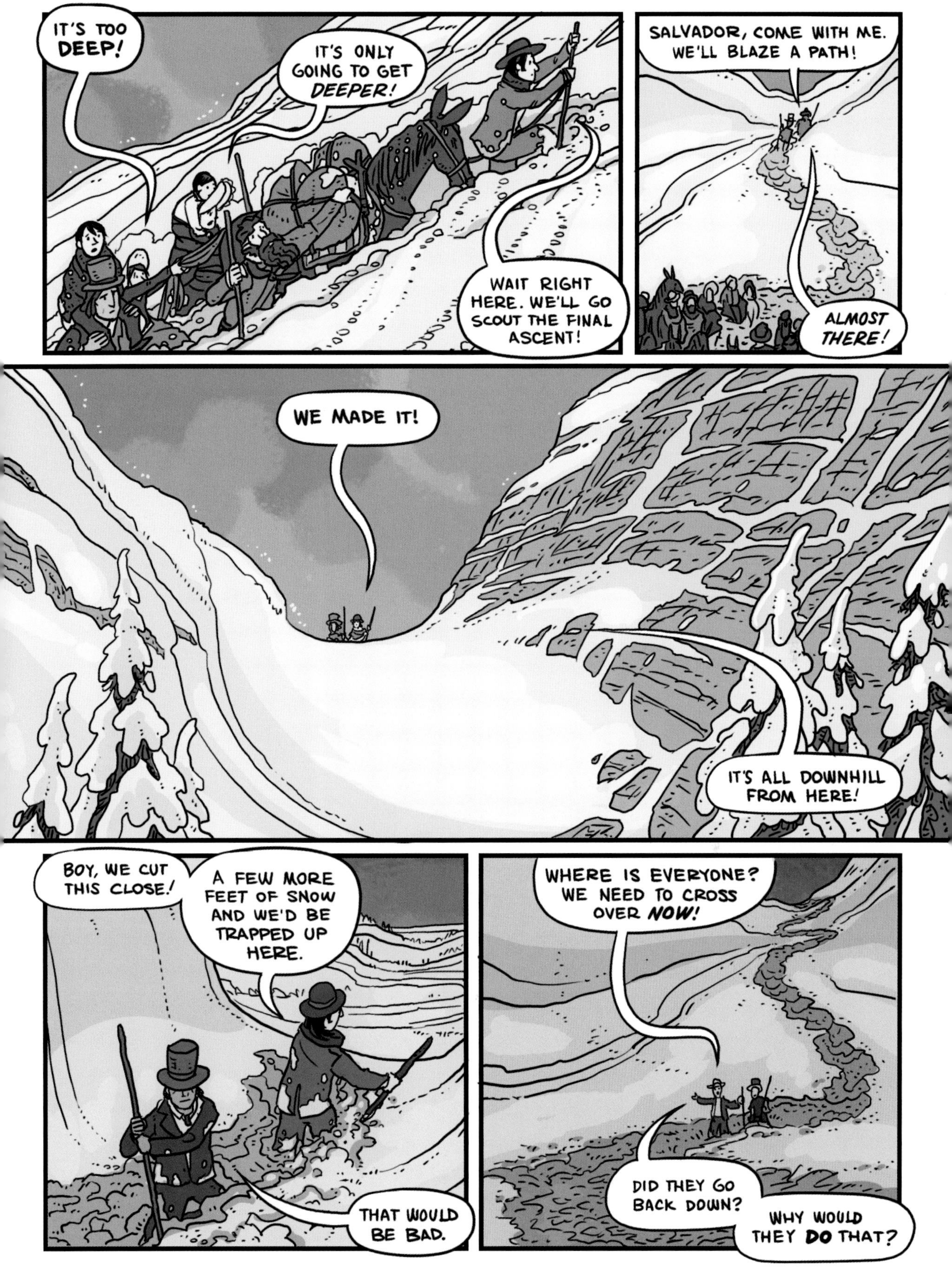
IT'S TOO DEEP!
IT'S ONLY GOING TO GET DEEPER!
WAIT RIGHT HERE. WE'LL GO SCOUT THE FINAL ASCENT!
SALVADOR, COME WITH ME. WE'LL BLAZE A PATH!
ALMOST THERE!
WE MADE IT!
IT'S ALL DOWNHILL FROM HERE!
BOY, WE CUT THIS CLOSE!
A FEW MORE FEET OF SNOW AND WE'D BE TRAPPED UP HERE.
THAT WOULD BE BAD.
WHERE IS EVERYONE? WE NEED TO CROSS OVER NOW!
DID THEY GO BACK DOWN?
WHY WOULD THEY DO THAT?

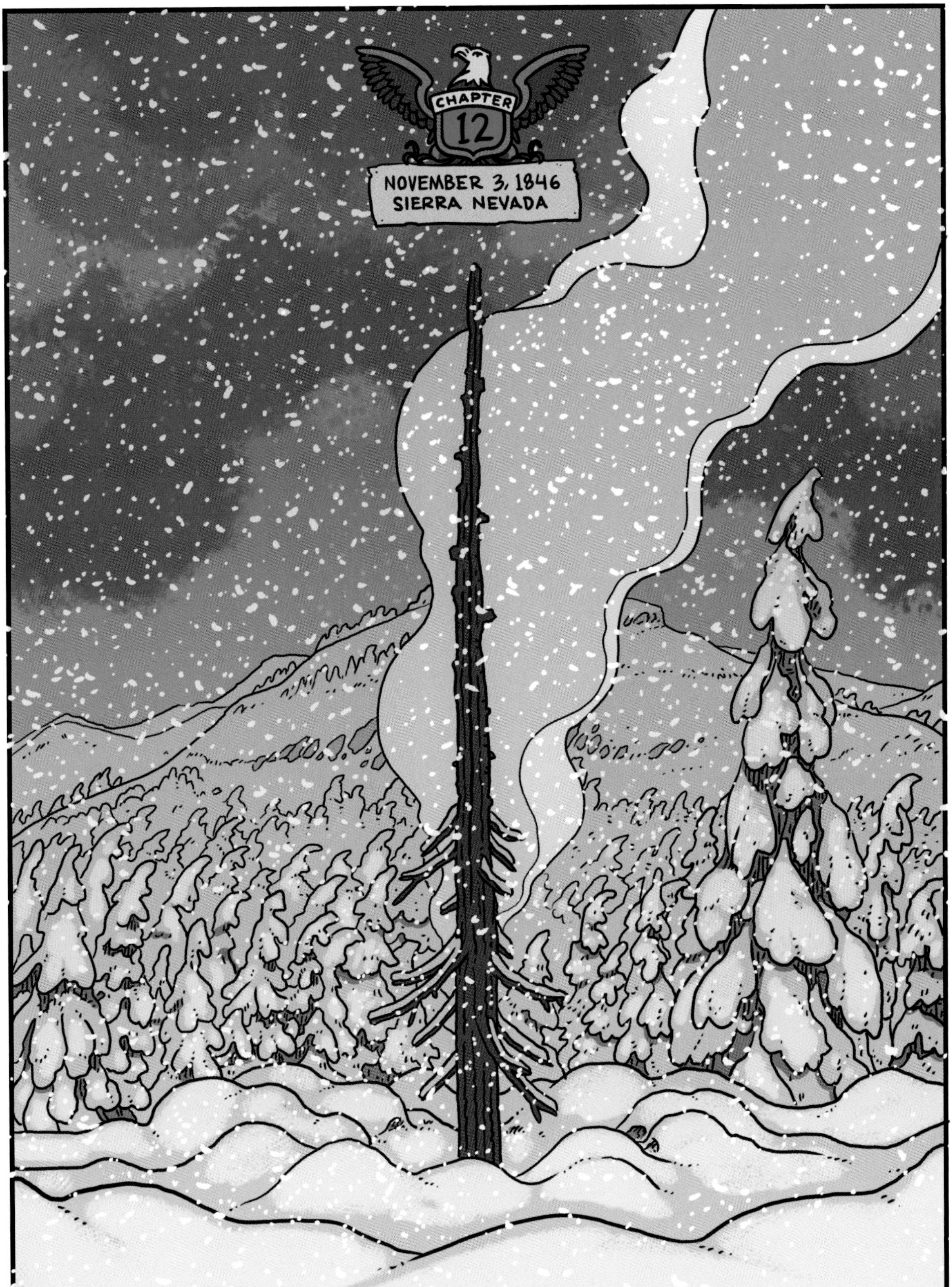
CHAPTER
12
NOVEMBER 3, 1846
SIERRA NEVADA

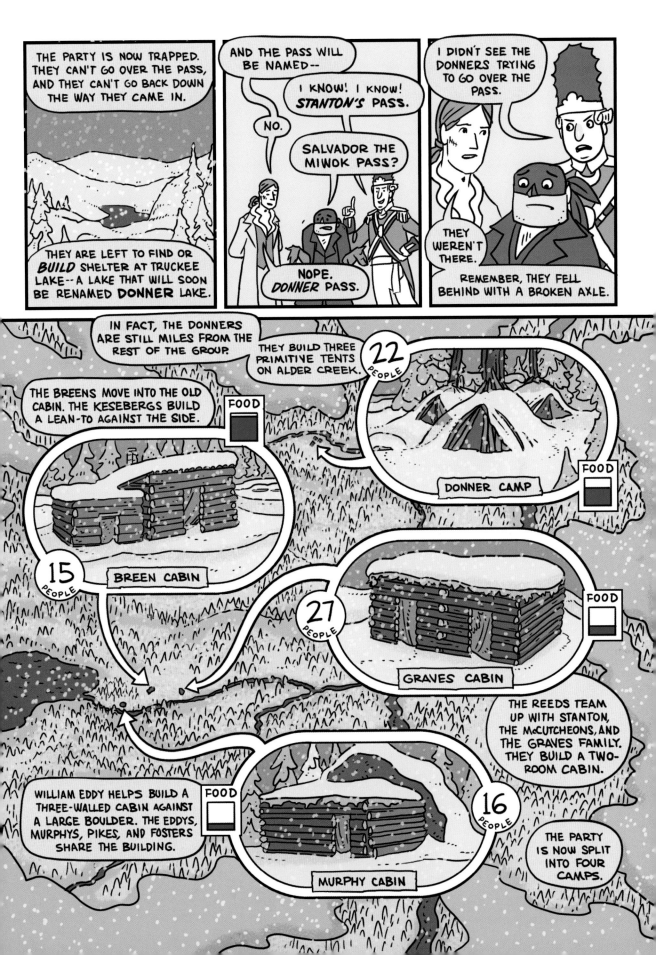

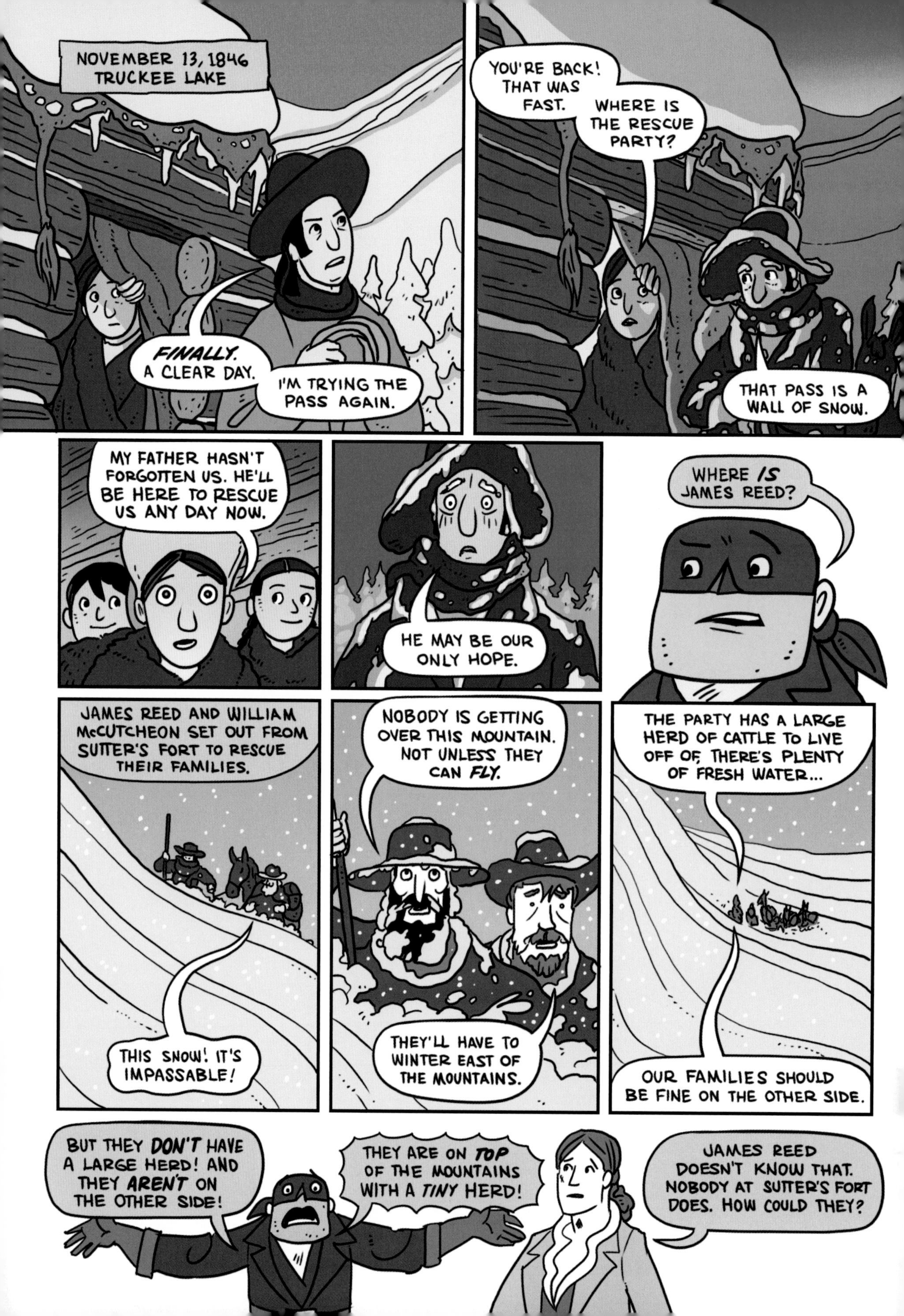
NOVEMBER 13, 1846
TRUCKEE LAKE
FINALLY. A CLEAR DAY.
I'M TRYING THE PASS AGAIN.
YOU'RE BACK! THAT WAS FAST.
WHERE IS THE RESCUE PARTY?
THAT PASS IS A WALL OF SNOW.
MY FATHER HASN'T FORGOTTEN US. HE'LL BE HERE TO RESCUE US ANY DAY NOW.
HE MAY BE OUR ONLY HOPE.
WHERE *IS* JAMES REED?
JAMES REED AND WILLIAM McCUTCHEON SET OUT FROM SUTTER'S FORT TO RESCUE THEIR FAMILIES.
THIS SNOW! IT'S IMPASSABLE!
NOBODY IS GETTING OVER THIS MOUNTAIN. NOT UNLESS THEY CAN *FLY*.
THEY'LL HAVE TO WINTER EAST OF THE MOUNTAINS.
THE PARTY HAS A LARGE HERD OF CATTLE TO LIVE OFF OF, THERE'S PLENTY OF FRESH WATER...
OUR FAMILIES SHOULD BE FINE ON THE OTHER SIDE.
BUT THEY *DON'T* HAVE A LARGE HERD! AND THEY *AREN'T* ON THE OTHER SIDE!
THEY ARE ON *TOP* OF THE MOUNTAINS WITH A *TINY* HERD!
JAMES REED DOESN'T KNOW THAT. NOBODY AT SUTTER'S FORT DOES. HOW COULD THEY?

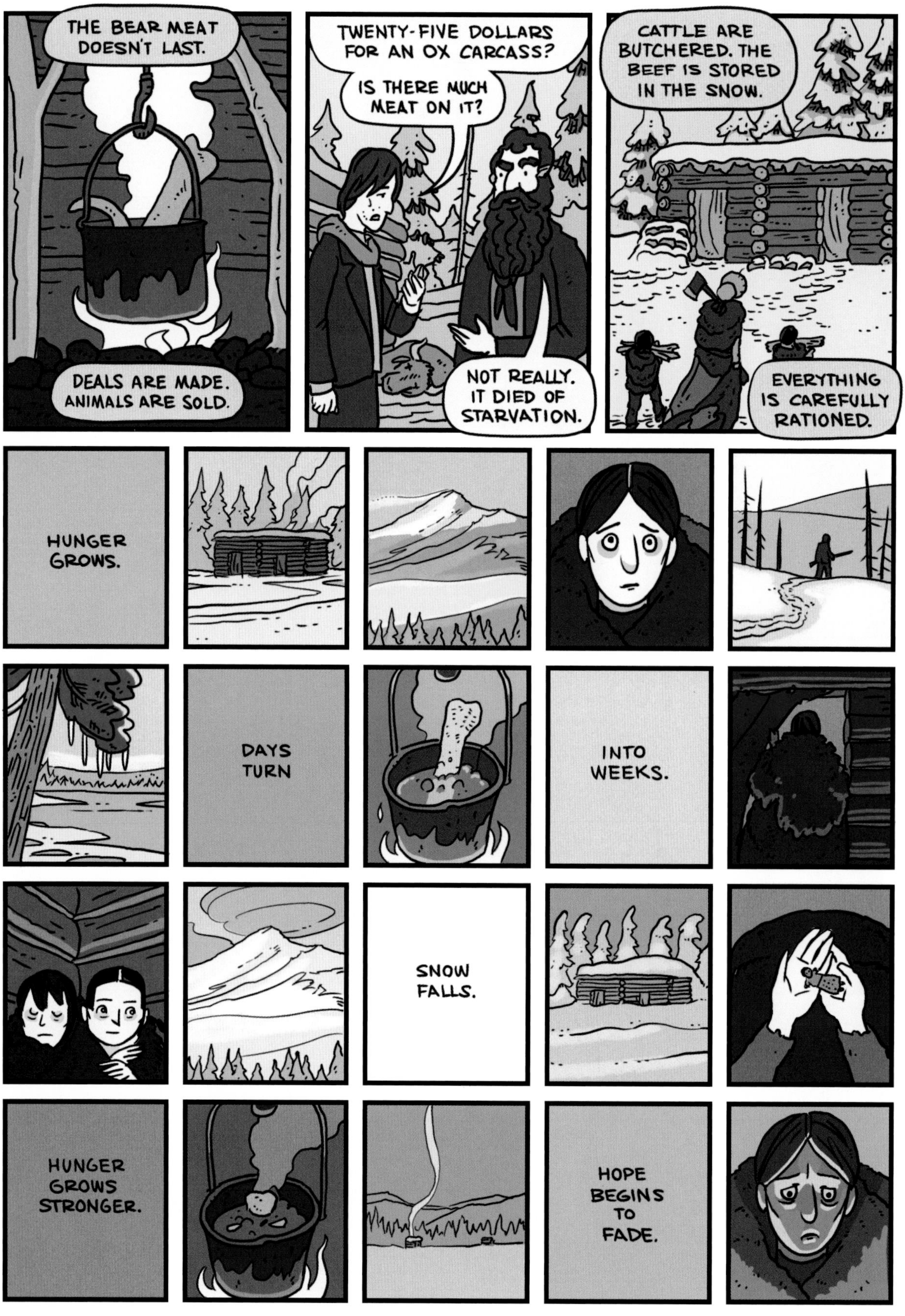
THE BEAR MEAT DOESN'T LAST.
DEALS ARE MADE. ANIMALS ARE SOLD.
TWENTY-FIVE DOLLARS FOR AN OX CARCASS?
IS THERE MUCH MEAT ON IT?
NOT REALLY. IT DIED OF STARVATION.
CATTLE ARE BUTCHERED. THE BEEF IS STORED IN THE SNOW.
EVERYTHING IS CAREFULLY RATIONED.
HUNGER GROWS.
DAYS TURN
INTO WEEKS.
SNOW FALLS.
HUNGER GROWS STRONGER.
HOPE BEGINS TO FADE.

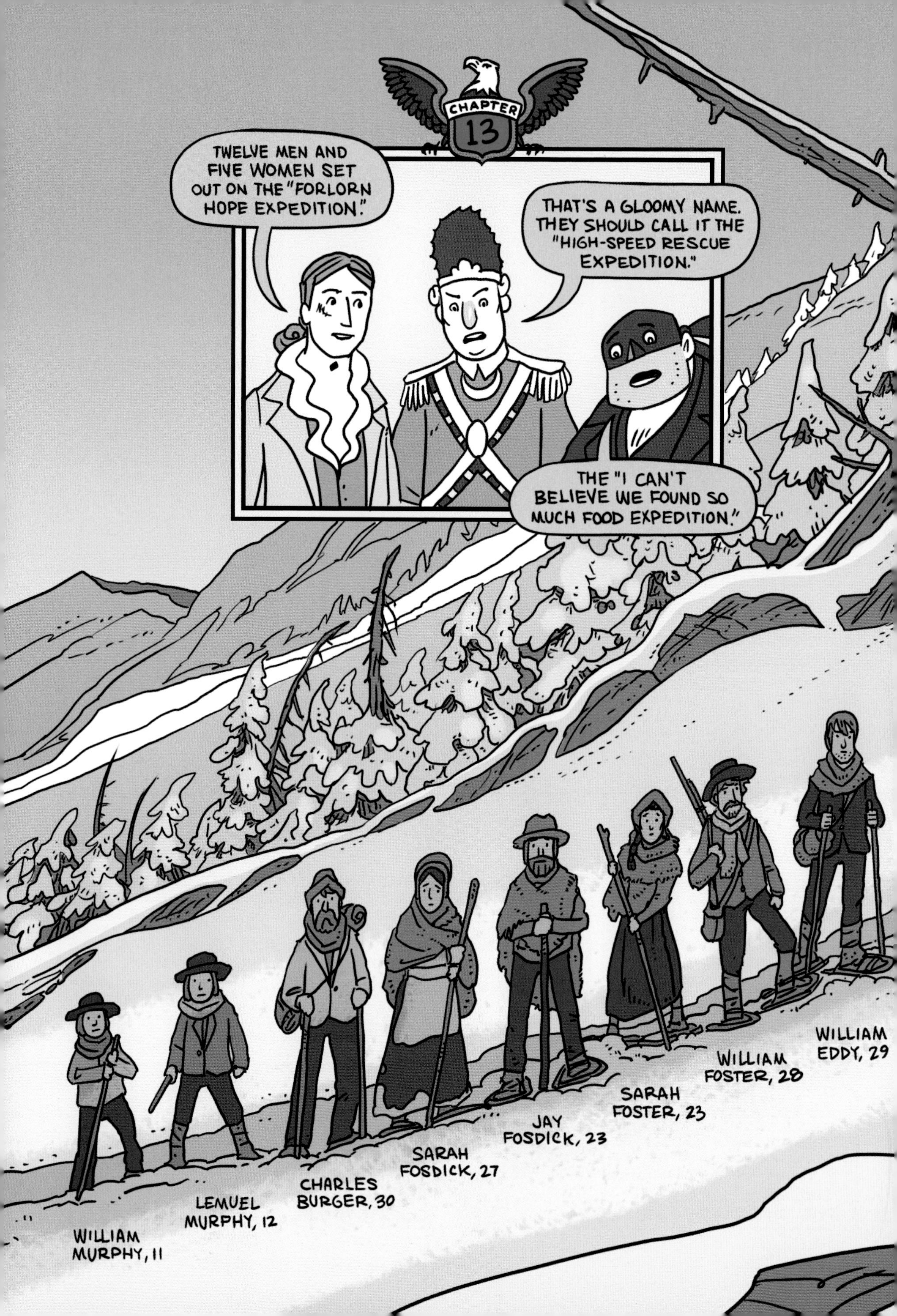
CHAPTER
13
TWELVE MEN AND FIVE WOMEN SET OUT ON THE "FORLORN HOPE EXPEDITION."
THAT'S A GLOOMY NAME. THEY SHOULD CALL IT THE "HIGH-SPEED RESCUE EXPEDITION."
THE "I CAN'T BELIEVE WE FOUND SO MUCH FOOD EXPEDITION."
WILLIAM MURPHY, 11
LEMUEL MURPHY, 12
CHARLES BURGER, 30
SARAH FOSDICK, 27
JAY FOSDICK, 23
SARAH FOSTER, 23
WILLIAM FOSTER, 28
WILLIAM EDDY, 29

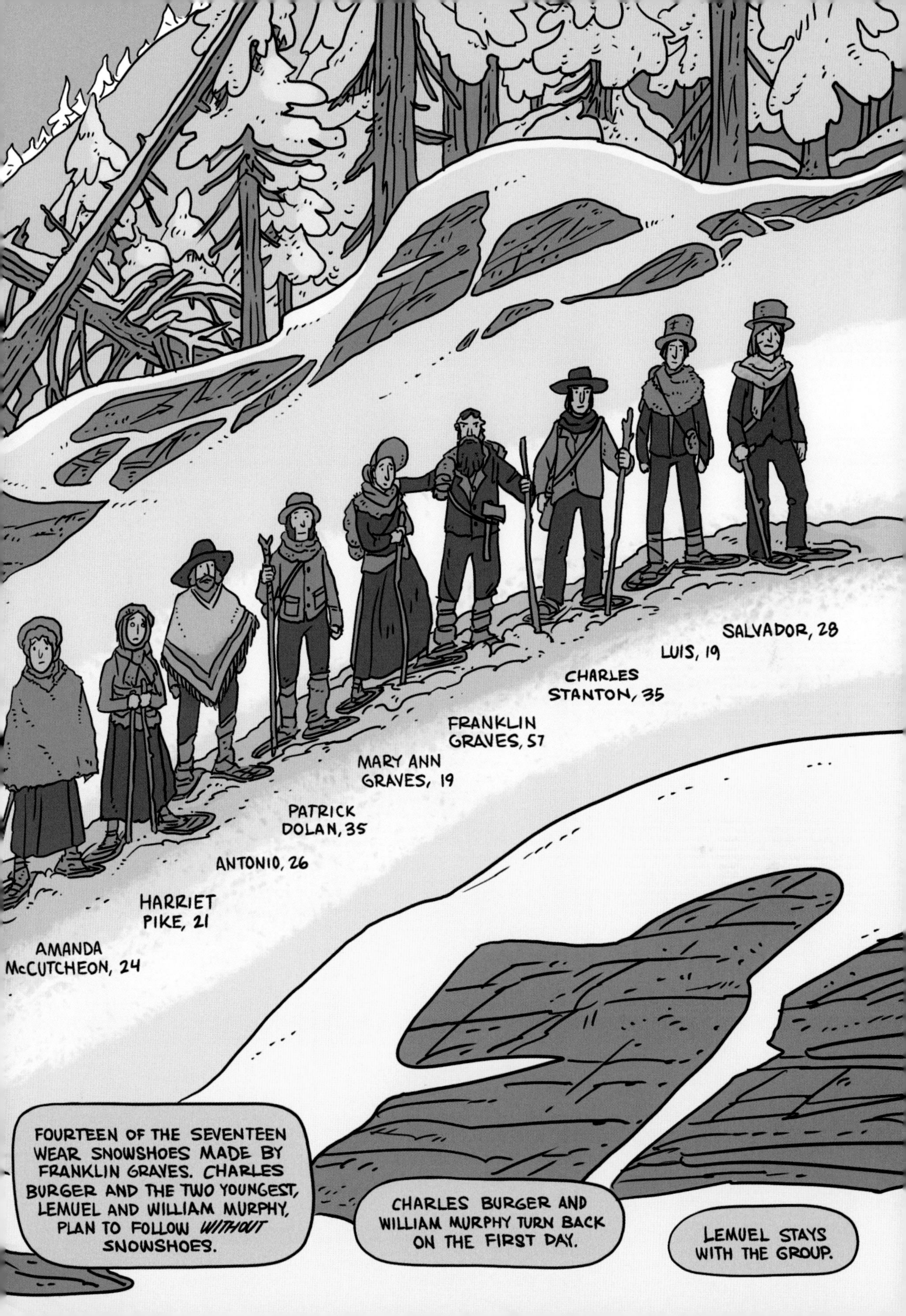
SALVADOR, 28
LUIS, 19
CHARLES STANTON, 35
FRANKLIN GRAVES, 57
MARY ANN GRAVES, 19
PATRICK DOLAN, 35
ANTONIO, 26
HARRIET PIKE, 21
AMANDA McCUTCHEON, 24
FOURTEEN OF THE SEVENTEEN WEAR SNOWSHOES MADE BY FRANKLIN GRAVES. CHARLES BURGER AND THE TWO YOUNGEST, LEMUEL AND WILLIAM MURPHY, PLAN TO FOLLOW *WITHOUT* SNOWSHOES.
CHARLES BURGER AND WILLIAM MURPHY TURN BACK ON THE FIRST DAY.
LEMUEL STAYS WITH THE GROUP.

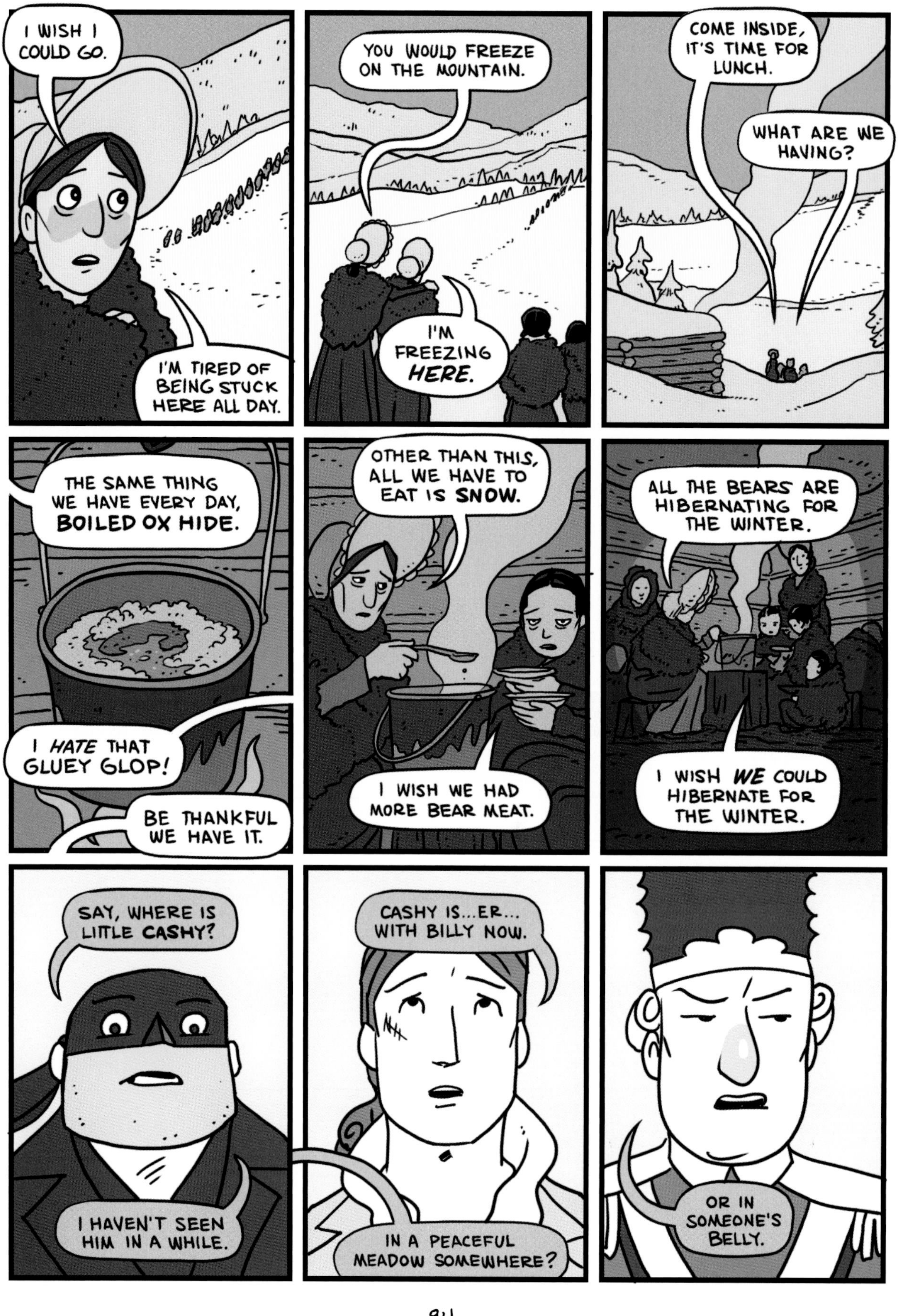
I WISH I COULD GO.
I'M TIRED OF BEING STUCK HERE ALL DAY.
YOU WOULD FREEZE ON THE MOUNTAIN.
I'M FREEZING HERE.
COME INSIDE, IT'S TIME FOR LUNCH.
WHAT ARE WE HAVING?
THE SAME THING WE HAVE EVERY DAY, BOILED OX HIDE.
I HATE THAT GLUEY GLOP!
BE THANKFUL WE HAVE IT.
OTHER THAN THIS, ALL WE HAVE TO EAT IS SNOW.
I WISH WE HAD MORE BEAR MEAT.
ALL THE BEARS ARE HIBERNATING FOR THE WINTER.
I WISH WE COULD HIBERNATE FOR THE WINTER.
SAY, WHERE IS LITTLE CASHY?
I HAVEN'T SEEN HIM IN A WHILE.
CASHY IS...ER... WITH BILLY NOW.
IN A PEACEFUL MEADOW SOMEWHERE?
OR IN SOMEONE'S BELLY.

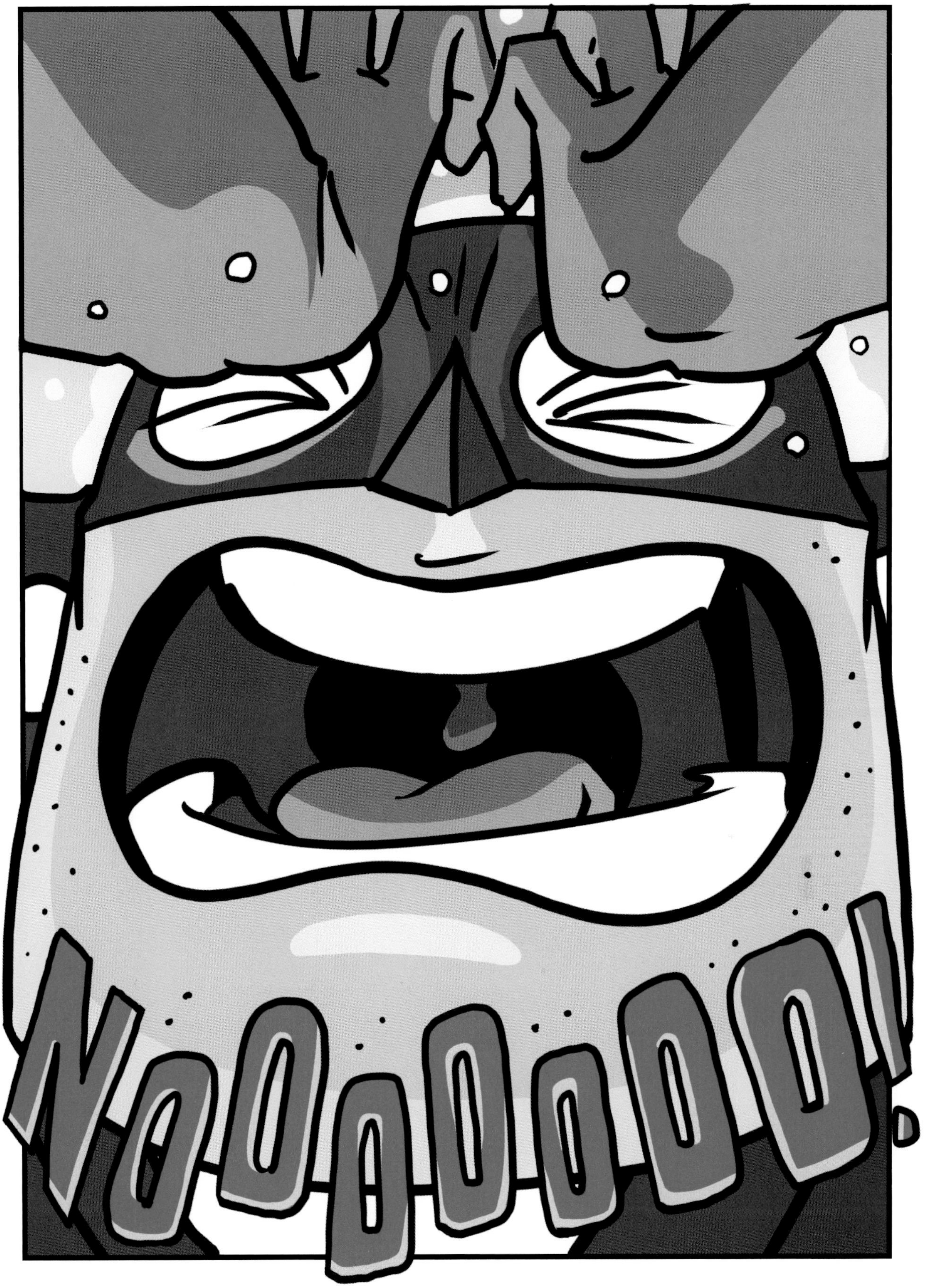
NOOOOOOO!!

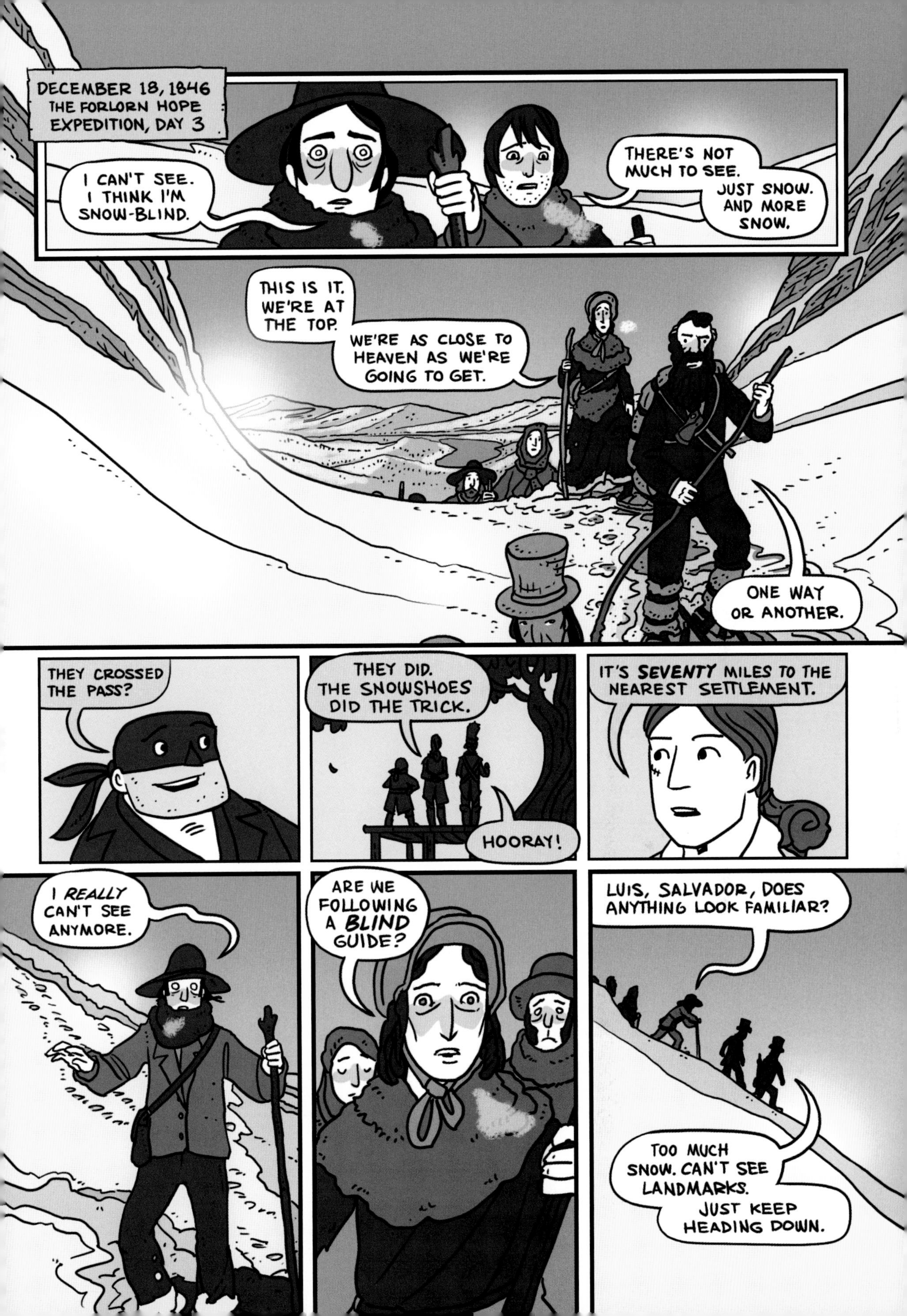
DECEMBER 18, 1846
THE FORLORN HOPE
EXPEDITION, DAY 3
I CAN'T SEE. I THINK I'M SNOW-BLIND.
THERE'S NOT MUCH TO SEE.
JUST SNOW. AND MORE SNOW.
THIS IS IT. WE'RE AT THE TOP.
WE'RE AS CLOSE TO HEAVEN AS WE'RE GOING TO GET.
ONE WAY OR ANOTHER.
THEY CROSSED THE PASS?
THEY DID. THE SNOWSHOES DID THE TRICK.
HOORAY!
IT'S SEVENTY MILES TO THE NEAREST SETTLEMENT.
I REALLY CAN'T SEE ANYMORE.
ARE WE FOLLOWING A BLIND GUIDE?
LUIS, SALVADOR, DOES ANYTHING LOOK FAMILIAR?
TOO MUCH SNOW. CAN'T SEE LANDMARKS.
JUST KEEP HEADING DOWN.

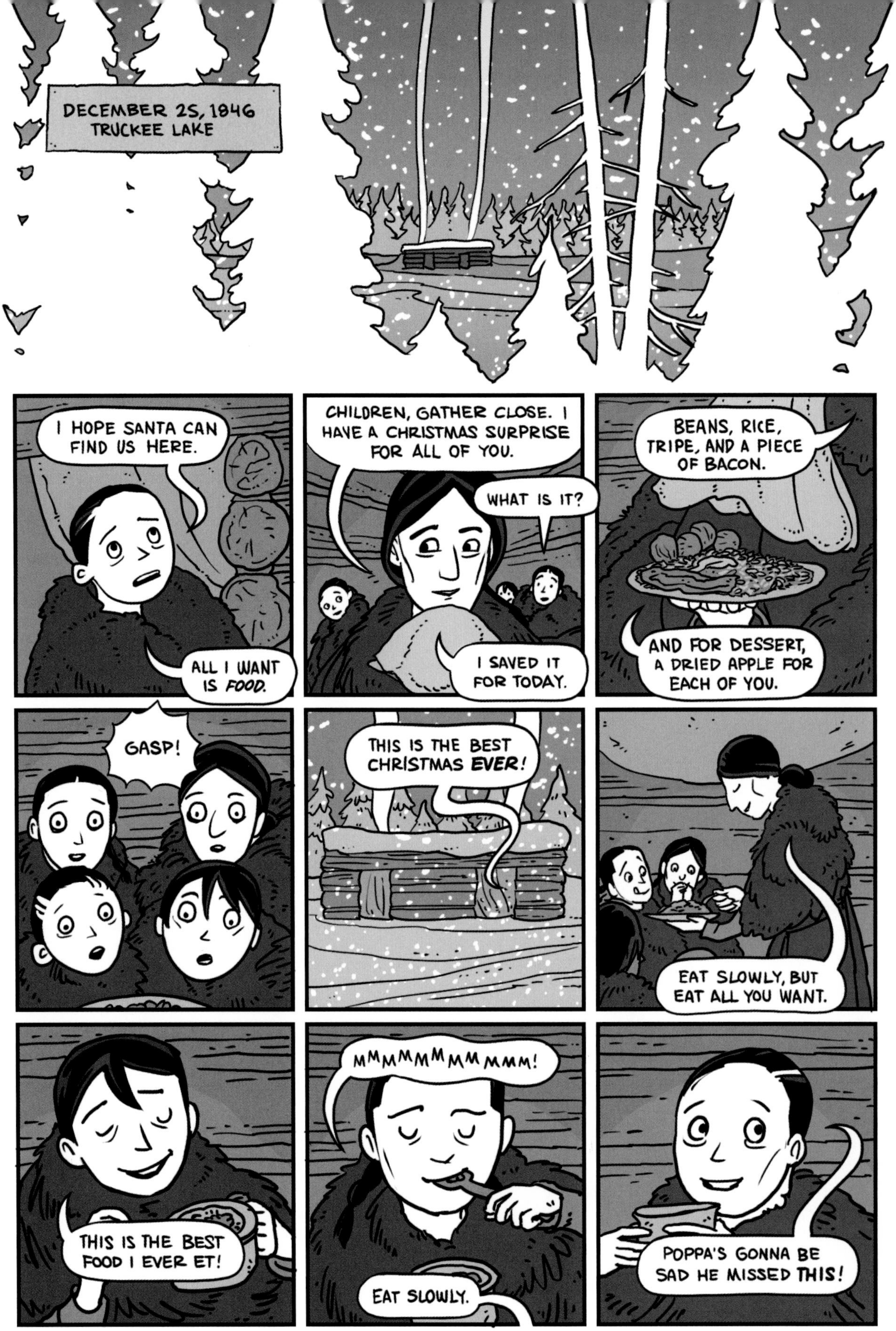
DECEMBER 25, 1846
TRUCKEE LAKE
I HOPE SANTA CAN FIND US HERE.
ALL I WANT IS *FOOD.*
CHILDREN, GATHER CLOSE. I HAVE A CHRISTMAS SURPRISE FOR ALL OF YOU.
WHAT IS IT?
I SAVED IT FOR TODAY.
BEANS, RICE, TRIPE, AND A PIECE OF BACON.
AND FOR DESSERT, A DRIED APPLE FOR EACH OF YOU.
GASP!
THIS IS THE BEST CHRISTMAS **EVER**!
EAT SLOWLY, BUT EAT ALL YOU WANT.
THIS IS THE BEST FOOD I EVER ET!
MMMMMMMMMMM!
EAT SLOWLY.
POPPA'S GONNA BE SAD HE MISSED **THIS**!

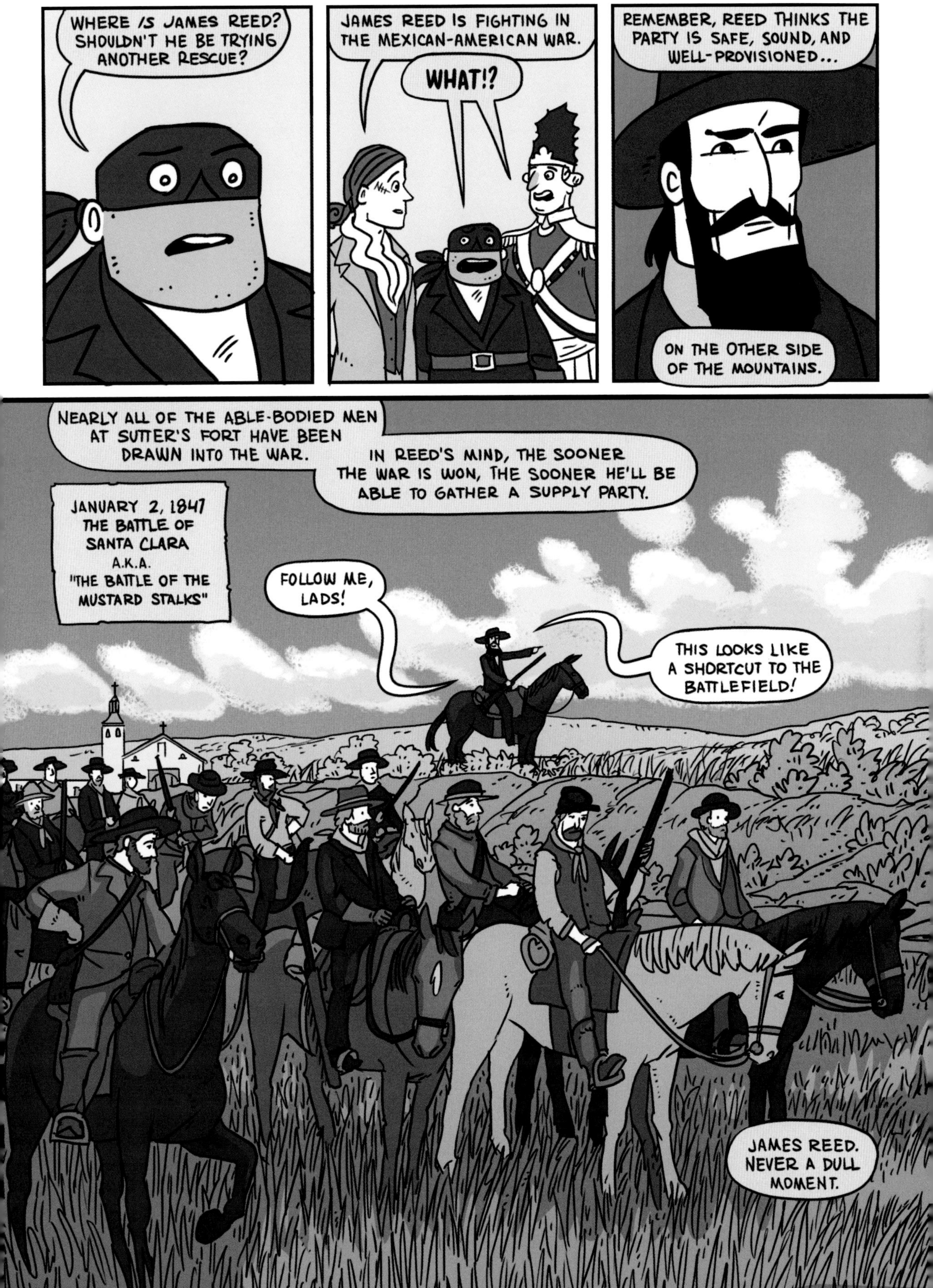
WHERE IS JAMES REED? SHOULDN'T HE BE TRYING ANOTHER RESCUE?
JAMES REED IS FIGHTING IN THE MEXICAN-AMERICAN WAR.
WHAT!?
REMEMBER, REED THINKS THE PARTY IS SAFE, SOUND, AND WELL-PROVISIONED...
ON THE OTHER SIDE OF THE MOUNTAINS.
NEARLY ALL OF THE ABLE-BODIED MEN AT SUTTER'S FORT HAVE BEEN DRAWN INTO THE WAR.
IN REED'S MIND, THE SOONER THE WAR IS WON, THE SOONER HE'LL BE ABLE TO GATHER A SUPPLY PARTY.
JANUARY 2, 1847 THE BATTLE OF SANTA CLARA A.K.A. "THE BATTLE OF THE MUSTARD STALKS"
FOLLOW ME, LADS!
THIS LOOKS LIKE A SHORTCUT TO THE BATTLEFIELD!
JAMES REED. NEVER A DULL MOMENT.

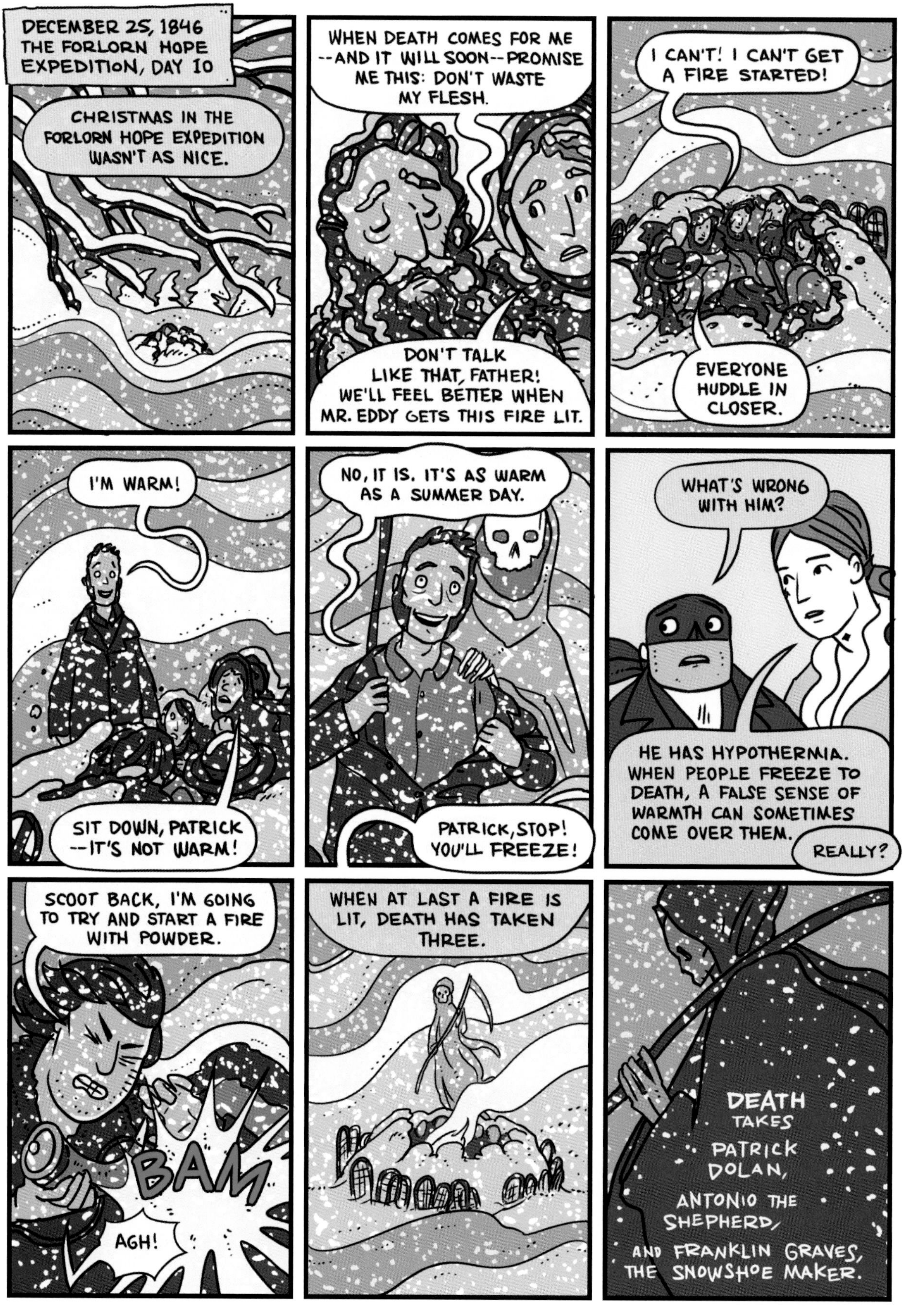
DECEMBER 25, 1846
THE FORLORN HOPE EXPEDITION, DAY 10
CHRISTMAS IN THE FORLORN HOPE EXPEDITION WASN'T AS NICE.
WHEN DEATH COMES FOR ME --AND IT WILL SOON--PROMISE ME THIS: DON'T WASTE MY FLESH.
DON'T TALK LIKE THAT, FATHER! WE'LL FEEL BETTER WHEN MR. EDDY GETS THIS FIRE LIT.
I CAN'T! I CAN'T GET A FIRE STARTED!
EVERYONE HUDDLE IN CLOSER.
I'M WARM!
SIT DOWN, PATRICK --IT'S NOT WARM!
NO, IT IS. IT'S AS WARM AS A SUMMER DAY.
PATRICK, STOP! YOU'LL FREEZE!
WHAT'S WRONG WITH HIM?
HE HAS HYPOTHERMIA. WHEN PEOPLE FREEZE TO DEATH, A FALSE SENSE OF WARMTH CAN SOMETIMES COME OVER THEM.
REALLY?
SCOOT BACK, I'M GOING TO TRY AND START A FIRE WITH POWDER.
BAM
AGH!
WHEN AT LAST A FIRE IS LIT, DEATH HAS TAKEN THREE.
DEATH TAKES PATRICK DOLAN, ANTONIO THE SHEPHERD, AND FRANKLIN GRAVES, THE SNOWSHOE MAKER.

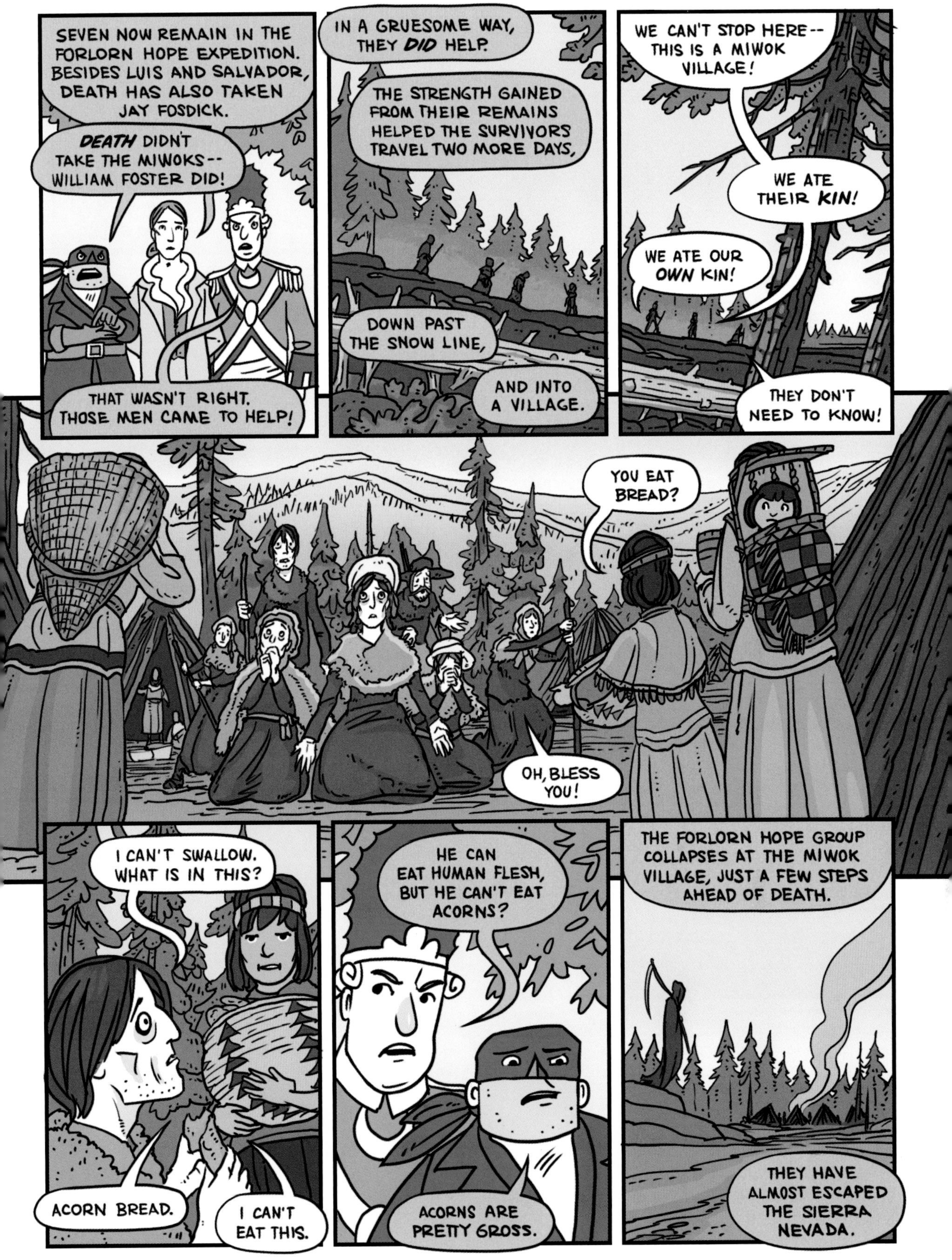
SEVEN NOW REMAIN IN THE FORLORN HOPE EXPEDITION. BESIDES LUIS AND SALVADOR, DEATH HAS ALSO TAKEN JAY FOSDICK.
DEATH DIDN'T TAKE THE MIWOKS-- WILLIAM FOSTER DID!
THAT WASN'T RIGHT. THOSE MEN CAME TO HELP!
IN A GRUESOME WAY, THEY DID HELP.
THE STRENGTH GAINED FROM THEIR REMAINS HELPED THE SURVIVORS TRAVEL TWO MORE DAYS,
DOWN PAST THE SNOW LINE,
AND INTO A VILLAGE.
WE CAN'T STOP HERE-- THIS IS A MIWOK VILLAGE!
WE ATE THEIR KIN!
WE ATE OUR OWN KIN!
THEY DON'T NEED TO KNOW!
YOU EAT BREAD?
OH, BLESS YOU!
I CAN'T SWALLOW. WHAT IS IN THIS?
ACORN BREAD.
I CAN'T EAT THIS.
HE CAN EAT HUMAN FLESH, BUT HE CAN'T EAT ACORNS?
ACORNS ARE PRETTY GROSS.
THE FORLORN HOPE GROUP COLLAPSES AT THE MIWOK VILLAGE, JUST A FEW STEPS AHEAD OF DEATH.
THEY HAVE ALMOST ESCAPED THE SIERRA NEVADA.

111

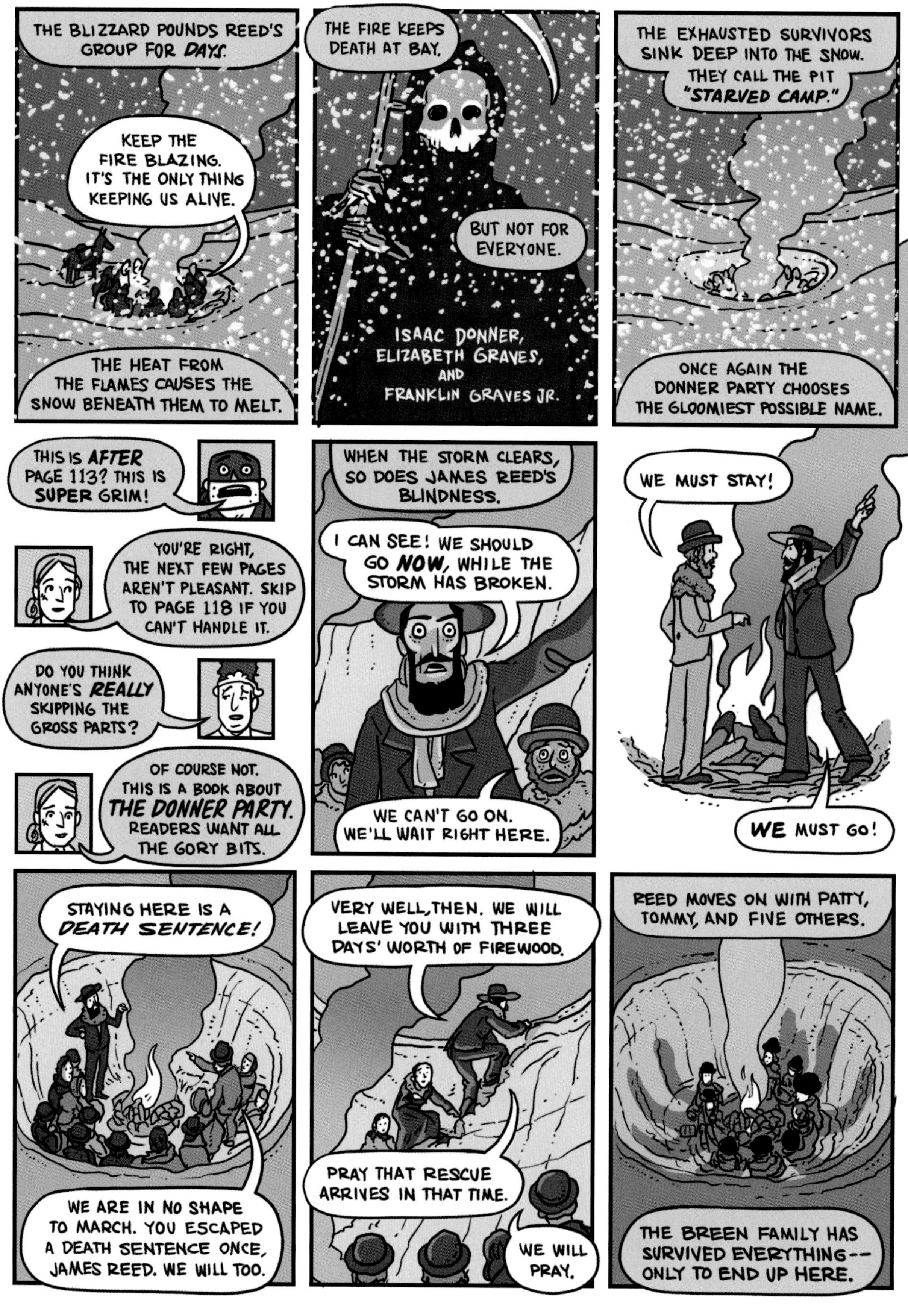

THE BLIZZARD POUNDS REED'S GROUP FOR DAYS.
KEEP THE FIRE BLAZING. IT'S THE ONLY THING KEEPING US ALIVE.
THE HEAT FROM THE FLAMES CAUSES THE SNOW BENEATH THEM TO MELT.
THE FIRE KEEPS DEATH AT BAY.
BUT NOT FOR EVERYONE.
ISAAC DONNER, ELIZABETH GRAVES, AND FRANKLIN GRAVES JR.
THE EXHAUSTED SURVIVORS SINK DEEP INTO THE SNOW. THEY CALL THE PIT "STARVED CAMP."
ONCE AGAIN THE DONNER PARTY CHOOSES THE GLOOMIEST POSSIBLE NAME.
THIS IS AFTER PAGE 113? THIS IS SUPER GRIM!
YOU'RE RIGHT, THE NEXT FEW PAGES AREN'T PLEASANT. SKIP TO PAGE 118 IF YOU CAN'T HANDLE IT.
DO YOU THINK ANYONE'S REALLY SKIPPING THE GROSS PARTS?
OF COURSE NOT. THIS IS A BOOK ABOUT THE DONNER PARTY. READERS WANT ALL THE GORY BITS.
WHEN THE STORM CLEARS, SO DOES JAMES REED'S BLINDNESS.
I CAN SEE! WE SHOULD GO NOW, WHILE THE STORM HAS BROKEN.
WE CAN'T GO ON. WE'LL WAIT RIGHT HERE.
WE MUST STAY!
WE MUST GO!
STAYING HERE IS A DEATH SENTENCE!
WE ARE IN NO SHAPE TO MARCH. YOU ESCAPED A DEATH SENTENCE ONCE, JAMES REED. WE WILL TOO.
VERY WELL, THEN. WE WILL LEAVE YOU WITH THREE DAYS' WORTH OF FIREWOOD.
PRAY THAT RESCUE ARRIVES IN THAT TIME.
WE WILL PRAY.
REED MOVES ON WITH PATTY, TOMMY, AND FIVE OTHERS.
THE BREEN FAMILY HAS SURVIVED EVERYTHING-- ONLY TO END UP HERE.

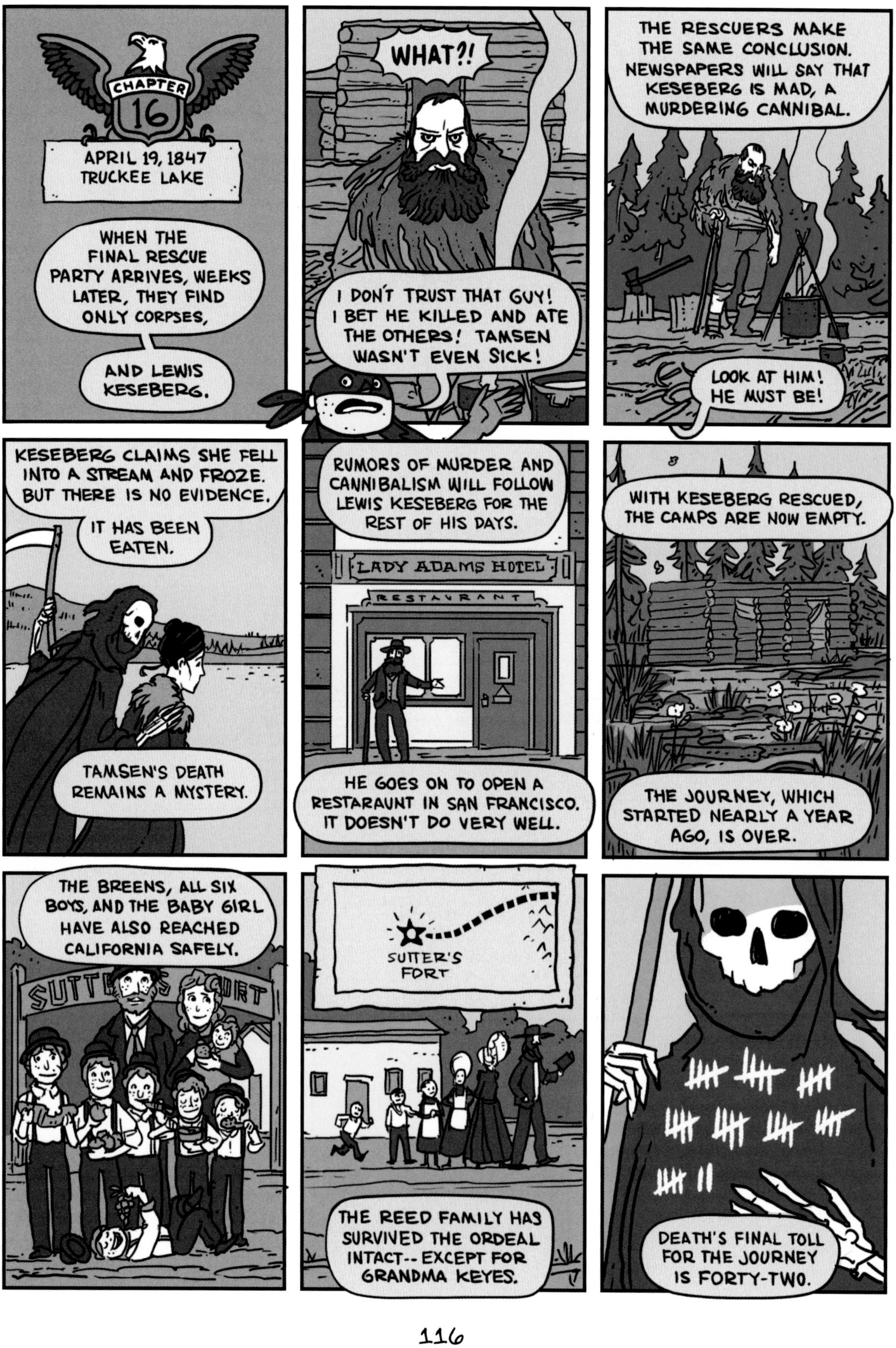
CHAPTER
16
APRIL 19, 1847
TRUCKEE LAKE
WHEN THE FINAL RESCUE PARTY ARRIVES, WEEKS LATER, THEY FIND ONLY CORPSES,
AND LEWIS KESEBERG.
WHAT?!
I DON'T TRUST THAT GUY! I BET HE KILLED AND ATE THE OTHERS! TAMSEN WASN'T EVEN SICK!
THE RESCUERS MAKE THE SAME CONCLUSION. NEWSPAPERS WILL SAY THAT KESEBERG IS MAD, A MURDERING CANNIBAL.
LOOK AT HIM! HE MUST BE!
KESEBERG CLAIMS SHE FELL INTO A STREAM AND FROZE. BUT THERE IS NO EVIDENCE.
IT HAS BEEN EATEN.
TAMSEN'S DEATH REMAINS A MYSTERY.
RUMORS OF MURDER AND CANNIBALISM WILL FOLLOW LEWIS KESEBERG FOR THE REST OF HIS DAYS.
LADY ADAMS HOTEL
RESTAURANT
HE GOES ON TO OPEN A RESTARAUNT IN SAN FRANCISCO. IT DOESN'T DO VERY WELL.
WITH KESEBERG RESCUED, THE CAMPS ARE NOW EMPTY.
THE JOURNEY, WHICH STARTED NEARLY A YEAR AGO, IS OVER.
THE BREENS, ALL SIX BOYS, AND THE BABY GIRL HAVE ALSO REACHED CALIFORNIA SAFELY.
SUTTER'S FORT
THE REED FAMILY HAS SURVIVED THE ORDEAL INTACT-- EXCEPT FOR GRANDMA KEYES.
DEATH'S FINAL TOLL FOR THE JOURNEY IS FORTY-TWO.

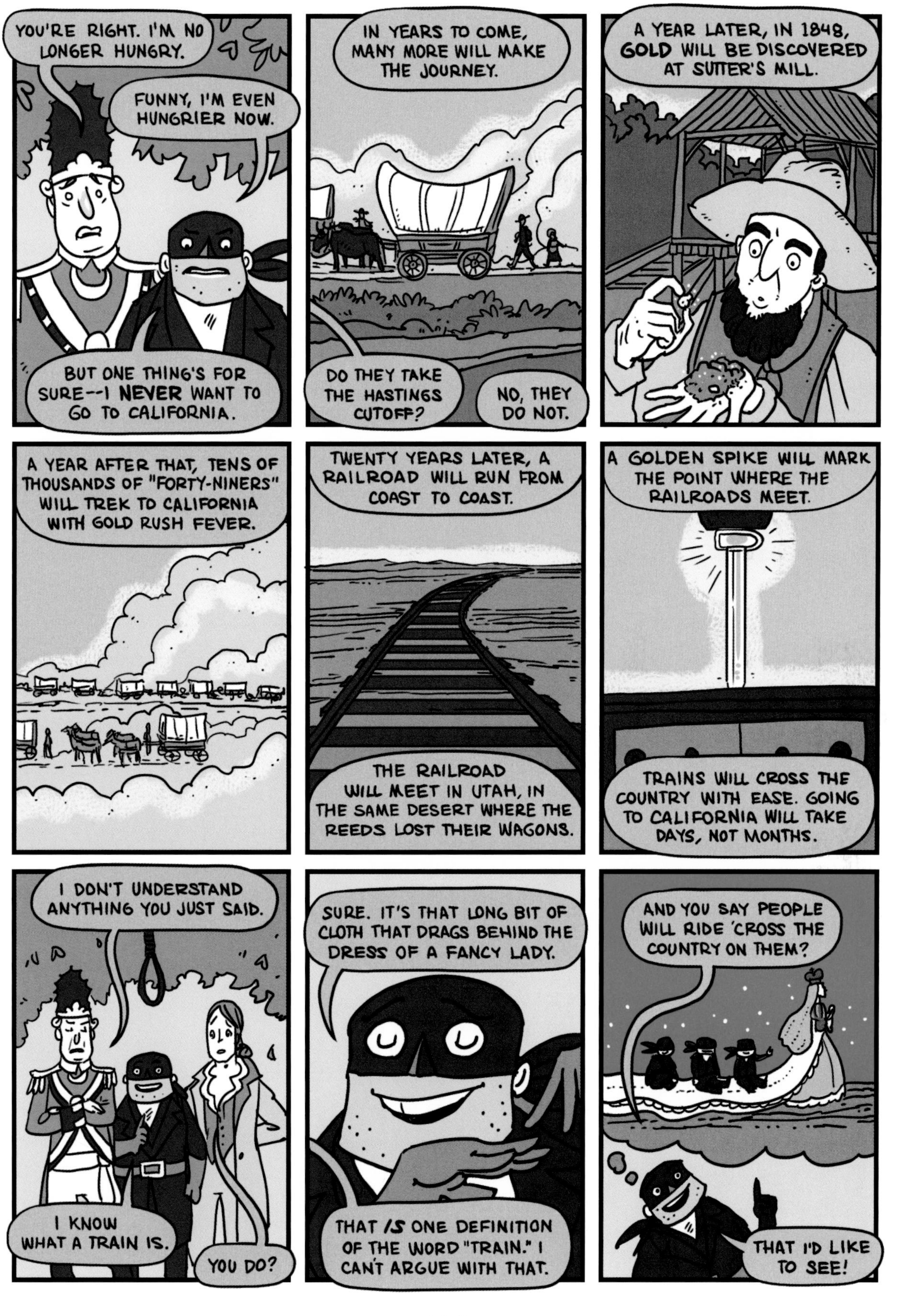
YOU'RE RIGHT. I'M NO LONGER HUNGRY.
FUNNY, I'M EVEN HUNGRIER NOW.
BUT ONE THING'S FOR SURE--I **NEVER** WANT TO GO TO CALIFORNIA.
IN YEARS TO COME, MANY MORE WILL MAKE THE JOURNEY.
DO THEY TAKE THE HASTINGS CUTOFF?
NO, THEY DO NOT.
A YEAR LATER, IN 1848, **GOLD** WILL BE DISCOVERED AT SUTTER'S MILL.
A YEAR AFTER THAT, TENS OF THOUSANDS OF "FORTY-NINERS" WILL TREK TO CALIFORNIA WITH GOLD RUSH FEVER.
TWENTY YEARS LATER, A RAILROAD WILL RUN FROM COAST TO COAST.
THE RAILROAD WILL MEET IN UTAH, IN THE SAME DESERT WHERE THE REEDS LOST THEIR WAGONS.
A GOLDEN SPIKE WILL MARK THE POINT WHERE THE RAILROADS MEET.
TRAINS WILL CROSS THE COUNTRY WITH EASE. GOING TO CALIFORNIA WILL TAKE DAYS, NOT MONTHS.
I DON'T UNDERSTAND ANYTHING YOU JUST SAID.
I KNOW WHAT A TRAIN IS.
YOU DO?
SURE. IT'S THAT LONG BIT OF CLOTH THAT DRAGS BEHIND THE DRESS OF A FANCY LADY.
THAT *IS* ONE DEFINITION OF THE WORD "TRAIN." I CAN'T ARGUE WITH THAT.
AND YOU SAY PEOPLE WILL RIDE 'CROSS THE COUNTRY ON THEM?
THAT I'D LIKE TO SEE!

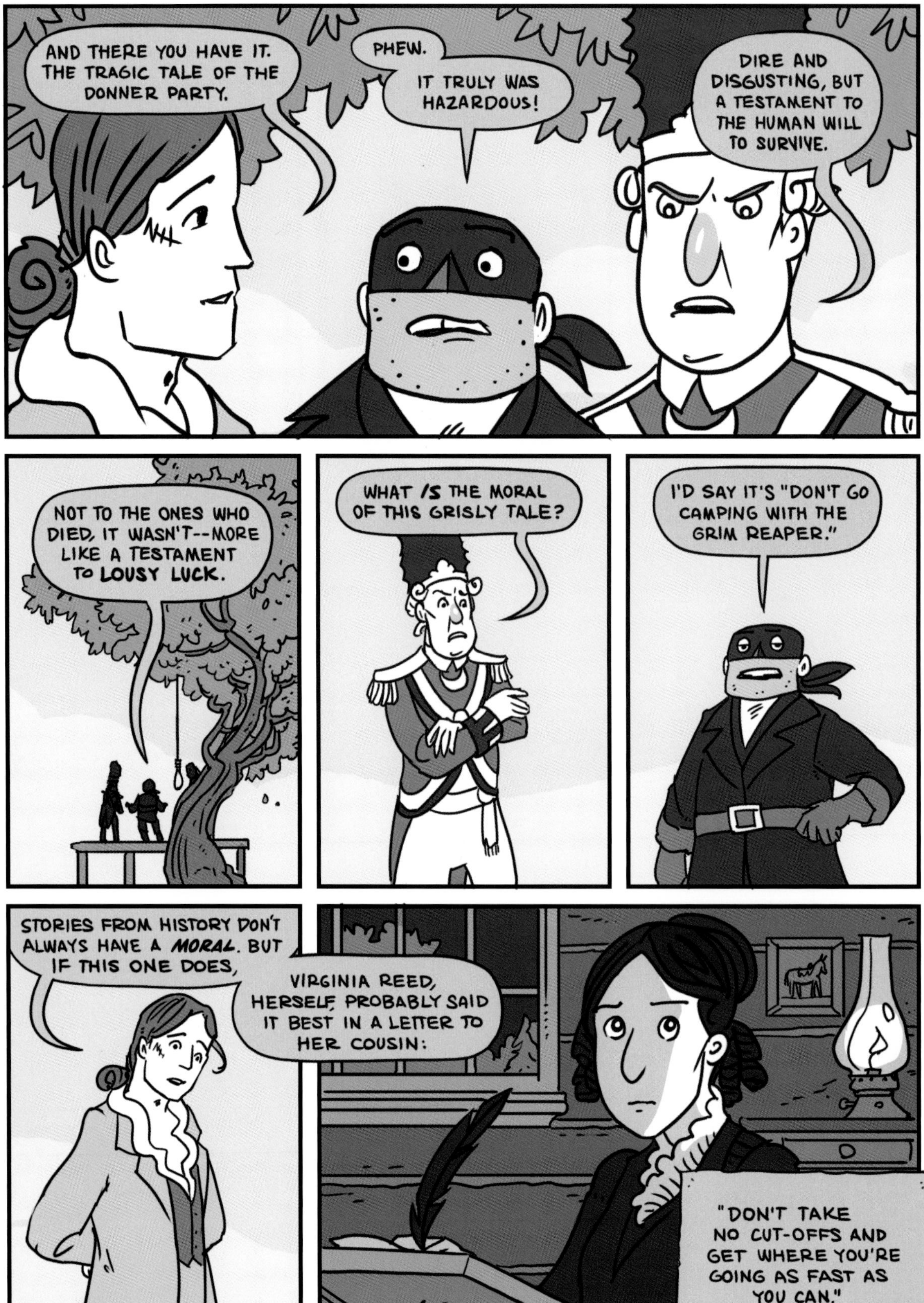
AND THERE YOU HAVE IT. THE TRAGIC TALE OF THE DONNER PARTY.
PHEW.
IT TRULY WAS HAZARDOUS!
DIRE AND DISGUSTING, BUT A TESTAMENT TO THE HUMAN WILL TO SURVIVE.
NOT TO THE ONES WHO DIED, IT WASN'T--MORE LIKE A TESTAMENT TO LOUSY LUCK.
WHAT IS THE MORAL OF THIS GRISLY TALE?
I'D SAY IT'S "DON'T GO CAMPING WITH THE GRIM REAPER."
STORIES FROM HISTORY DON'T ALWAYS HAVE A MORAL. BUT IF THIS ONE DOES,
VIRGINIA REED, HERSELF, PROBABLY SAID IT BEST IN A LETTER TO HER COUSIN:
"DON'T TAKE NO CUT-OFFS AND GET WHERE YOU'RE GOING AS FAST AS YOU CAN."

NATHAN HALE'S HAZARDOUS TALES

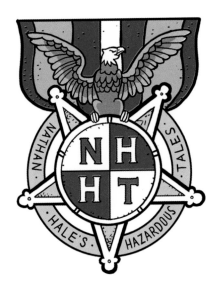

WHO DIED AND WHO SURVIVED

KEY: STARVATION/EXPOSURE ACCIDENTAL SHOOTING

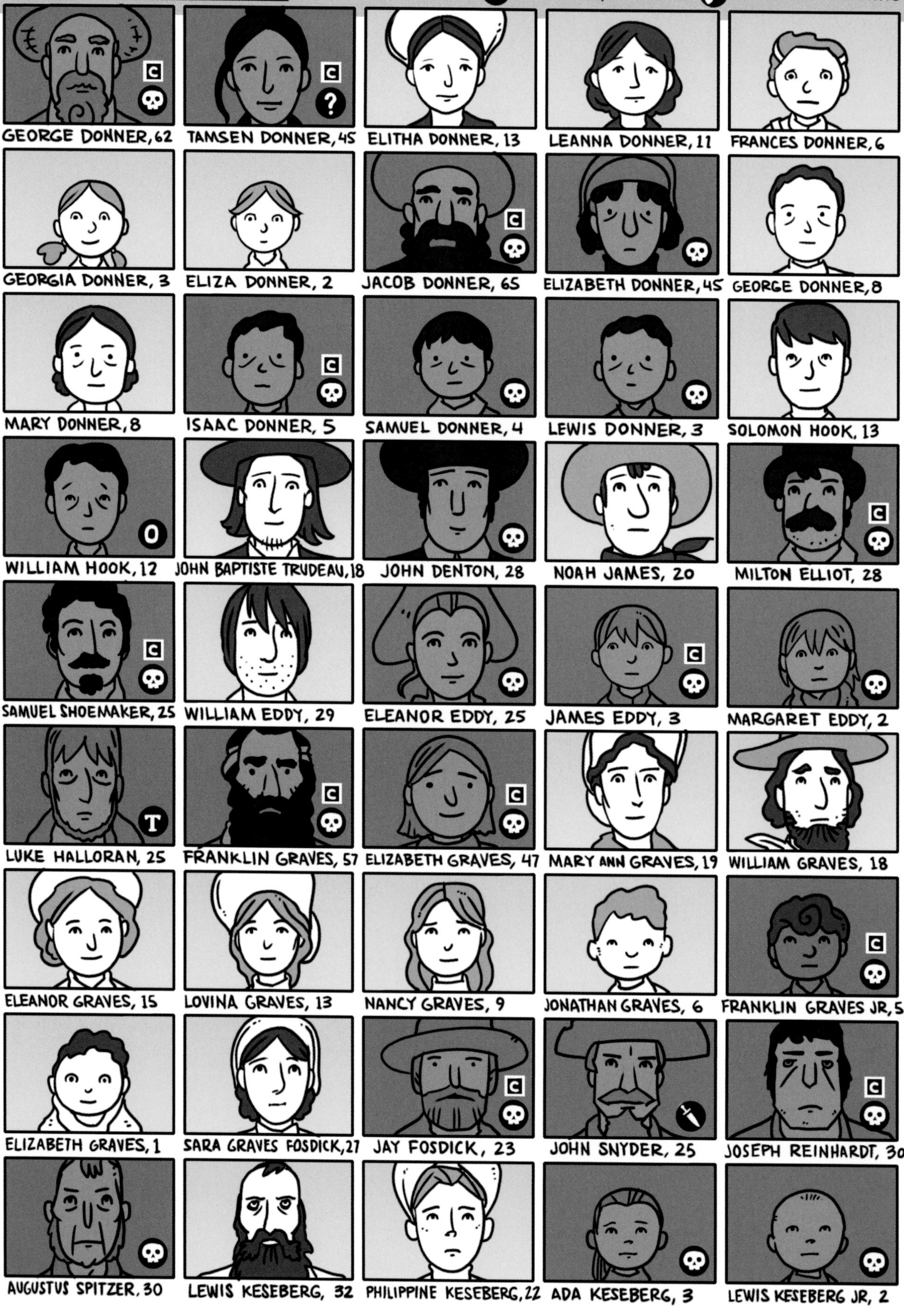

GEORGE DONNER, 62
TAMSEN DONNER, 45
ELITHA DONNER, 13
LEANNA DONNER, 11
FRANCES DONNER, 6
GEORGIA DONNER, 3
ELIZA DONNER, 2
JACOB DONNER, 65
ELIZABETH DONNER, 45
GEORGE DONNER, 8
MARY DONNER, 8
ISAAC DONNER, 5
SAMUEL DONNER, 4
LEWIS DONNER, 3
SOLOMON HOOK, 13
WILLIAM HOOK, 12
JOHN BAPTISTE TRUDEAU, 18
JOHN DENTON, 28
NOAH JAMES, 20
MILTON ELLIOT, 28
SAMUEL SHOEMAKER, 25
WILLIAM EDDY, 29
ELEANOR EDDY, 25
JAMES EDDY, 3
MARGARET EDDY, 2
LUKE HALLORAN, 25
FRANKLIN GRAVES, 57
ELIZABETH GRAVES, 47
MARY ANN GRAVES, 19
WILLIAM GRAVES, 18
ELEANOR GRAVES, 15
LOVINA GRAVES, 13
NANCY GRAVES, 9
JONATHAN GRAVES, 6
FRANKLIN GRAVES JR, 5
ELIZABETH GRAVES, 1
SARA GRAVES FOSDICK, 27
JAY FOSDICK, 23
JOHN SNYDER, 25
JOSEPH REINHARDT, 30
AUGUSTUS SPITZER, 30
LEWIS KESEBERG, 32
PHILIPPINE KESEBERG, 22
ADA KESEBERG, 3
LEWIS KESEBERG JR, 2

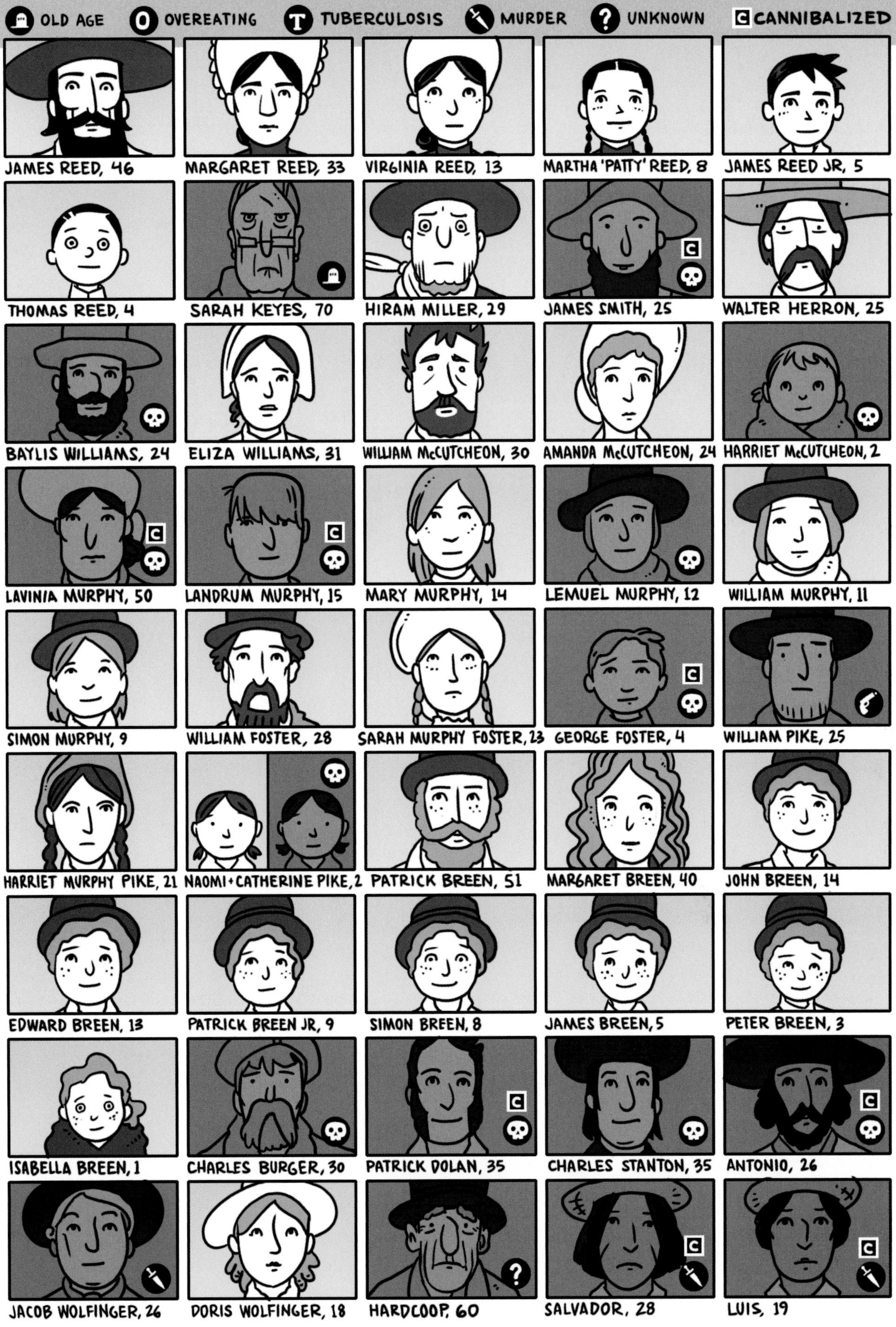
OLD AGE
O OVEREATING
T TUBERCULOSIS
MURDER
? UNKNOWN
C CANNIBALIZED
JAMES REED, 46
MARGARET REED, 33
VIRGINIA REED, 13
MARTHA 'PATTY' REED, 8
JAMES REED JR, 5
THOMAS REED, 4
SARAH KEYES, 70
HIRAM MILLER, 29
C
JAMES SMITH, 25
WALTER HERRON, 25
BAYLIS WILLIAMS, 24
ELIZA WILLIAMS, 31
WILLIAM McCUTCHEON, 30
AMANDA McCUTCHEON, 24
HARRIET McCUTCHEON, 2
C
LAVINIA MURPHY, 50
C
LANDRUM MURPHY, 15
MARY MURPHY, 14
LEMUEL MURPHY, 12
WILLIAM MURPHY, 11
SIMON MURPHY, 9
WILLIAM FOSTER, 28
SARAH MURPHY FOSTER, 23
C
GEORGE FOSTER, 4
WILLIAM PIKE, 25
HARRIET MURPHY PIKE, 21
NAOMI + CATHERINE PIKE, 2
PATRICK BREEN, 51
MARGARET BREEN, 40
JOHN BREEN, 14
EDWARD BREEN, 13
PATRICK BREEN JR, 9
SIMON BREEN, 8
JAMES BREEN, 5
PETER BREEN, 3
ISABELLA BREEN, 1
CHARLES BURGER, 30
C
PATRICK DOLAN, 35
CHARLES STANTON, 35
C
ANTONIO, 26
JACOB WOLFINGER, 26
DORIS WOLFINGER, 18
?
HARDCOOP, 60
C
SALVADOR, 28
C
LUIS, 19

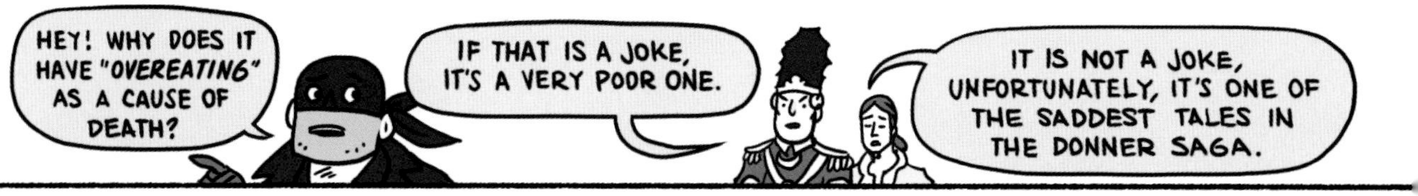
HEY! WHY DOES IT HAVE "OVEREATING" AS A CAUSE OF DEATH?
IF THAT IS A JOKE, IT'S A VERY POOR ONE.
IT IS NOT A JOKE, UNFORTUNATELY. IT'S ONE OF THE SADDEST TALES IN THE DONNER SAGA.

THE SAD, SAD STORY OF WILLIAM HOOK

THE BOY WHO ATE TOO MUCH

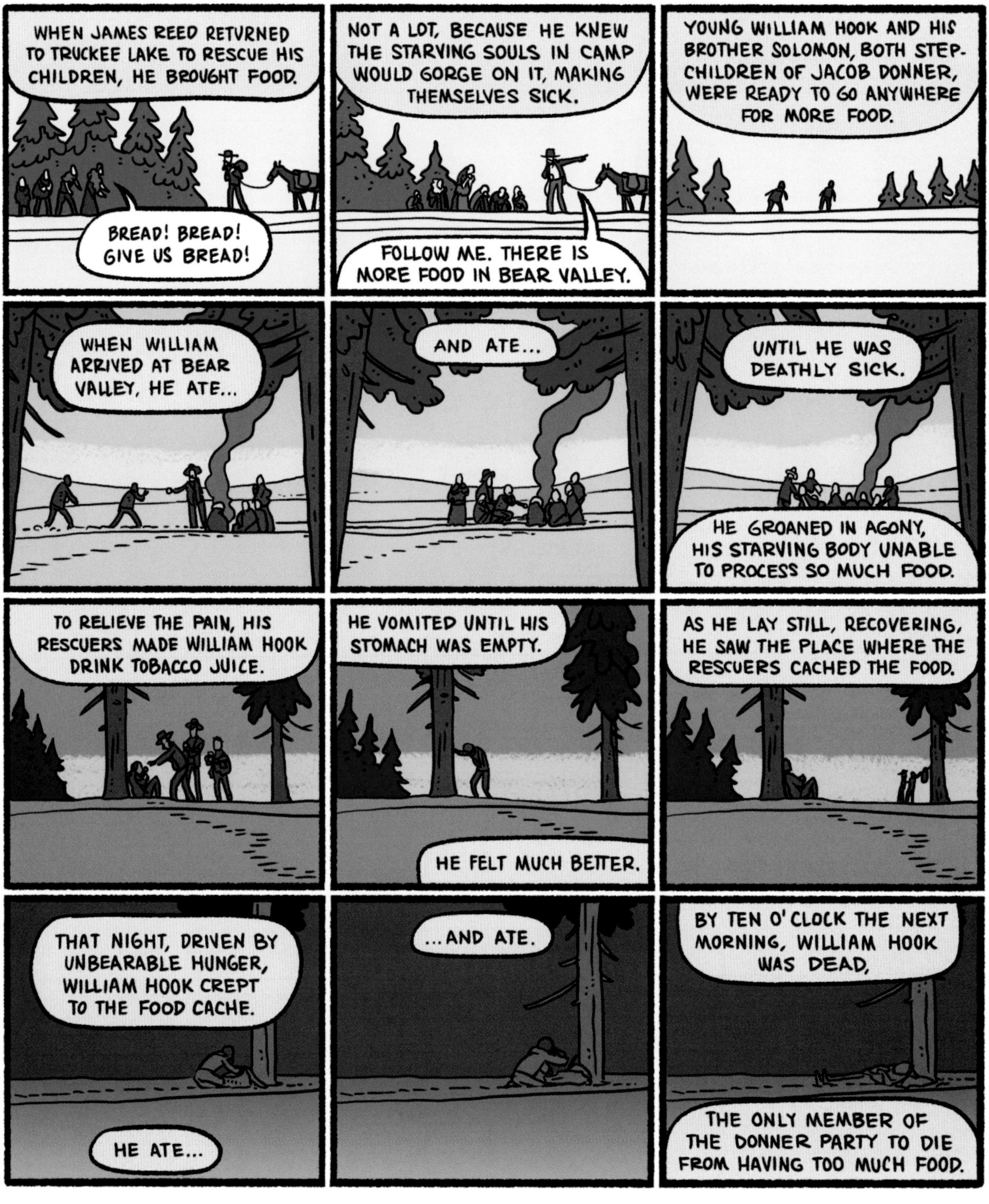
WHEN JAMES REED RETURNED TO TRUCKEE LAKE TO RESCUE HIS CHILDREN, HE BROUGHT FOOD.
BREAD! BREAD! GIVE US BREAD!
NOT A LOT, BECAUSE HE KNEW THE STARVING SOULS IN CAMP WOULD GORGE ON IT, MAKING THEMSELVES SICK.
FOLLOW ME. THERE IS MORE FOOD IN BEAR VALLEY.
YOUNG WILLIAM HOOK AND HIS BROTHER SOLOMON, BOTH STEP-CHILDREN OF JACOB DONNER, WERE READY TO GO ANYWHERE FOR MORE FOOD.
WHEN WILLIAM ARRIVED AT BEAR VALLEY, HE ATE...
AND ATE...
UNTIL HE WAS DEATHLY SICK.
HE GROANED IN AGONY, HIS STARVING BODY UNABLE TO PROCESS SO MUCH FOOD.
TO RELIEVE THE PAIN, HIS RESCUERS MADE WILLIAM HOOK DRINK TOBACCO JUICE.
HE VOMITED UNTIL HIS STOMACH WAS EMPTY.
HE FELT MUCH BETTER.
AS HE LAY STILL, RECOVERING, HE SAW THE PLACE WHERE THE RESCUERS CACHED THE FOOD.
THAT NIGHT, DRIVEN BY UNBEARABLE HUNGER, WILLIAM HOOK CREPT TO THE FOOD CACHE.
HE ATE...
...AND ATE.
BY TEN O'CLOCK THE NEXT MORNING, WILLIAM HOOK WAS DEAD,
THE ONLY MEMBER OF THE DONNER PARTY TO DIE FROM HAVING TOO MUCH FOOD.

JAMES AND MARGARET REED

THE REED FAMILY SETTLED IN SAN JOSE, WHERE JAMES BECAME A RANCHER. HE ALSO SAT ON THE FIRST TOWN COUNCIL AND WAS CHIEF OF POLICE.

VIRGINIA WROTE A MEMOIR OF HER JOURNEY CALLED *ACROSS THE PLAINS IN THE DONNER PARTY 1846*. HER DESCRIPTIONS WERE USED EXTENSIVELY WHEN RESEARCHING THIS BOOK. BILL THE PONY, SCARING SIOUX BRAVES WITH A TELESCOPE, TAKING HER FATHER'S GUNS --THESE ARE STORIES FROM VIRGINIA'S TALE.

PATTY'S TINY DOLL, NAMED "DOLLY," ALSO SURVIVED THE TRIP. DOLLY CAN BE SEEN AT SUTTER'S FORT STATE HISTORIC PARK, CA.

MARTHA "PATTY" REED

THERE WERE TWO DONNER FAMILIES--THE **GEORGE** DONNER FAMILY AND THE **JACOB** DONNER FAMILY. THE ONLY DONNERS TO MAKE IT SAFELY OVER THE PASS WERE ORPHANS; ALL FOUR DONNER PARENTS DIED AT TRUCKEE LAKE. THE DONNER ORPHANS FOUND FAMILIES IN CALIFORNIA TO LIVE WITH. MARY AND FRANCES DONNER LIVED WITH THE REEDS IN SAN JOSE. THE DONNER NAME IS NOW A PERMANENT PART OF THE LANDSCAPE OF THE AMERICAN WEST; DONNER LAKE AND DONNER PASS ARE JUST TWO OF MANY LOCATIONS NAMED FOR THE FAMILY.

ALL OF THE BREENS SURVIVED. **ALL SEVEN CHILDREN**, RANGING FROM AGES 1 TO 14, MADE IT THROUGH THE DEADLY WINTER OF 1846-47. THEY ARRIVED AT SUTTER'S FORT WITH NOTHING BUT THE CLOTHES ON THEIR BACKS. THEY WERE THE FIRST AMERICANS TO SETTLE IN SAN JUAN BAUTISTA. THEY LIVED HAPPILY EVER AFTER.

"I WAS BORN UNDER AN EVIL STAR!" LEWIS KESEBERG WOULD LATER SAY OF HIS ORDEAL WITH THE DONNER PARTY. THE FINAL MEMBER TO BE RESCUED FROM TRUCKEE LAKE, HE WAS OFTEN PAINTED BY THE MEDIA AS A VILLAIN, ESPECIALLY CONCERNING THE MYSTERIOUS FATE OF TAMSEN DONNER. SOME STORIES CLAIM HE MURDERED AND ATE HER. HE WAS PLAGUED BY CANNIBAL JOKES AND RUMORS FOR THE REST OF HIS LIFE. HIS BAD LUCK CONTINUED WHEN HIS BUSINESS, A HOTEL/RESTAURANT CALLED THE LADY ADAMS, BURNED DOWN AND HIS SECOND BUSINESS, A BREWERY, WAS DESTROYED IN A FLOOD.

"DOLLY"
(FOR MORE ON DOLLY, SEE PAGE 60.)

LEWIS KESEBERG

TO THE END OF HIS DAYS, **LANSFORD HASTINGS** INSISTED THAT HIS CUTOFF WAS THE SUPERIOR, EASIER ROUTE TO CALIFORNIA. AFTER FIGHTING IN THE MEXICAN-AMERICAN WAR, HE OFFERED TO GUIDE OTHER PIONEER GROUPS TO THE WEST. NOBODY ACCEPTED. DURING THE CIVIL WAR, HE HATCHED A PLOT TO JOIN CALIFORNIA WITH THE **SOUTH**. NOBODY ACCEPTED THAT, EITHER. HE HAD PLANS TO SET UP A COLONY IN BRAZIL FOR EXPATRIATE CONFEDERATES. ONCE AGAIN, NOBODY ACCEPTED. HE DIED ON A SHIP EN ROUTE TO BRAZIL.

CALABRO, MARIAN *THE PERILOUS JOURNEY OF THE DONNER PARTY* NEW YORK: CLARION, 1999

ALTER, J. CECIL *JIM BRIDGER*. NORMAN: UNIVERSITY OF OKLAHOMA PRESS, 1962

MULLEN JR., FRANK
THE DONNER PARTY CHRONICLES: A DAY BY DAY ACCOUNT OF A DOOMED WAGON TRAIN
RENO: A HALCYON IMPRINT OF THE NEVADA HUMANITIES COMMITTEE, 1997

HAFEN, LeROY R., ed. *TRAPPERS OF THE FAR WEST: SIXTEEN BIOGRAPHICAL SKETCHES*
LINCOLN: UNIVERSITY OF NEBRASKA PRESS, 1983

HOUGHTON, ELIZA POOR DONNER,
THE EXPEDITION OF THE DONNER PARTY AND ITS TRAGIC FATE CHICAGO: A.C. McCLURG, 1911

JOHNSON, KRISTEN, ed. *UNFORTUNATE EMIGRANTS: NARRATIVES OF THE DONNER PARTY*
LOGAN: UTAH STATE UNIVERSITY PRESS, 1996

JONES, EVAN *TRAPPERS AND MOUNTAIN MEN* NEW YORK: AMERICAN HERITAGE, 1961

McGLASHAN, C.F.
HISTORY OF THE DONNER PARTY: A TRAGEDY OF THE SIERRA
TRUCKEE, CALIF.: CROWLEY & McGLASHAN, 1879

MILLS, BRONWYN *THE MEXICAN WAR*
NEW YORK: FACTS ON FILE, 1992

NARDO, DON. *THE MEXICAN-AMERICAN WAR*
SAN DIEGO: LUCENT BOOKS, 1991

RARICK, ETHAN
DESPERATE PASSAGE: THE DONNER PARTY'S PERILOUS JOURNEY WEST
NEW YORK: OXFORD UNIVERSITY PRESS, 2008

STEWART, GEORGE R. *ORDEAL BY HUNGER: THE STORY OF THE DONNER PARTY* NEW YORK: HOLT, 1936

TUNIS, EDWIN *FRONTIER LIVING* CLEVELAND, WORLD PUB., 1961

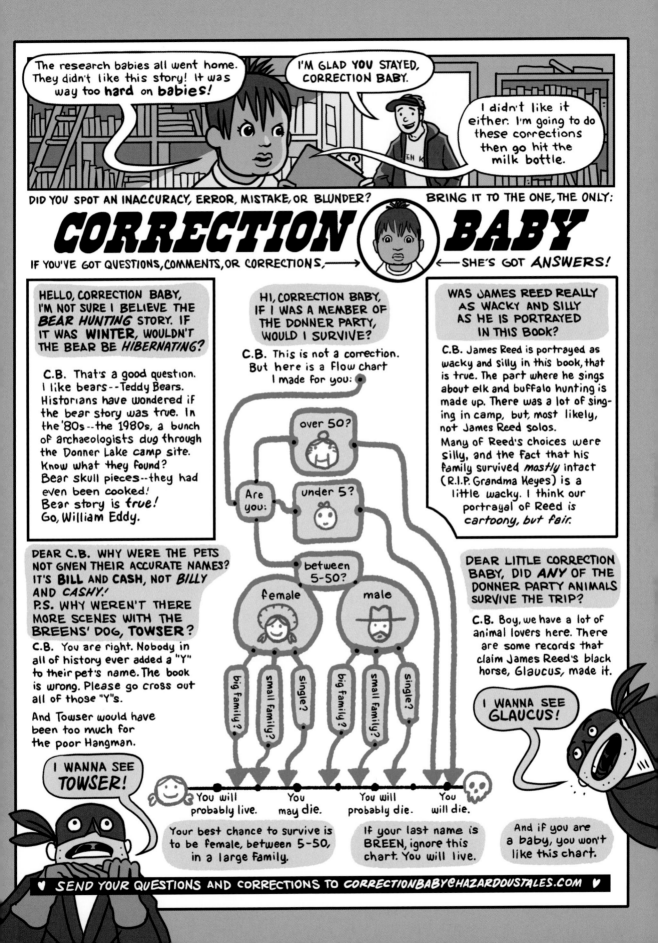

The research babies all went home. They didn't like this story! It was way too **hard** on **babies**!

I'M GLAD **YOU** STAYED, CORRECTION BABY.

I didn't like it either. I'm going to do these corrections then go hit the milk bottle.

DID YOU SPOT AN INACCURACY, ERROR, MISTAKE, OR BLUNDER? BRING IT TO THE ONE, THE ONLY:

CORRECTION BABY

IF YOU'VE GOT QUESTIONS, COMMENTS, OR CORRECTIONS, → ← SHE'S GOT **ANSWERS**!

HELLO, CORRECTION BABY, I'M NOT SURE I BELIEVE THE *BEAR HUNTING* STORY. IF IT WAS **WINTER**, WOULDN'T THE BEAR BE *HIBERNATING*?

C.B. That's a good question. I like bears--Teddy Bears. Historians have wondered if the bear story was true. In the '80s--the 1980s, a bunch of archaeologists dug through the Donner Lake camp site. Know what they found? Bear skull pieces--they had even been cooked! Bear story is *true*! Go, William Eddy.

HI, CORRECTION BABY, IF I WAS A MEMBER OF THE DONNER PARTY, WOULD I SURVIVE?

C.B. This is not a correction. But here is a flow chart I made for you:

over 50?

Are you:

under 5?

between 5-50?

female

male

big family?
small family?
single?
big family?
small family?
single?

WAS JAMES REED REALLY AS WACKY AND SILLY AS HE IS PORTRAYED IN THIS BOOK?

C.B. James Reed is portrayed as wacky and silly in this book, that is true. The part where he sings about elk and buffalo hunting is made up. There was a lot of singing in camp, but, most likely, not James Reed solos.
Many of Reed's choices were silly, and the fact that his family survived *mostly* intact (R.I.P. Grandma Keyes) is a little wacky. I think our portrayal of Reed is *cartoony, but fair*.

DEAR C.B. WHY WERE THE PETS NOT GIVEN THEIR ACCURATE NAMES? IT'S **BILL** AND **CASH**, NOT *BILLY* AND *CASHY*!
P.S. WHY WEREN'T THERE MORE SCENES WITH THE BREENS' DOG, **TOWSER**?

C.B. You are right. Nobody in all of history ever added a "Y" to their pet's name. The book is wrong. Please go cross out all of those "Y"s.

And Towser would have been too much for the poor Hangman.

I WANNA SEE **TOWSER**!

DEAR LITTLE CORRECTION BABY, DID *ANY* OF THE DONNER PARTY ANIMALS SURVIVE THE TRIP?

C.B. Boy, we have a lot of animal lovers here. There are some records that claim James Reed's black horse, Glaucus, made it.

I WANNA SEE **GLAUCUS**!

You will probably live.

You may die.

You will probably die.

You will die.

Your best chance to survive is to be female, between 5-50, in a large family.

If your last name is BREEN, ignore this chart. You will live.

And if you are a baby, you won't like this chart.

♥ SEND YOUR QUESTIONS AND CORRECTIONS TO *CORRECTIONBABY@HAZARDOUSTALES.COM* ♥

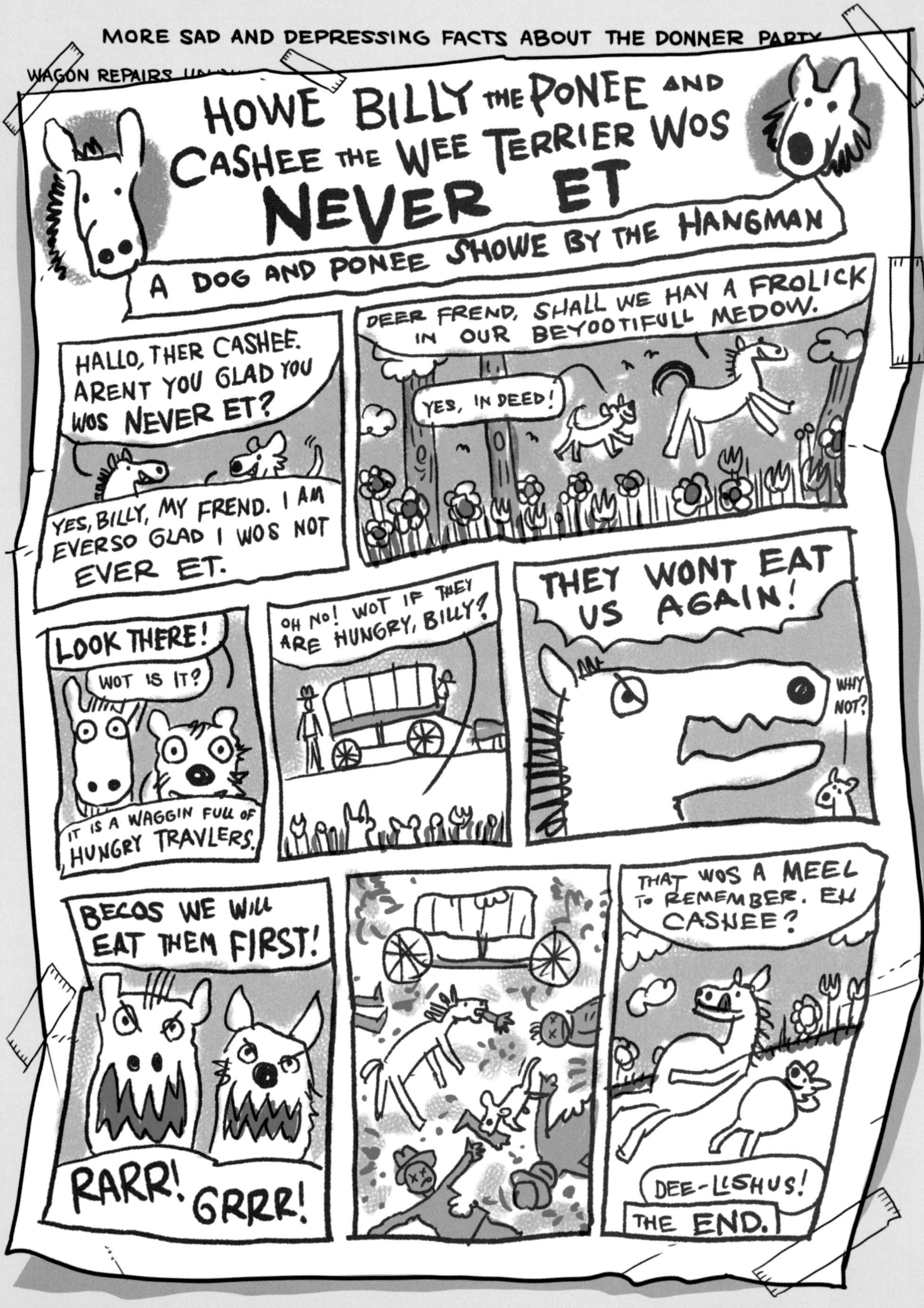
MORE SAD AND DEPRESSING FACTS ABOUT THE DONNER PARTY
HOWE BILLY THE PONEE AND CASHEE THE WEE TERRIER WOS NEVER ET
A DOG AND PONEE SHOWE BY THE HANGMAN
HALLO, THER CASHEE. ARENT YOU GLAD YOU WOS NEVER ET?
YES, BILLY, MY FREND. I AM EVERSO GLAD I WOS NOT EVER ET.
DEER FREND, SHALL WE HAV A FROLICK IN OUR BEYOOTIFULL MEDOW.
YES, IN DEED!
LOOK THERE!
WOT IS IT?
IT IS A WAGGIN FULL OF HUNGRY TRAVLERS.
OH NO! WOT IF THEY ARE HUNGRY, BILLY?
THEY WONT EAT US AGAIN!
WHY NOT?
BECOS WE WILL EAT THEM FIRST!
RARR!
GRRR!
THAT WOS A MEEL TO REMEMBER. EH CASHEE?
DEE-LISHUS!
THE END.

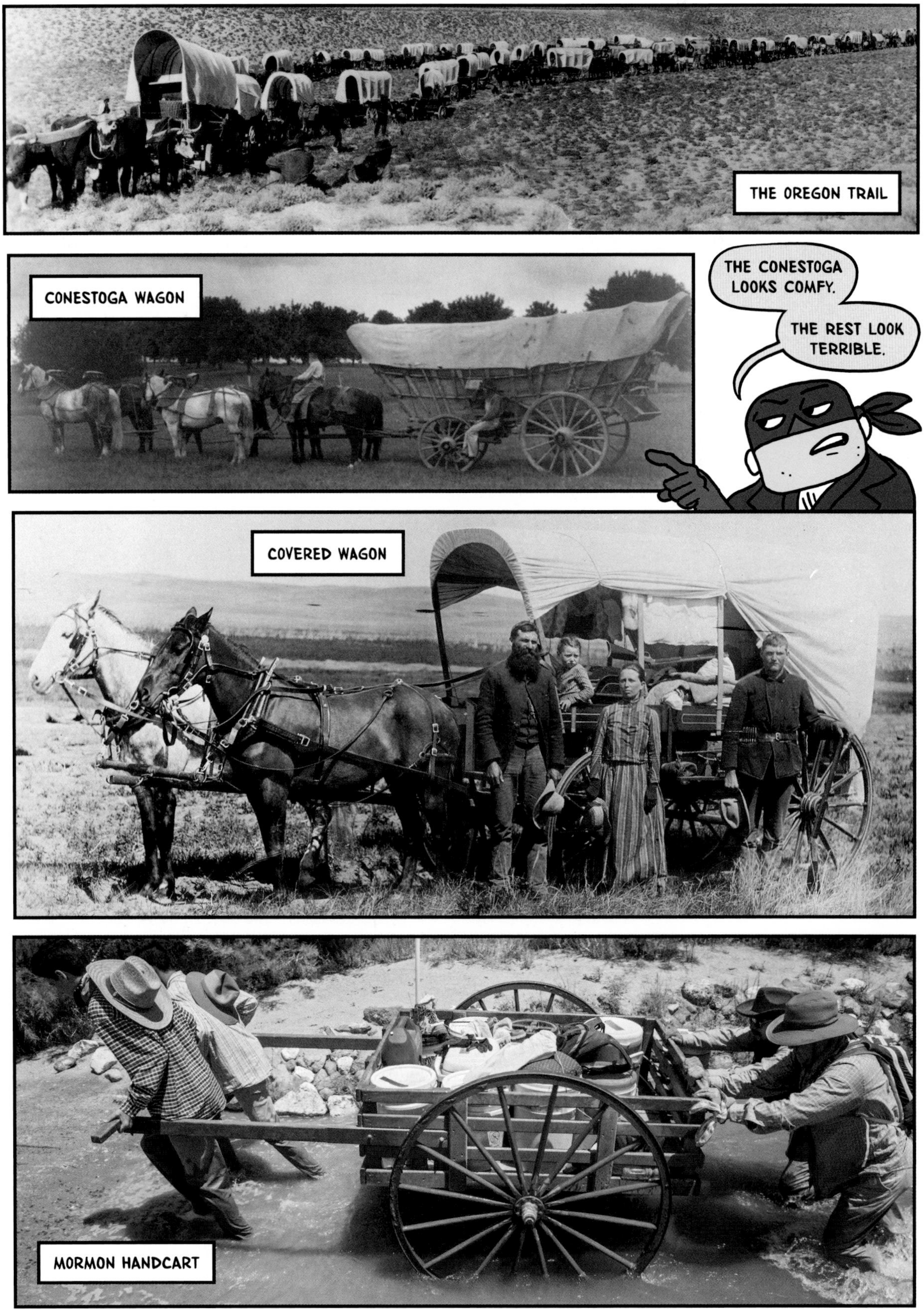
THE OREGON TRAIL
CONESTOGA WAGON
THE CONESTOGA LOOKS COMFY.
THE REST LOOK TERRIBLE.
COVERED WAGON
MORMON HANDCART

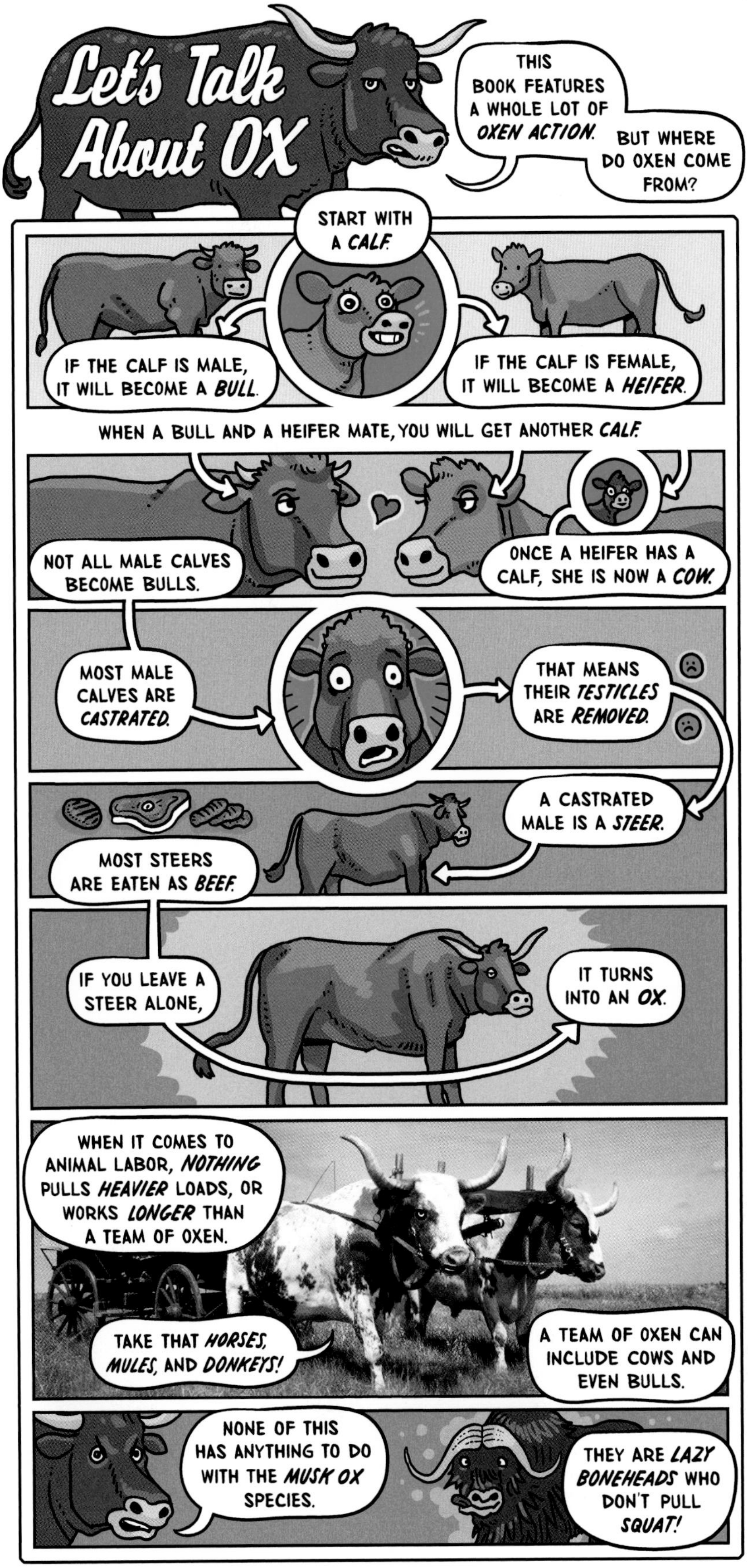
Let's Talk About OX
THIS BOOK FEATURES A WHOLE LOT OF OXEN ACTION.
BUT WHERE DO OXEN COME FROM?
START WITH A CALF.
IF THE CALF IS MALE, IT WILL BECOME A BULL.
IF THE CALF IS FEMALE, IT WILL BECOME A HEIFER.
WHEN A BULL AND A HEIFER MATE, YOU WILL GET ANOTHER CALF.
ONCE A HEIFER HAS A CALF, SHE IS NOW A COW.
NOT ALL MALE CALVES BECOME BULLS.
MOST MALE CALVES ARE CASTRATED.
THAT MEANS THEIR TESTICLES ARE REMOVED.
A CASTRATED MALE IS A STEER.
MOST STEERS ARE EATEN AS BEEF.
IF YOU LEAVE A STEER ALONE,
IT TURNS INTO AN OX.
WHEN IT COMES TO ANIMAL LABOR, NOTHING PULLS HEAVIER LOADS, OR WORKS LONGER THAN A TEAM OF OXEN.
TAKE THAT HORSES, MULES, AND DONKEYS!
A TEAM OF OXEN CAN INCLUDE COWS AND EVEN BULLS.
NONE OF THIS HAS ANYTHING TO DO WITH THE MUSK OX SPECIES.
THEY ARE LAZY BONEHEADS WHO DON'T PULL SQUAT!

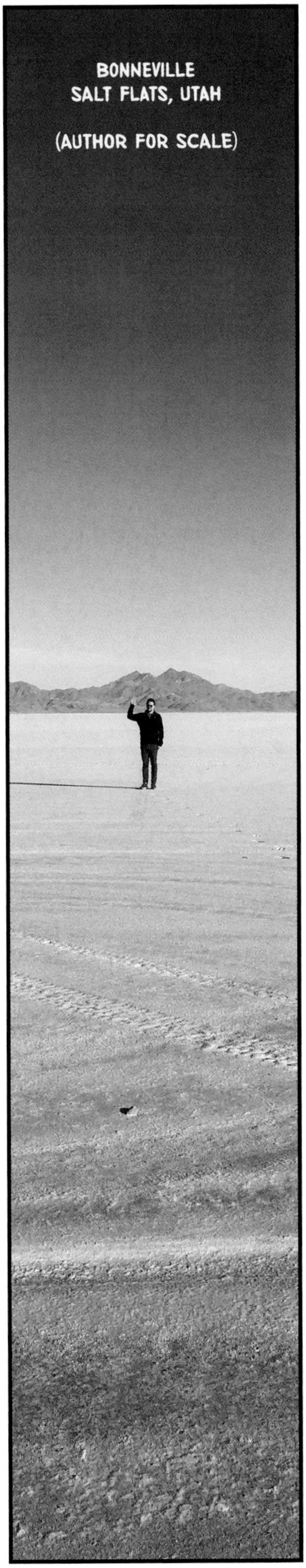
BONNEVILLE SALT FLATS, UTAH
(AUTHOR FOR SCALE)

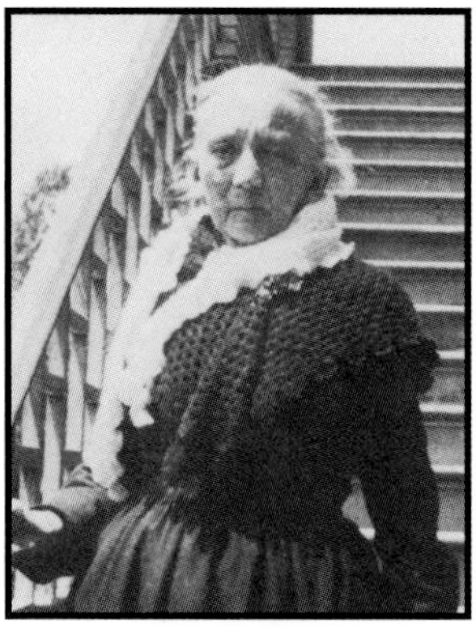

PATTY REED

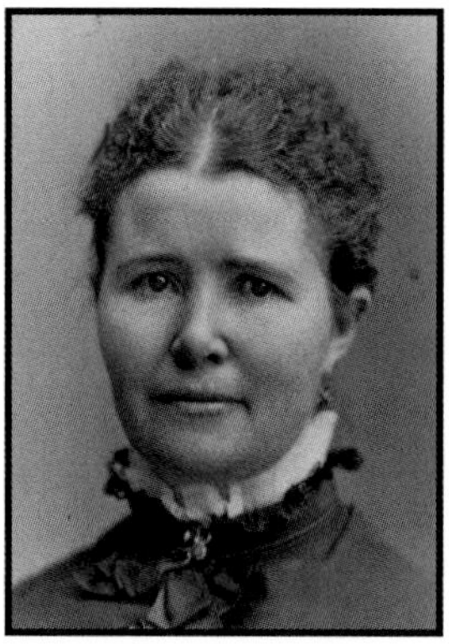

GEORGIA DONNER

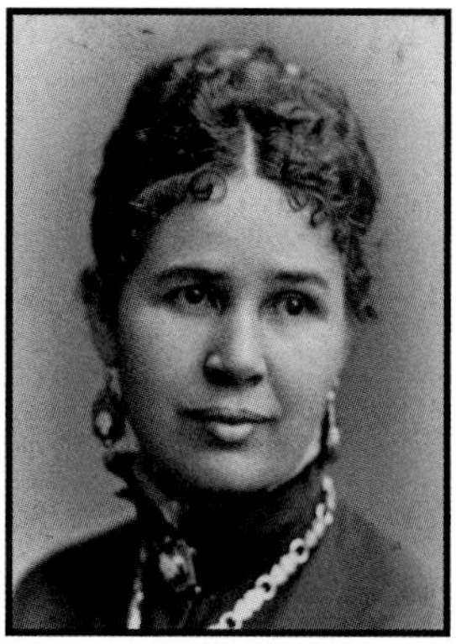

ELIZA DONNER

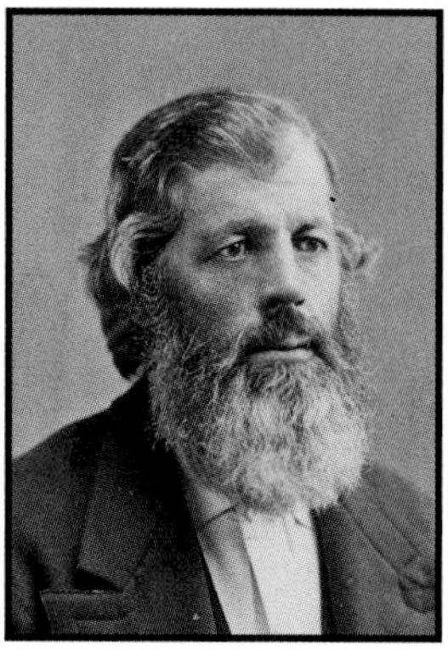

WILLIAM GRAVES

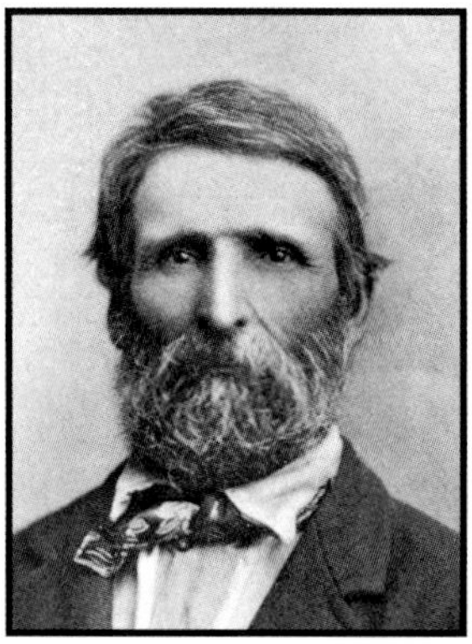

JEAN BAPTISTE TRUDEAU

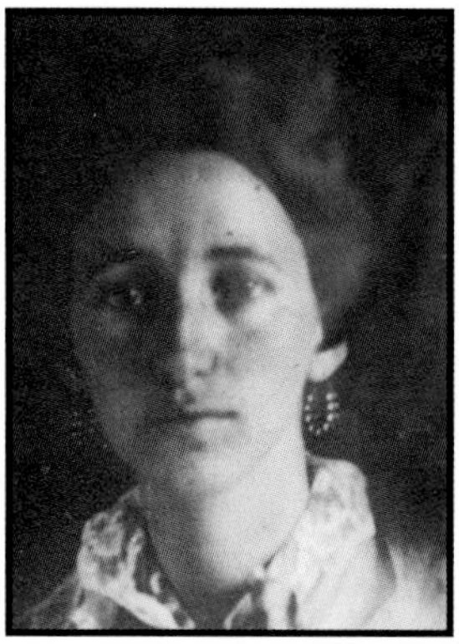

MARY MURPHY

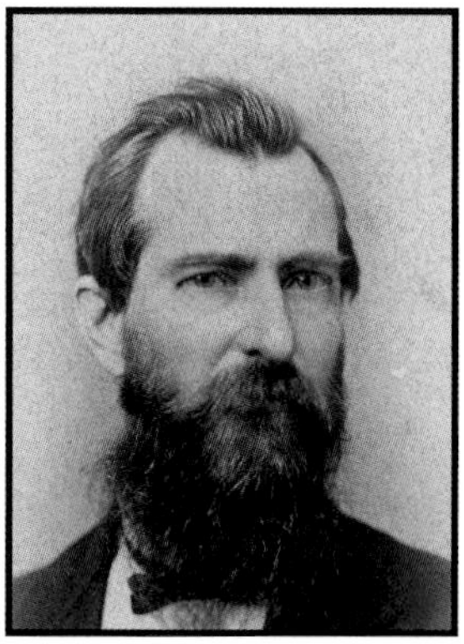

WILLIAM MURPHY

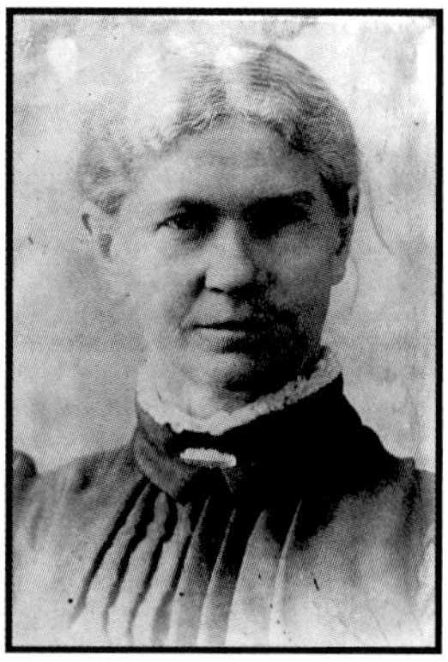

NANCY BLAISDELL GRAVES

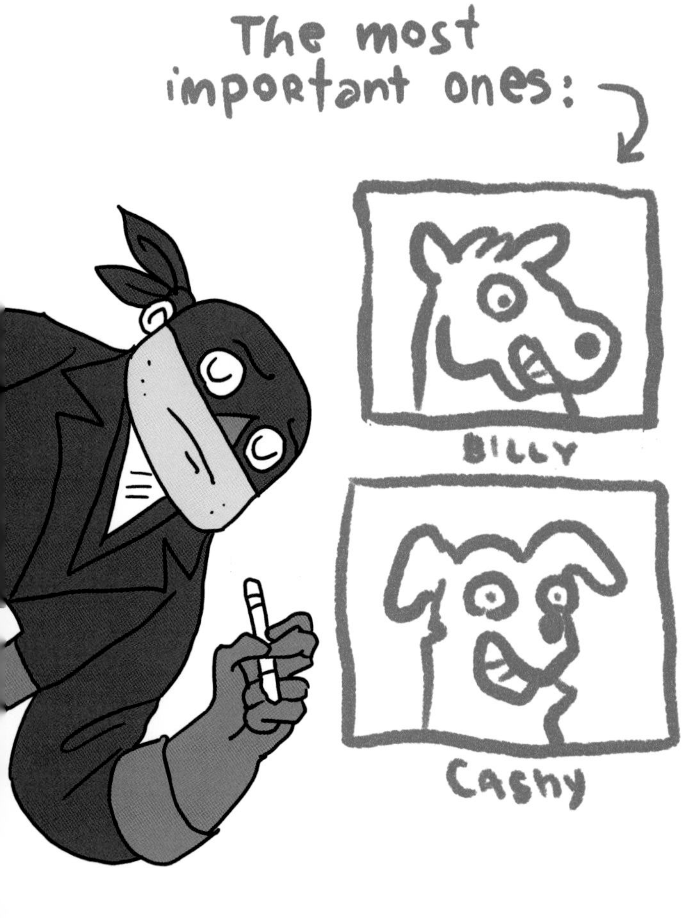
The most important ones:
BILLY
Cashy

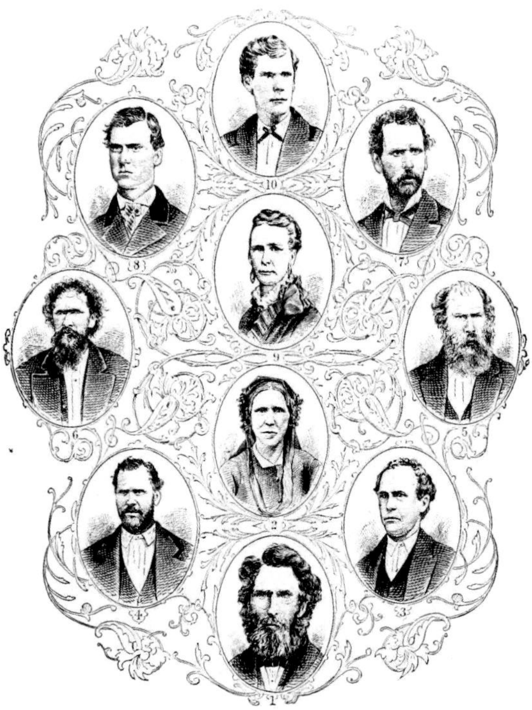

THE BREEN FAMILY.

1. PATRICK, Sr. 2. MARGARET. 3. JOHN. 4. EDWARD P. 5. PATRICK, Jr. 6. SIMON P. 7. JAMES F. 8. PETER. 9. BELLA M. 10. WILLIAM M.

CHIEF BLACK HAWK

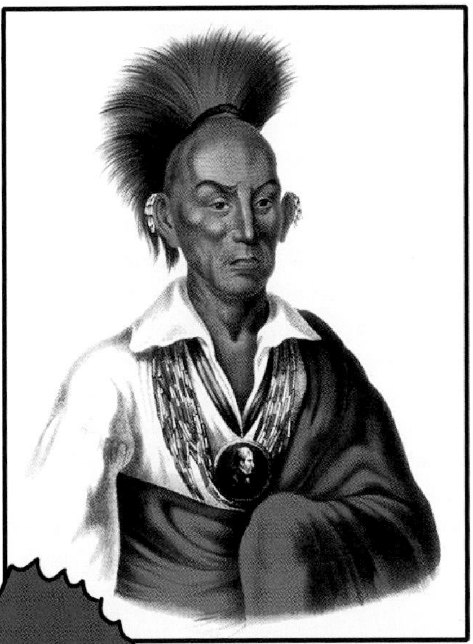

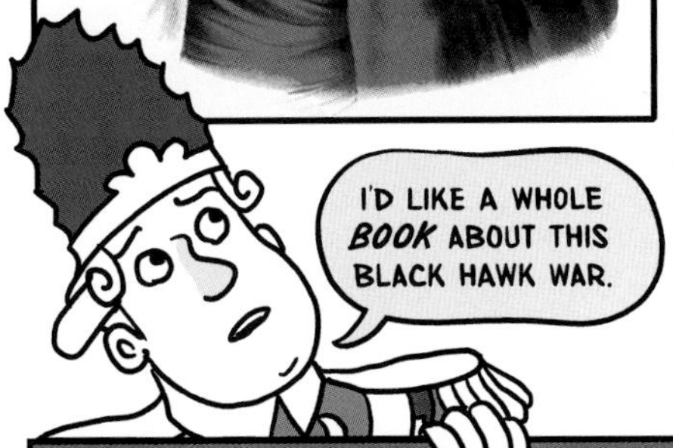
I'D LIKE A WHOLE *BOOK* ABOUT THIS BLACK HAWK WAR.

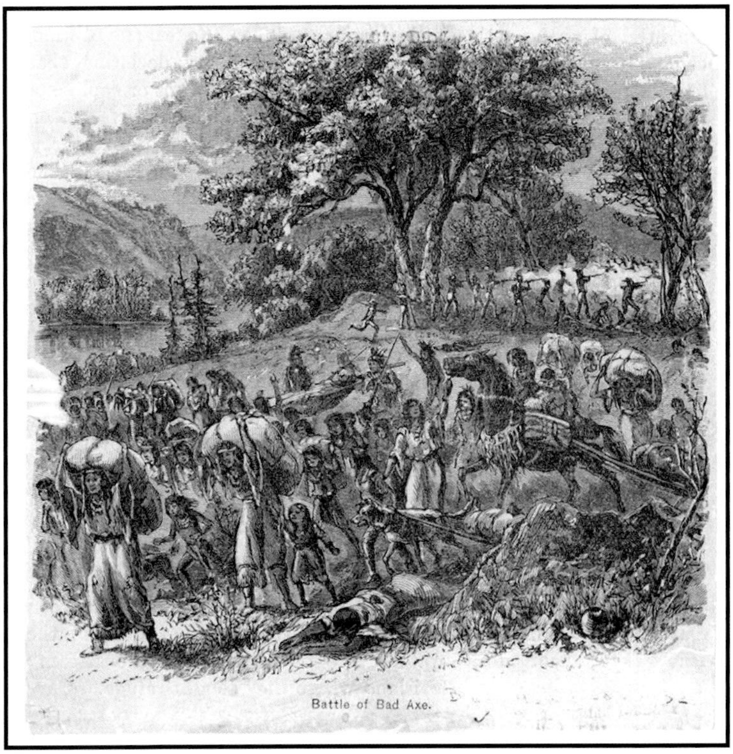
Battle of Bad Axe.

THE BATTLE OF BAD AXE, THE FINAL BATTLE OF THE BLACK HAWK WAR

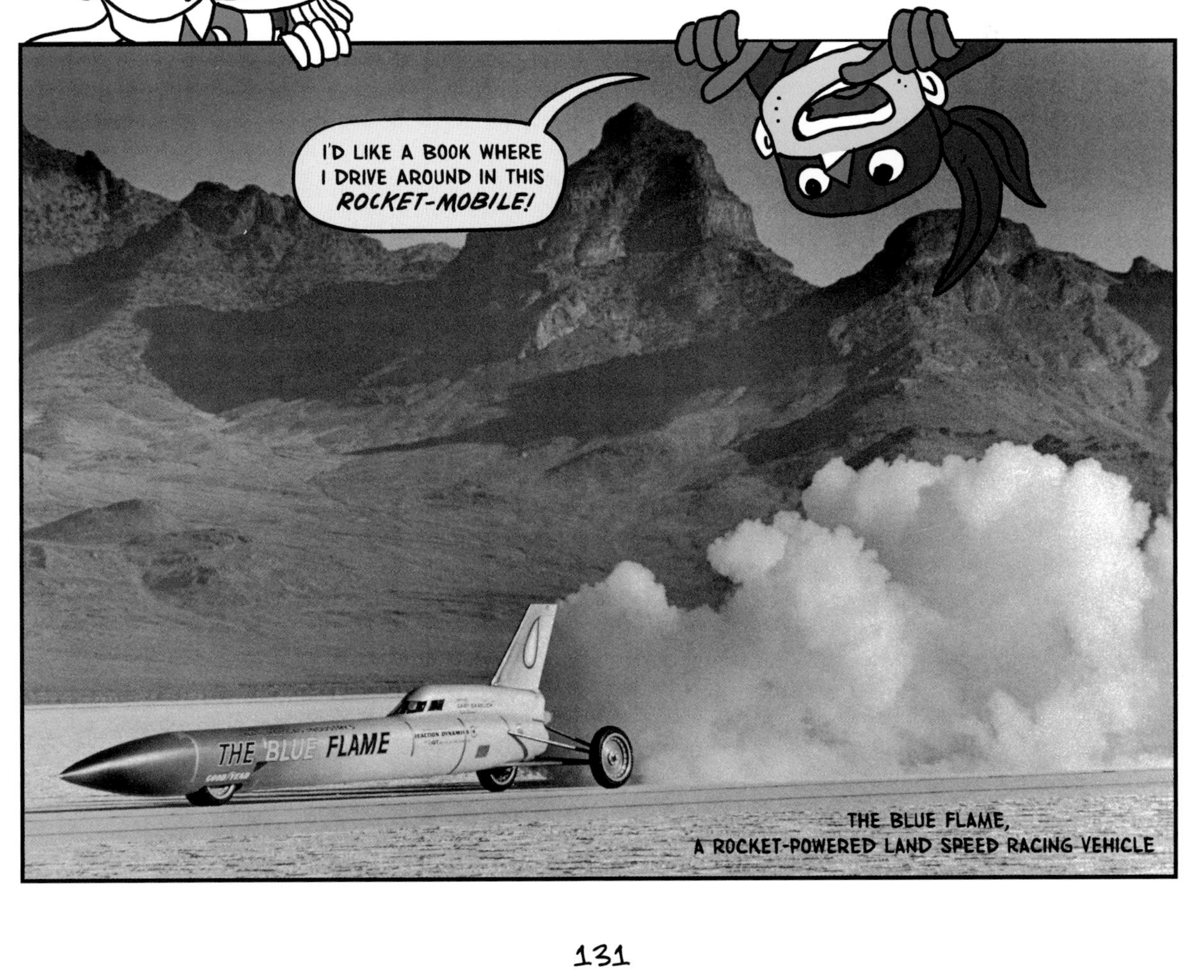
I'D LIKE A BOOK WHERE I DRIVE AROUND IN THIS *ROCKET-MOBILE!*
THE BLUE FLAME

THE BLUE FLAME,
A ROCKET-POWERED LAND SPEED RACING VEHICLE

Eph Hanks and the HANDCART PEOPLE

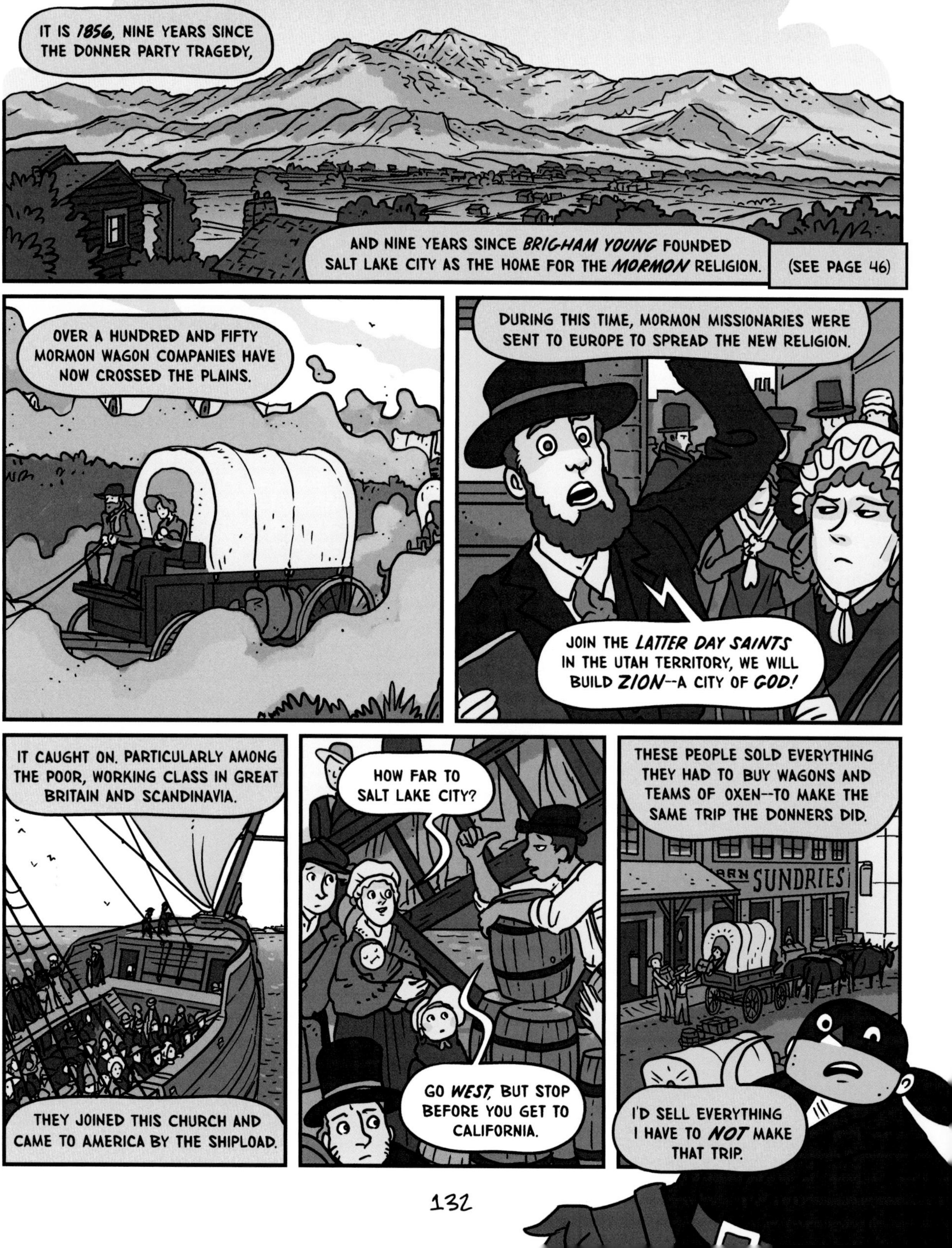

IT IS 1856, NINE YEARS SINCE THE DONNER PARTY TRAGEDY,
AND NINE YEARS SINCE BRIGHAM YOUNG FOUNDED SALT LAKE CITY AS THE HOME FOR THE MORMON RELIGION.
(SEE PAGE 46)
OVER A HUNDRED AND FIFTY MORMON WAGON COMPANIES HAVE NOW CROSSED THE PLAINS.
DURING THIS TIME, MORMON MISSIONARIES WERE SENT TO EUROPE TO SPREAD THE NEW RELIGION.
JOIN THE LATTER DAY SAINTS IN THE UTAH TERRITORY, WE WILL BUILD ZION--A CITY OF GOD!
IT CAUGHT ON. PARTICULARLY AMONG THE POOR, WORKING CLASS IN GREAT BRITAIN AND SCANDINAVIA.
THEY JOINED THIS CHURCH AND CAME TO AMERICA BY THE SHIPLOAD.
HOW FAR TO SALT LAKE CITY?
GO WEST, BUT STOP BEFORE YOU GET TO CALIFORNIA.
THESE PEOPLE SOLD EVERYTHING THEY HAD TO BUY WAGONS AND TEAMS OF OXEN--TO MAKE THE SAME TRIP THE DONNERS DID.
SUNDRIES
I'D SELL EVERYTHING I HAVE TO NOT MAKE THAT TRIP.

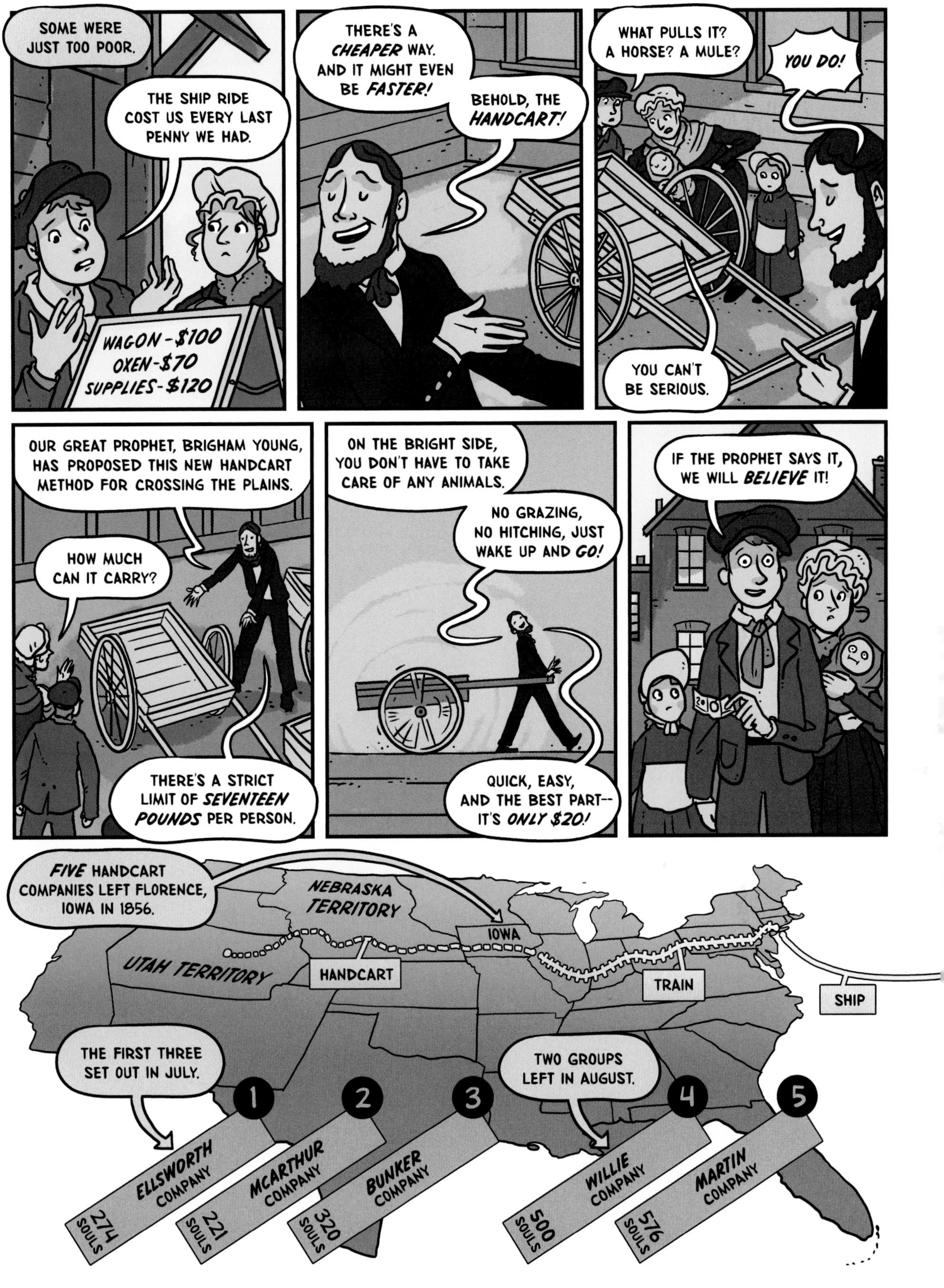
SOME WERE JUST TOO POOR.
THE SHIP RIDE COST US EVERY LAST PENNY WE HAD.
WAGON-$100
OXEN-$70
SUPPLIES-$120
THERE'S A CHEAPER WAY. AND IT MIGHT EVEN BE FASTER!
BEHOLD, THE HANDCART!
WHAT PULLS IT? A HORSE? A MULE?
YOU DO!
YOU CAN'T BE SERIOUS.
OUR GREAT PROPHET, BRIGHAM YOUNG, HAS PROPOSED THIS NEW HANDCART METHOD FOR CROSSING THE PLAINS.
HOW MUCH CAN IT CARRY?
THERE'S A STRICT LIMIT OF SEVENTEEN POUNDS PER PERSON.
ON THE BRIGHT SIDE, YOU DON'T HAVE TO TAKE CARE OF ANY ANIMALS.
NO GRAZING, NO HITCHING, JUST WAKE UP AND GO!
QUICK, EASY, AND THE BEST PART-- IT'S ONLY $20!
IF THE PROPHET SAYS IT, WE WILL BELIEVE IT!
FIVE HANDCART COMPANIES LEFT FLORENCE, IOWA IN 1856.
NEBRASKA TERRITORY
IOWA
UTAH TERRITORY
HANDCART
TRAIN
SHIP
THE FIRST THREE SET OUT IN JULY.
TWO GROUPS LEFT IN AUGUST.
1
ELLSWORTH COMPANY
274 SOULS
2
MCARTHUR COMPANY
221 SOULS
3
BUNKER COMPANY
320 SOULS
4
WILLIE COMPANY
500 SOULS
5
MARTIN COMPANY
576 SOULS

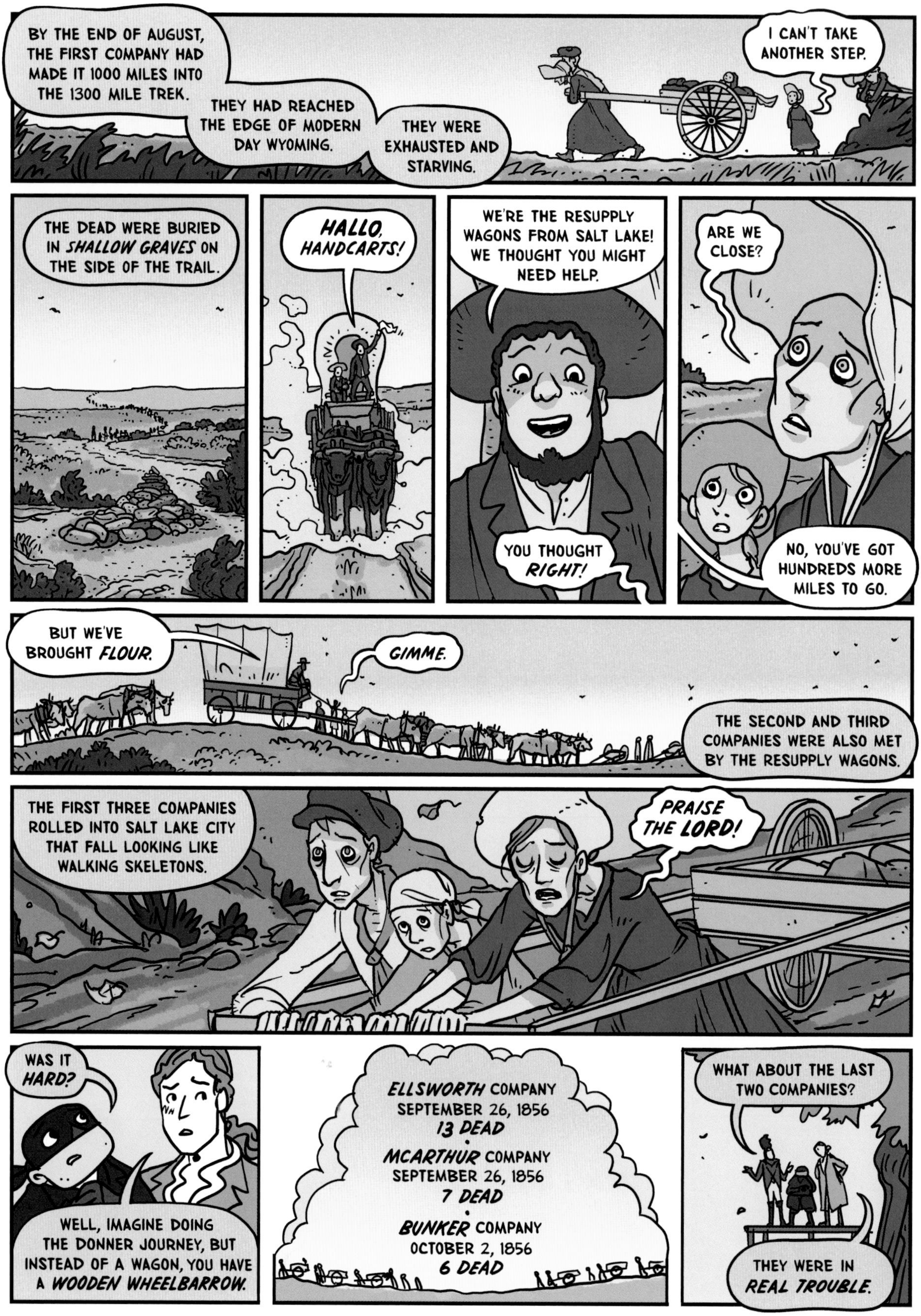
BY THE END OF AUGUST, THE FIRST COMPANY HAD MADE IT 1000 MILES INTO THE 1300 MILE TREK.
THEY HAD REACHED THE EDGE OF MODERN DAY WYOMING.
THEY WERE EXHAUSTED AND STARVING.
I CAN'T TAKE ANOTHER STEP.
THE DEAD WERE BURIED IN SHALLOW GRAVES ON THE SIDE OF THE TRAIL.
HALLO, HANDCARTS!
WE'RE THE RESUPPLY WAGONS FROM SALT LAKE! WE THOUGHT YOU MIGHT NEED HELP.
YOU THOUGHT RIGHT!
ARE WE CLOSE?
NO, YOU'VE GOT HUNDREDS MORE MILES TO GO.
BUT WE'VE BROUGHT FLOUR.
GIMME.
THE SECOND AND THIRD COMPANIES WERE ALSO MET BY THE RESUPPLY WAGONS.
THE FIRST THREE COMPANIES ROLLED INTO SALT LAKE CITY THAT FALL LOOKING LIKE WALKING SKELETONS.
PRAISE THE LORD!
WAS IT HARD?
WELL, IMAGINE DOING THE DONNER JOURNEY, BUT INSTEAD OF A WAGON, YOU HAVE A WOODEN WHEELBARROW.
ELLSWORTH COMPANY
SEPTEMBER 26, 1856
13 DEAD
MCARTHUR COMPANY
SEPTEMBER 26, 1856
7 DEAD
BUNKER COMPANY
OCTOBER 2, 1856
6 DEAD
WHAT ABOUT THE LAST TWO COMPANIES?
THEY WERE IN REAL TROUBLE.

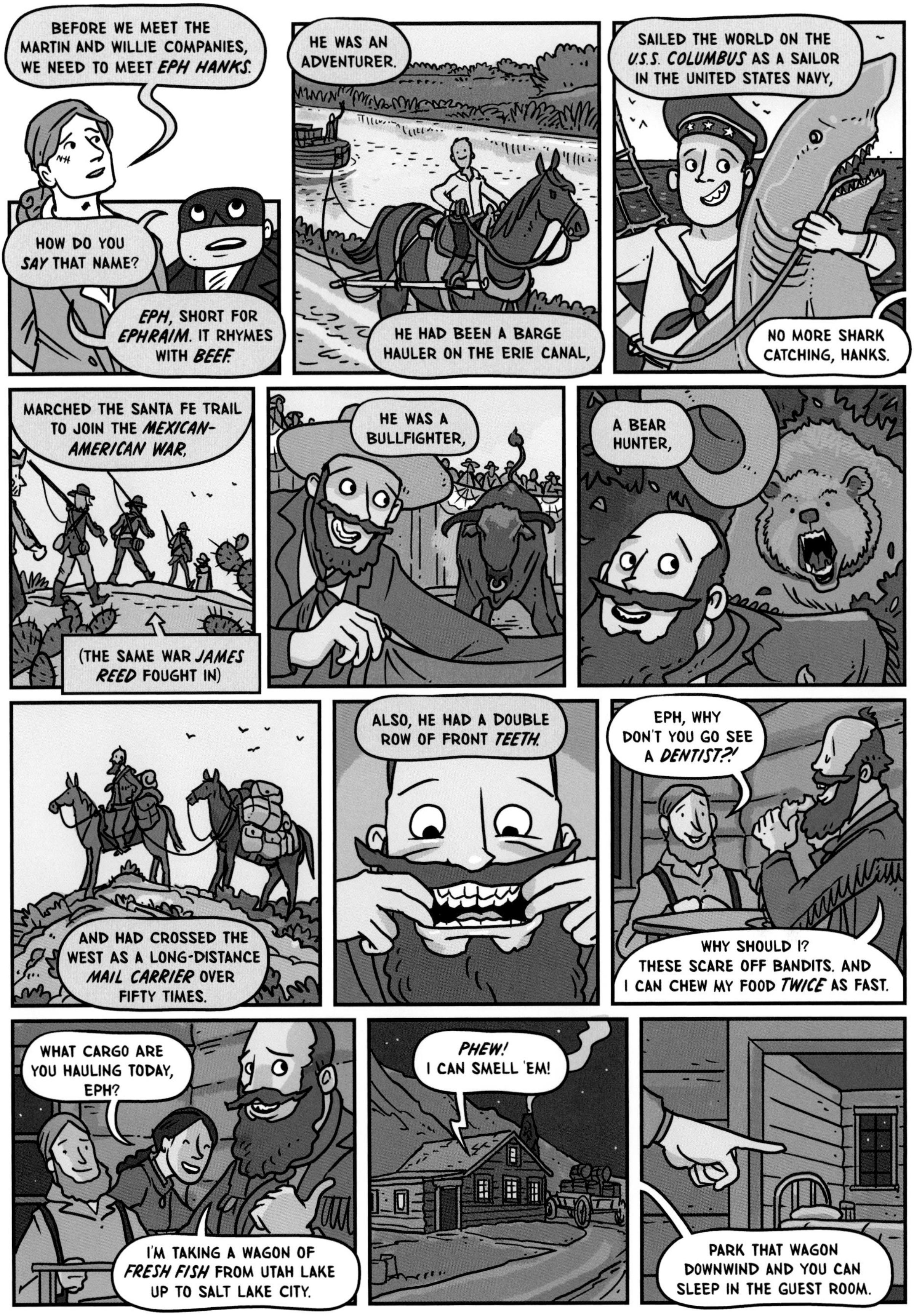
BEFORE WE MEET THE MARTIN AND WILLIE COMPANIES, WE NEED TO MEET *EPH HANKS*.
HOW DO YOU *SAY* THAT NAME?
EPH, SHORT FOR *EPHRAIM*. IT RHYMES WITH *BEEF*.
HE WAS AN ADVENTURER.
HE HAD BEEN A BARGE HAULER ON THE ERIE CANAL,
SAILED THE WORLD ON THE *U.S.S. COLUMBUS* AS A SAILOR IN THE UNITED STATES NAVY,
NO MORE SHARK CATCHING, HANKS.
MARCHED THE SANTA FE TRAIL TO JOIN THE *MEXICAN-AMERICAN WAR*,
(THE SAME WAR *JAMES REED* FOUGHT IN)
HE WAS A BULLFIGHTER,
A BEAR HUNTER,
AND HAD CROSSED THE WEST AS A LONG-DISTANCE *MAIL CARRIER* OVER FIFTY TIMES.
ALSO, HE HAD A DOUBLE ROW OF FRONT *TEETH*.
EPH, WHY DON'T YOU GO SEE A *DENTIST?!*
WHY SHOULD I? THESE SCARE OFF BANDITS. AND I CAN CHEW MY FOOD *TWICE* AS FAST.
WHAT CARGO ARE YOU HAULING TODAY, EPH?
I'M TAKING A WAGON OF *FRESH FISH* FROM UTAH LAKE UP TO SALT LAKE CITY.
PHEW! I CAN SMELL 'EM!
PARK THAT WAGON DOWNWIND AND YOU CAN SLEEP IN THE GUEST ROOM.

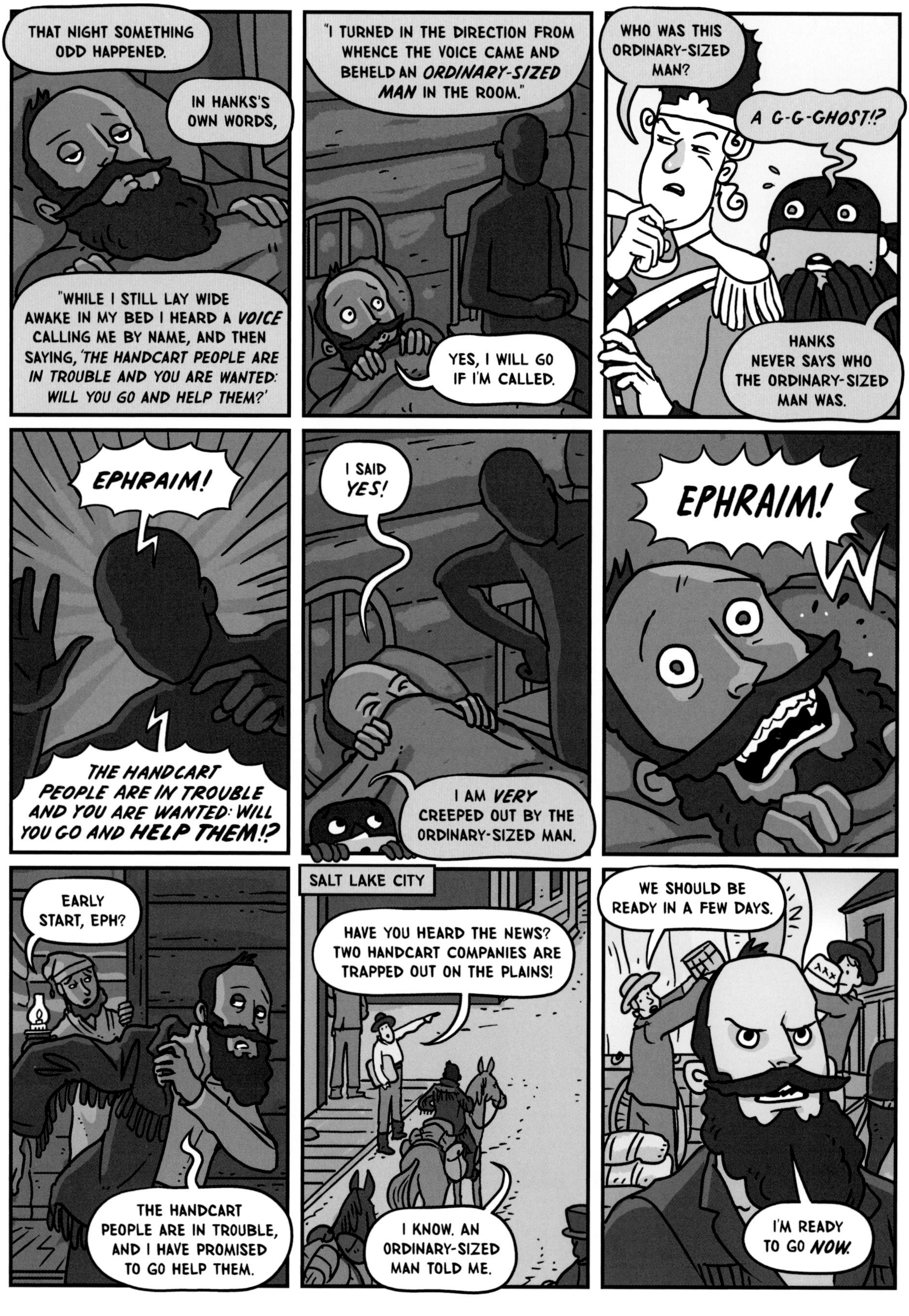
THAT NIGHT SOMETHING ODD HAPPENED.
IN HANKS'S OWN WORDS,
"WHILE I STILL LAY WIDE AWAKE IN MY BED I HEARD A *VOICE* CALLING ME BY NAME, AND THEN SAYING, '*THE HANDCART PEOPLE ARE IN TROUBLE AND YOU ARE WANTED: WILL YOU GO AND HELP THEM?*'
"I TURNED IN THE DIRECTION FROM WHENCE THE VOICE CAME AND BEHELD AN *ORDINARY-SIZED MAN* IN THE ROOM."
YES, I WILL GO IF I'M CALLED.
WHO WAS THIS ORDINARY-SIZED MAN?
A G-G-GHOST!?
HANKS NEVER SAYS WHO THE ORDINARY-SIZED MAN WAS.
EPHRAIM!
THE HANDCART PEOPLE ARE IN TROUBLE AND YOU ARE WANTED: WILL YOU GO AND HELP THEM!?
I SAID *YES!*
I AM *VERY* CREEPED OUT BY THE ORDINARY-SIZED MAN.
EPHRAIM!
EARLY START, EPH?
THE HANDCART PEOPLE ARE IN TROUBLE, AND I HAVE PROMISED TO GO HELP THEM.
SALT LAKE CITY
HAVE YOU HEARD THE NEWS? TWO HANDCART COMPANIES ARE TRAPPED OUT ON THE PLAINS!
I KNOW. AN ORDINARY-SIZED MAN TOLD ME.
WE SHOULD BE READY IN A FEW DAYS.
I'M READY TO GO *NOW.*

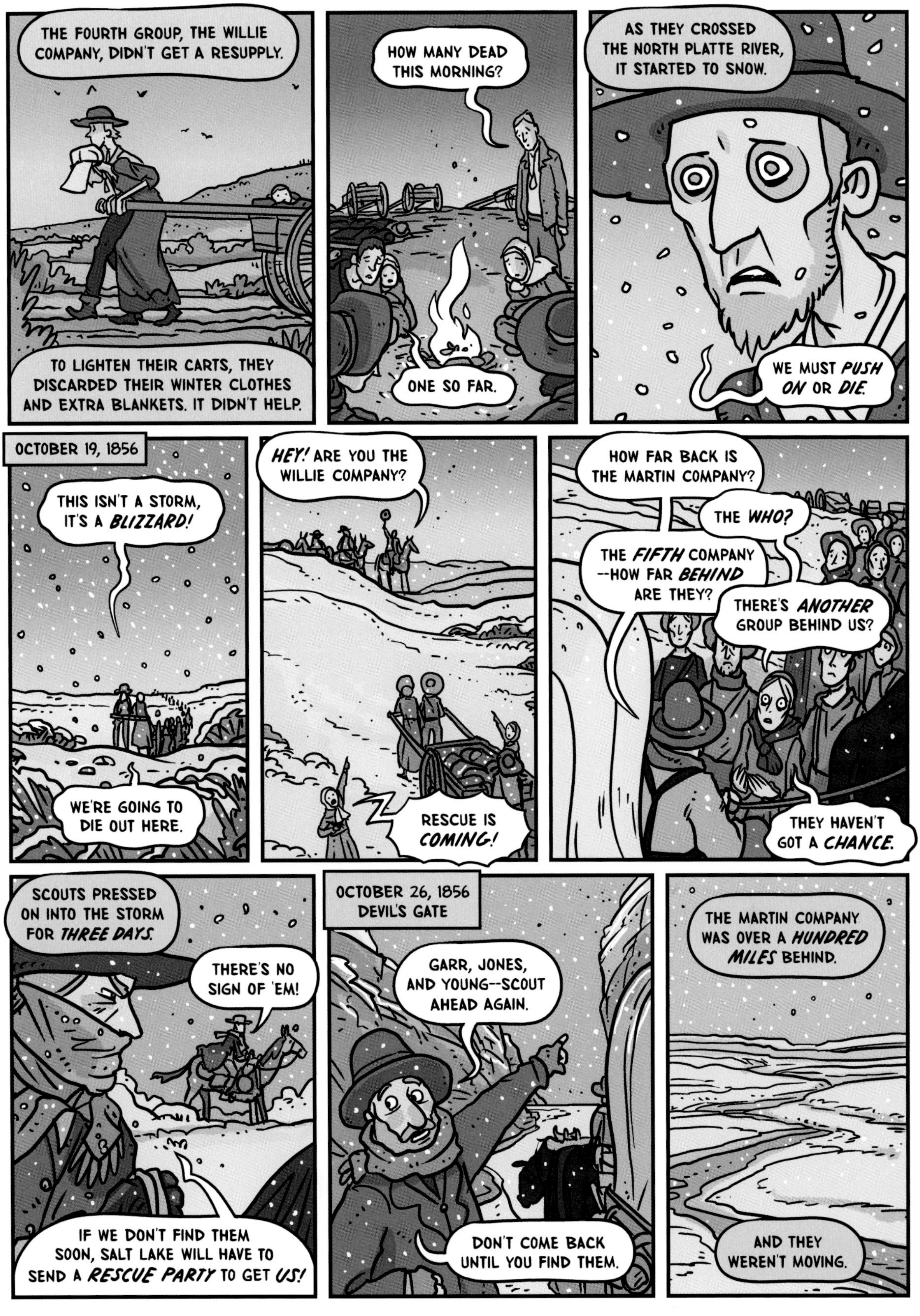
THE FOURTH GROUP, THE WILLIE COMPANY, DIDN'T GET A RESUPPLY.
TO LIGHTEN THEIR CARTS, THEY DISCARDED THEIR WINTER CLOTHES AND EXTRA BLANKETS. IT DIDN'T HELP.
HOW MANY DEAD THIS MORNING?
ONE SO FAR.
AS THEY CROSSED THE NORTH PLATTE RIVER, IT STARTED TO SNOW.
WE MUST *PUSH ON* OR *DIE*.
OCTOBER 19, 1856
THIS ISN'T A STORM, IT'S A *BLIZZARD!*
WE'RE GOING TO DIE OUT HERE.
HEY! ARE YOU THE WILLIE COMPANY?
RESCUE IS *COMING!*
HOW FAR BACK IS THE MARTIN COMPANY?
THE *WHO?*
THE *FIFTH* COMPANY --HOW FAR *BEHIND* ARE THEY?
THERE'S *ANOTHER* GROUP BEHIND US?
THEY HAVEN'T GOT A *CHANCE*.
SCOUTS PRESSED ON INTO THE STORM FOR *THREE DAYS*.
THERE'S NO SIGN OF 'EM!
IF WE DON'T FIND THEM SOON, SALT LAKE WILL HAVE TO SEND A *RESCUE PARTY* TO GET *US!*
OCTOBER 26, 1856 DEVIL'S GATE
GARR, JONES, AND YOUNG--SCOUT AHEAD AGAIN.
DON'T COME BACK UNTIL YOU FIND THEM.
THE MARTIN COMPANY WAS OVER A *HUNDRED MILES* BEHIND.
AND THEY WEREN'T MOVING.

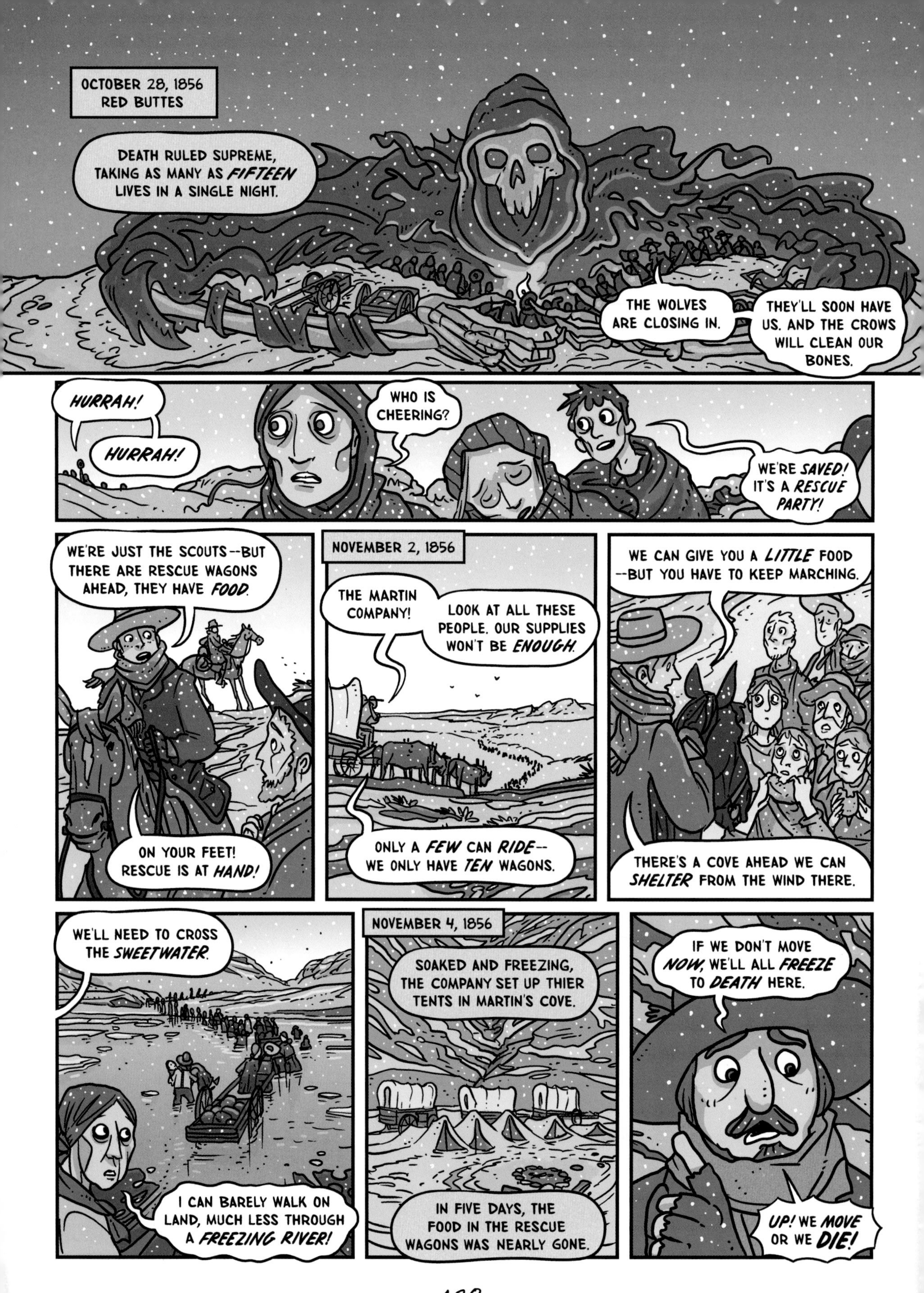
OCTOBER 28, 1856
RED BUTTES
DEATH RULED SUPREME, TAKING AS MANY AS FIFTEEN LIVES IN A SINGLE NIGHT.
THE WOLVES ARE CLOSING IN.
THEY'LL SOON HAVE US. AND THE CROWS WILL CLEAN OUR BONES.
HURRAH!
HURRAH!
WHO IS CHEERING?
WE'RE SAVED! IT'S A RESCUE PARTY!
WE'RE JUST THE SCOUTS--BUT THERE ARE RESCUE WAGONS AHEAD, THEY HAVE FOOD.
ON YOUR FEET! RESCUE IS AT HAND!
NOVEMBER 2, 1856
THE MARTIN COMPANY!
LOOK AT ALL THESE PEOPLE. OUR SUPPLIES WON'T BE ENOUGH.
ONLY A FEW CAN RIDE-- WE ONLY HAVE TEN WAGONS.
WE CAN GIVE YOU A LITTLE FOOD --BUT YOU HAVE TO KEEP MARCHING.
THERE'S A COVE AHEAD WE CAN SHELTER FROM THE WIND THERE.
WE'LL NEED TO CROSS THE SWEETWATER.
I CAN BARELY WALK ON LAND, MUCH LESS THROUGH A FREEZING RIVER!
NOVEMBER 4, 1856
SOAKED AND FREEZING, THE COMPANY SET UP THIER TENTS IN MARTIN'S COVE.
IN FIVE DAYS, THE FOOD IN THE RESCUE WAGONS WAS NEARLY GONE.
IF WE DON'T MOVE NOW, WE'LL ALL FREEZE TO DEATH HERE.
UP! WE MOVE OR WE DIE!

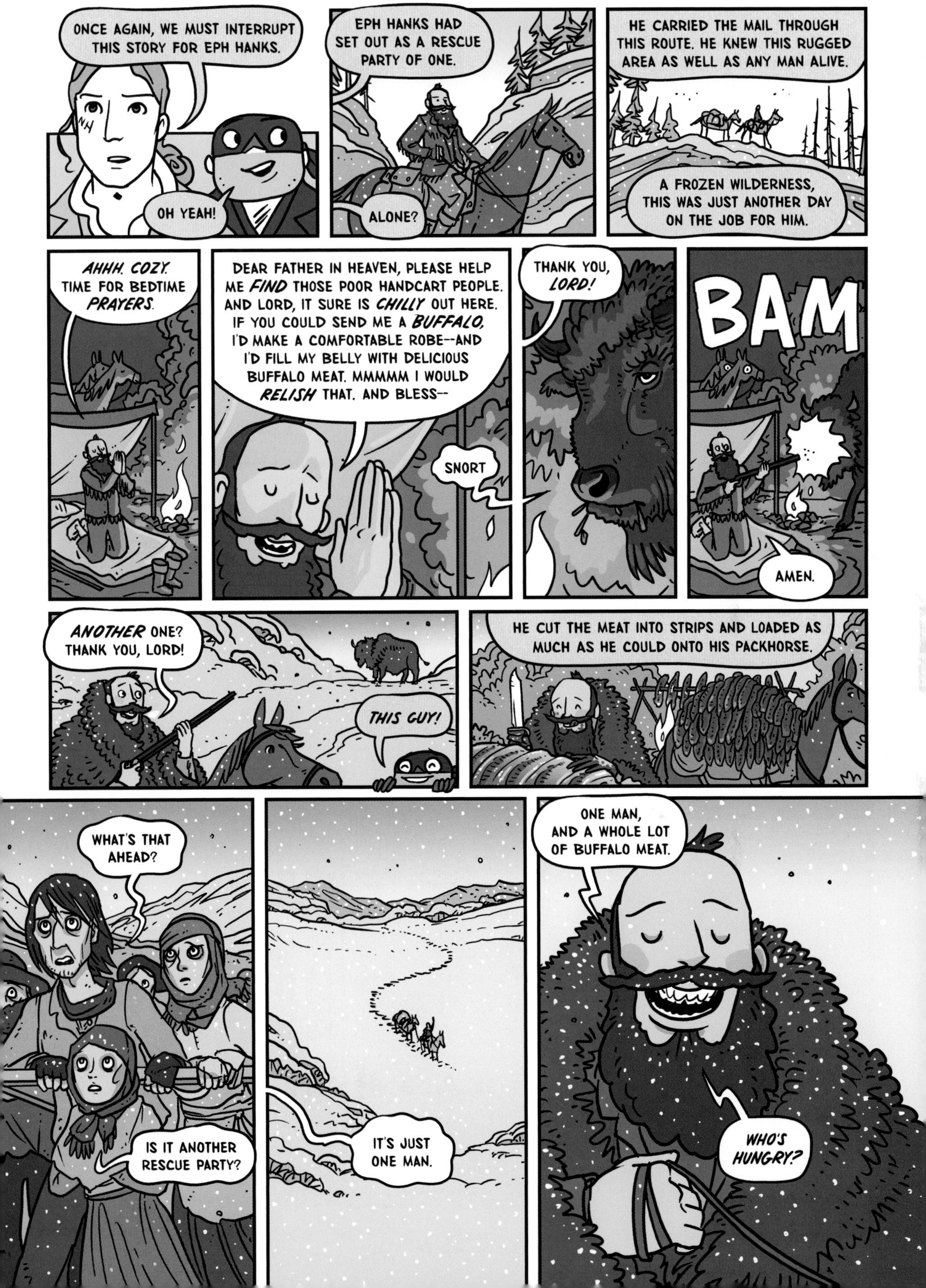
ONCE AGAIN, WE MUST INTERRUPT THIS STORY FOR EPH HANKS.
OH YEAH!
EPH HANKS HAD SET OUT AS A RESCUE PARTY OF ONE.
ALONE?
HE CARRIED THE MAIL THROUGH THIS ROUTE. HE KNEW THIS RUGGED AREA AS WELL AS ANY MAN ALIVE.
A FROZEN WILDERNESS, THIS WAS JUST ANOTHER DAY ON THE JOB FOR HIM.
AHHH. COZY. TIME FOR BEDTIME PRAYERS.
DEAR FATHER IN HEAVEN, PLEASE HELP ME FIND THOSE POOR HANDCART PEOPLE. AND LORD, IT SURE IS CHILLY OUT HERE. IF YOU COULD SEND ME A BUFFALO, I'D MAKE A COMFORTABLE ROBE--AND I'D FILL MY BELLY WITH DELICIOUS BUFFALO MEAT. MMMMM I WOULD RELISH THAT. AND BLESS--
THANK YOU, LORD!
SNORT
BAM
AMEN.
ANOTHER ONE? THANK YOU, LORD!
THIS GUY!
HE CUT THE MEAT INTO STRIPS AND LOADED AS MUCH AS HE COULD ONTO HIS PACKHORSE.
WHAT'S THAT AHEAD?
IS IT ANOTHER RESCUE PARTY?
IT'S JUST ONE MAN.
ONE MAN, AND A WHOLE LOT OF BUFFALO MEAT.
WHO'S HUNGRY?

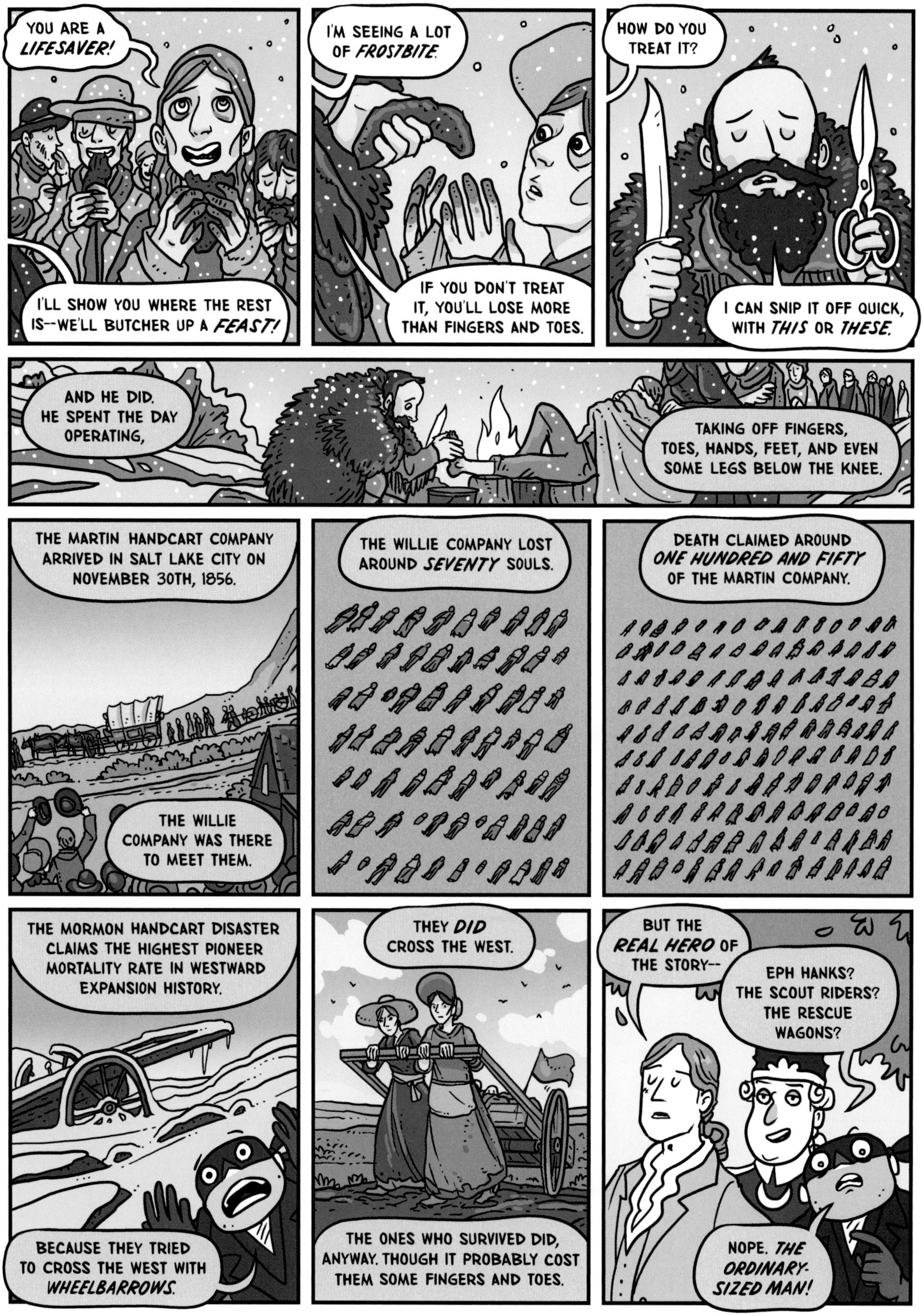
YOU ARE A *LIFESAVER!*
I'LL SHOW YOU WHERE THE REST IS--WE'LL BUTCHER UP A *FEAST!*
I'M SEEING A LOT OF *FROSTBITE.*
IF YOU DON'T TREAT IT, YOU'LL LOSE MORE THAN FINGERS AND TOES.
HOW DO YOU TREAT IT?
I CAN SNIP IT OFF QUICK, WITH *THIS* OR *THESE.*
AND HE DID. HE SPENT THE DAY OPERATING,
TAKING OFF FINGERS, TOES, HANDS, FEET, AND EVEN SOME LEGS BELOW THE KNEE.
THE MARTIN HANDCART COMPANY ARRIVED IN SALT LAKE CITY ON NOVEMBER 30TH, 1856.
THE WILLIE COMPANY WAS THERE TO MEET THEM.
THE WILLIE COMPANY LOST AROUND *SEVENTY* SOULS.
DEATH CLAIMED AROUND *ONE HUNDRED AND FIFTY* OF THE MARTIN COMPANY.
THE MORMON HANDCART DISASTER CLAIMS THE HIGHEST PIONEER MORTALITY RATE IN WESTWARD EXPANSION HISTORY.
BECAUSE THEY TRIED TO CROSS THE WEST WITH *WHEELBARROWS.*
THEY *DID* CROSS THE WEST.
THE ONES WHO SURVIVED DID, ANYWAY. THOUGH IT PROBABLY COST THEM SOME FINGERS AND TOES.
BUT THE *REAL HERO* OF THE STORY--
EPH HANKS? THE SCOUT RIDERS? THE RESCUE WAGONS?
NOPE. *THE ORDINARY-SIZED MAN!*

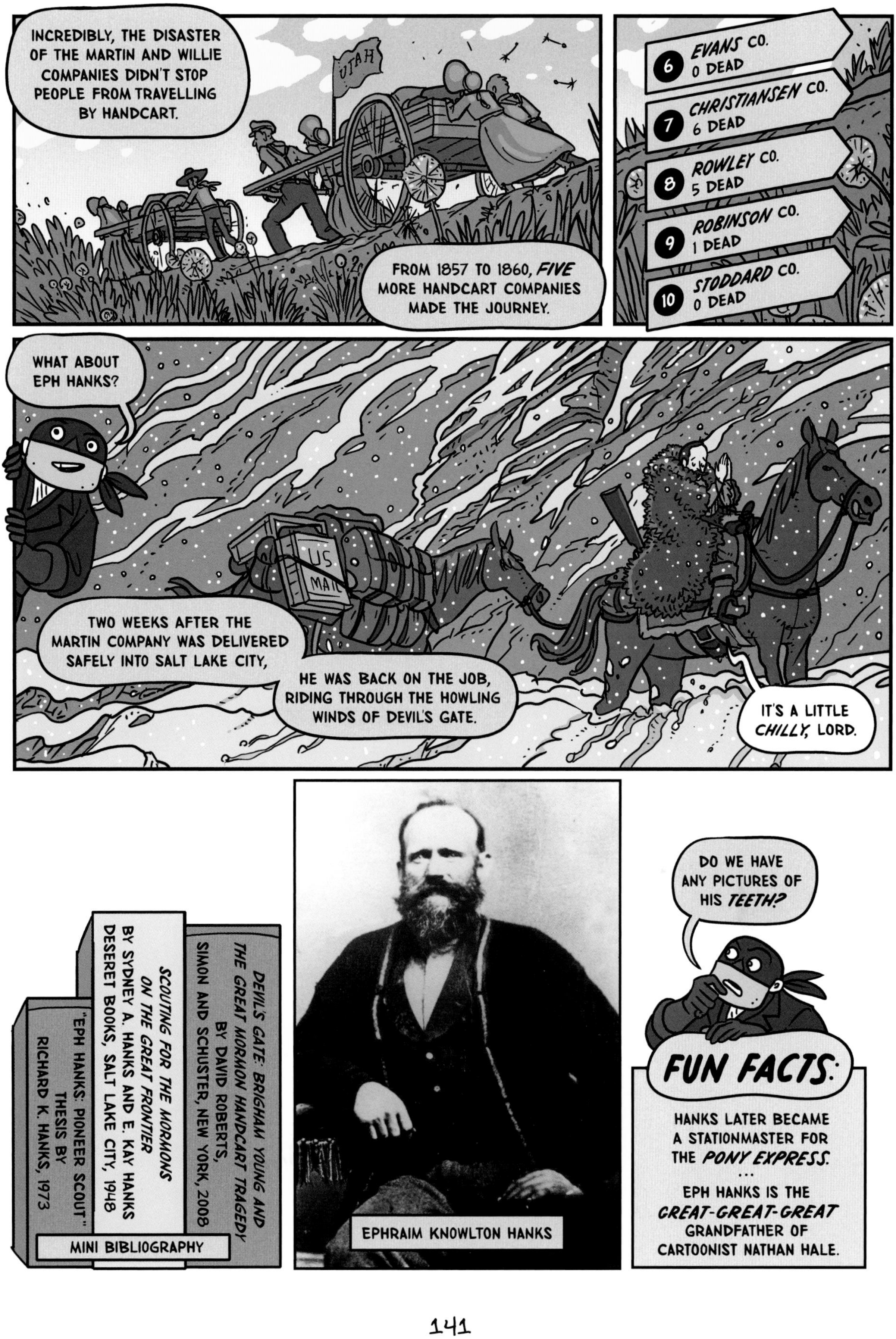
INCREDIBLY, THE DISASTER OF THE MARTIN AND WILLIE COMPANIES DIDN'T STOP PEOPLE FROM TRAVELLING BY HANDCART.
UTAH
FROM 1857 TO 1860, *FIVE* MORE HANDCART COMPANIES MADE THE JOURNEY.
6 *EVANS* CO. 0 DEAD
7 *CHRISTIANSEN* CO. 6 DEAD
8 *ROWLEY* CO. 5 DEAD
9 *ROBINSON* CO. 1 DEAD
10 *STODDARD* CO. 0 DEAD
WHAT ABOUT EPH HANKS?
US MAIL
TWO WEEKS AFTER THE MARTIN COMPANY WAS DELIVERED SAFELY INTO SALT LAKE CITY,
HE WAS BACK ON THE JOB, RIDING THROUGH THE HOWLING WINDS OF DEVIL'S GATE.
IT'S A LITTLE *CHILLY,* LORD.
DEVIL'S GATE: BRIGHAM YOUNG AND THE GREAT MORMON HANDCART TRAGEDY BY DAVID ROBERTS, SIMON AND SCHUSTER, NEW YORK, 2008
SCOUTING FOR THE MORMONS ON THE GREAT FRONTIER BY SYDNEY A. HANKS AND E. KAY HANKS DESERET BOOKS, SALT LAKE CITY, 1948
"EPH HANKS: PIONEER SCOUT" THESIS BY RICHARD K. HANKS, 1973
MINI BIBLIOGRAPHY
EPHRAIM KNOWLTON HANKS
DO WE HAVE ANY PICTURES OF HIS *TEETH?*
FUN FACTS:
HANKS LATER BECAME A STATIONMASTER FOR THE *PONY EXPRESS.*
...
EPH HANKS IS THE *GREAT-GREAT-GREAT* GRANDFATHER OF CARTOONIST NATHAN HALE.

HAZARDOUS TRAILS

OREGON TRAIL ☠☠

"THE **COWARDS** NEVER START AND THE **WEAK** DIE ALONG THE WAY." SAID **KIT CARSON** ABOUT THE **300,000+** EMIGRANTS WHO TRAVELED WEST ON THE OREGON TRAIL. PIONEERS FACED DEATH BY DROWNING, SCURVY, STAMPEDE, NATIVE AMERICAN ATTACK, AND **CHOLERA** ON THIS **2,000** MILE TRAIL.

1811 → 1869

CALIFORNIA TRAIL ☠☠

IN 1849, THE YEAR OF THE GOLD RUSH, **90,000** GOLD-HUNTERS BRAVED THE **2,000** MILE TREK. THESE PROSPECTORS WERE KNOWN AS "**FORTY-NINERS**." ONLY 40,000 ARRIVED, THE REST TURNED BACK--OR DIED ON THE WAY. A GROUP THAT DIDN'T LOSE AT LEAST ONE MEMBER WAS CONSIDERED LUCKY.

1841 → 1869

SANTA FE TRAIL ☠☠☠

900 MILES OF *RATTLESNAKE*-INFESTED DESERT. THE MAJOR TRADE ROUTE BETWEEN THE U.S. AND MEXICO. IT ALSO SERVED AS AN *INVASION ROUTE* DURING THE **MEXICAN-AMERICAN** WAR. THE TRAIL CROSSED HOSTILE **APACHE** AND **COMANCHE** TERRITORY AS WELL.

1821 → 1880

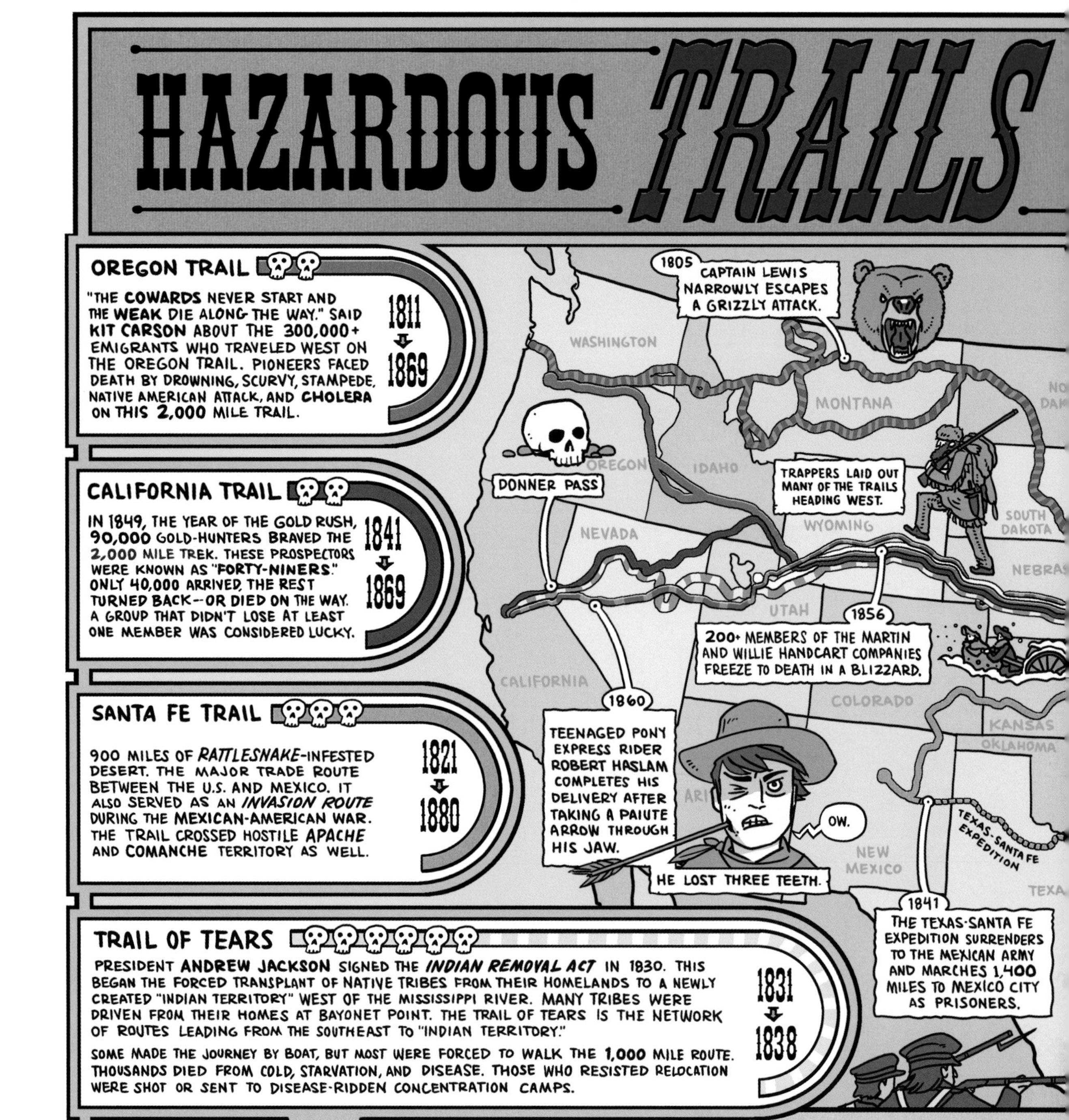
1805
CAPTAIN LEWIS NARROWLY ESCAPES A GRIZZLY ATTACK.
WASHINGTON
MONTANA
OREGON
IDAHO
DONNER PASS
TRAPPERS LAID OUT MANY OF THE TRAILS HEADING WEST.
NEVADA
WYOMING
SOUTH DAKOTA
UTAH
1856
200+ MEMBERS OF THE MARTIN AND WILLIE HANDCART COMPANIES FREEZE TO DEATH IN A BLIZZARD.
CALIFORNIA
1860
TEENAGED PONY EXPRESS RIDER ROBERT HASLAM COMPLETES HIS DELIVERY AFTER TAKING A PAIUTE ARROW THROUGH HIS JAW.
OW.
HE LOST THREE TEETH.
COLORADO
KANSAS
OKLAHOMA
TEXAS-SANTA FE EXPEDITION
NEW MEXICO
1841
THE TEXAS-SANTA FE EXPEDITION SURRENDERS TO THE MEXICAN ARMY AND MARCHES 1,400 MILES TO MEXICO CITY AS PRISONERS.

TRAIL OF TEARS ☠☠☠☠☠☠

PRESIDENT **ANDREW JACKSON** SIGNED THE ***INDIAN REMOVAL ACT*** IN 1830. THIS BEGAN THE FORCED TRANSPLANT OF NATIVE TRIBES FROM THEIR HOMELANDS TO A NEWLY CREATED "INDIAN TERRITORY" WEST OF THE MISSISSIPPI RIVER. MANY TRIBES WERE DRIVEN FROM THEIR HOMES AT BAYONET POINT. THE TRAIL OF TEARS IS THE NETWORK OF ROUTES LEADING FROM THE SOUTHEAST TO "INDIAN TERRITORY."

SOME MADE THE JOURNEY BY BOAT, BUT MOST WERE FORCED TO WALK THE **1,000** MILE ROUTE. THOUSANDS DIED FROM COLD, STARVATION, AND DISEASE. THOSE WHO RESISTED RELOCATION WERE SHOT OR SENT TO DISEASE-RIDDEN CONCENTRATION CAMPS.

1831 → 1838

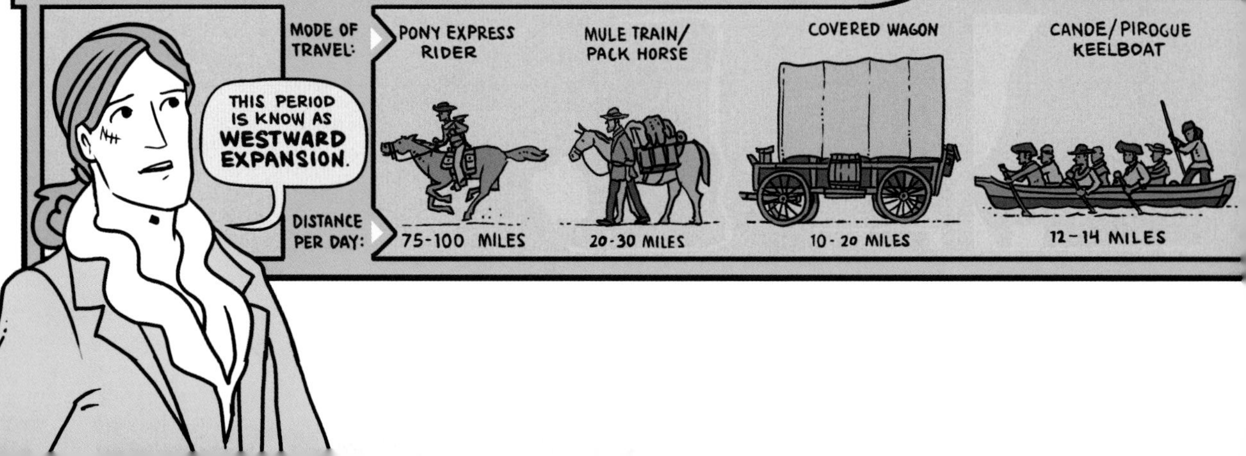
THIS PERIOD IS KNOW AS **WESTWARD EXPANSION**.
MODE OF TRAVEL:
PONY EXPRESS RIDER
MULE TRAIN/ PACK HORSE
COVERED WAGON
CANOE/PIROGUE KEELBOAT
DISTANCE PER DAY:
75-100 MILES
20-30 MILES
10-20 MILES
12-14 MILES

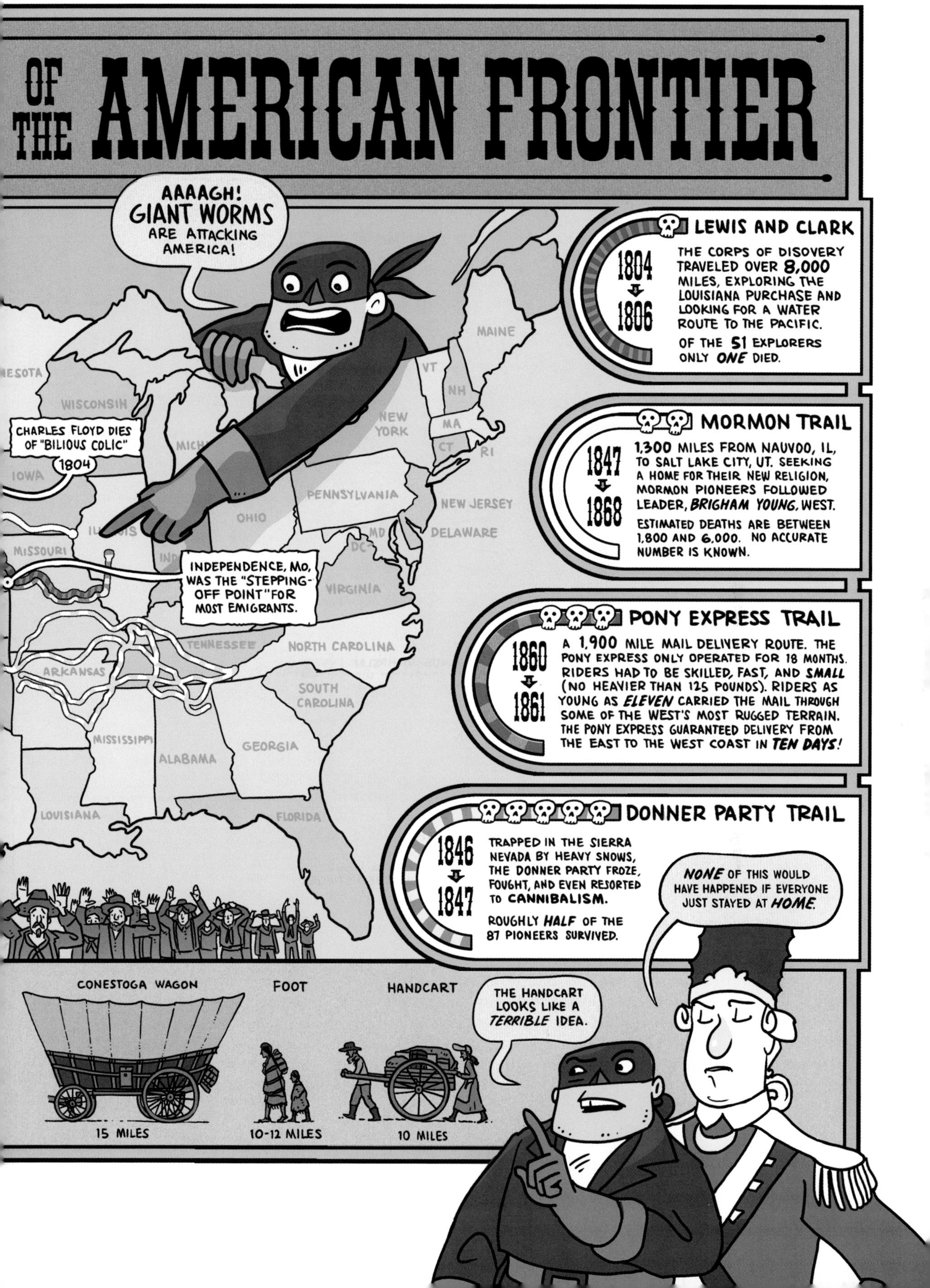
OF THE AMERICAN FRONTIER
AAAAGH! GIANT WORMS ARE ATTACKING AMERICA!
LEWIS AND CLARK
1804 1806
THE CORPS OF DISCOVERY TRAVELED OVER 8,000 MILES, EXPLORING THE LOUISIANA PURCHASE AND LOOKING FOR A WATER ROUTE TO THE PACIFIC.
OF THE 51 EXPLORERS ONLY ONE DIED.
MORMON TRAIL
1847 1868
1,300 MILES FROM NAUVOO, IL, TO SALT LAKE CITY, UT. SEEKING A HOME FOR THEIR NEW RELIGION, MORMON PIONEERS FOLLOWED LEADER, BRIGHAM YOUNG, WEST.
ESTIMATED DEATHS ARE BETWEEN 1,800 AND 6,000. NO ACCURATE NUMBER IS KNOWN.
PONY EXPRESS TRAIL
1860 1861
A 1,900 MILE MAIL DELIVERY ROUTE. THE PONY EXPRESS ONLY OPERATED FOR 18 MONTHS. RIDERS HAD TO BE SKILLED, FAST, AND SMALL (NO HEAVIER THAN 125 POUNDS). RIDERS AS YOUNG AS ELEVEN CARRIED THE MAIL THROUGH SOME OF THE WEST'S MOST RUGGED TERRAIN. THE PONY EXPRESS GUARANTEED DELIVERY FROM THE EAST TO THE WEST COAST IN TEN DAYS!
DONNER PARTY TRAIL
1846 1847
TRAPPED IN THE SIERRA NEVADA BY HEAVY SNOWS, THE DONNER PARTY FROZE, FOUGHT, AND EVEN RESORTED TO CANNIBALISM.
ROUGHLY HALF OF THE 87 PIONEERS SURVIVED.
NONE OF THIS WOULD HAVE HAPPENED IF EVERYONE JUST STAYED AT HOME.
CHARLES FLOYD DIES OF "BILIOUS COLIC"
1804
INDEPENDENCE, MO, WAS THE "STEPPING-OFF POINT" FOR MOST EMIGRANTS.
MAINE
VT
NH
MA
CT
RI
NEW YORK
PENNSYLVANIA
NEW JERSEY
DELAWARE
MD
DC
OHIO
VIRGINIA
NORTH CAROLINA
SOUTH CAROLINA
TENNESSEE
GEORGIA
ALABAMA
MISSISSIPPI
FLORIDA
LOUISIANA
ARKANSAS
MISSOURI
IOWA
WISCONSIN
CONESTOGA WAGON
15 MILES
FOOT
10-12 MILES
HANDCART
10 MILES
THE HANDCART LOOKS LIKE A TERRIBLE IDEA.

THE MYSTERIOUS LIBRARIAN'S TALE

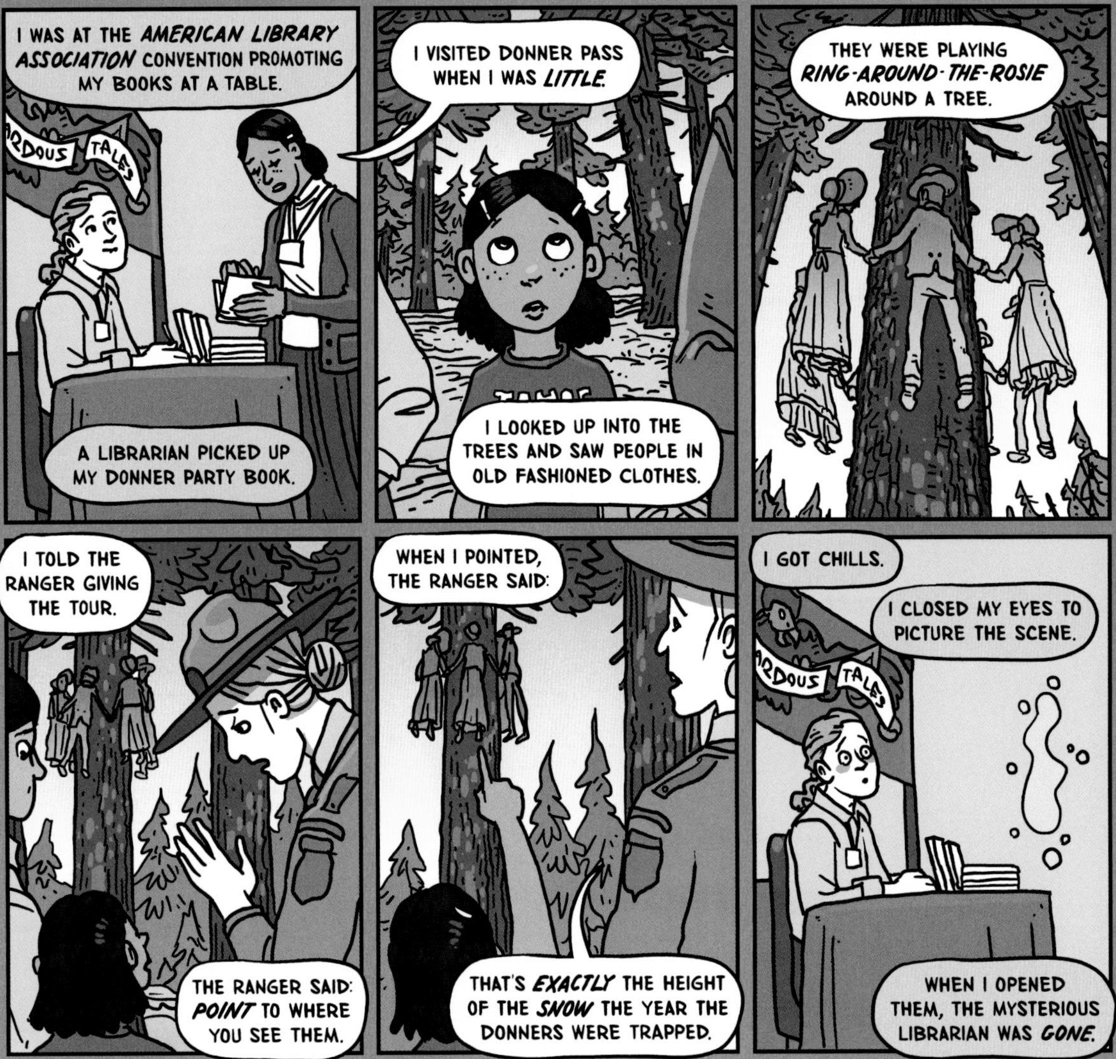

I WAS AT THE *AMERICAN LIBRARY ASSOCIATION* CONVENTION PROMOTING MY BOOKS AT A TABLE.
A LIBRARIAN PICKED UP MY DONNER PARTY BOOK.
I VISITED DONNER PASS WHEN I WAS *LITTLE*.
I LOOKED UP INTO THE TREES AND SAW PEOPLE IN OLD FASHIONED CLOTHES.
THEY WERE PLAYING *RING-AROUND-THE-ROSIE* AROUND A TREE.
I TOLD THE RANGER GIVING THE TOUR.
THE RANGER SAID: *POINT* TO WHERE YOU SEE THEM.
WHEN I POINTED, THE RANGER SAID:
THAT'S *EXACTLY* THE HEIGHT OF THE *SNOW* THE YEAR THE DONNERS WERE TRAPPED.
I GOT CHILLS.
I CLOSED MY EYES TO PICTURE THE SCENE.
WHEN I OPENED THEM, THE MYSTERIOUS LIBRARIAN WAS *GONE*.

IMAGE CREDITS

PAGE 121: *TOP:* CLASSICSTOCK/ALAMY. *SECOND:* COURTESY OF THE LIBRARY OF CONGRESS, LC--USZ62--24396. *BOTTOM:* JIM WEST/ALAMY.

PAGE 121: *BOTTOM LEFT:* GREG RYAN/ALAMY.

PAGE 123: *TOP ROW, LEFT:* COURTESY OF HISTORY SAN JOSE. *TOP ROW, CENTER LEFT:* COURTESY OF THE BANCROFT LIBRARY. *TOP ROW, CENTER RIGHT:* COURTESY OF THE BANCROFT LIBRARY. *TOP ROW, RIGHT:* COURTESY OF THE BANCROFT LIBRARY. *BOTTOM ROW, LEFT:* ELIZA P. DONNER HOUGHTON'S *THE EXPEDITION OF THE DONNER PARTY AND ITS TRAGIC FATE*, OPPOSITE P. 34; THIS COPY WAS PUBLISHED IN 1920. *BOTTOM ROW, CENTER LEFT:* THIS PHOTOGRAPH COURTESY OF THE YUBA COUNTY LIBRARY LOCAL HISTORY ARCHIVES. PLEASE CONTACT THE LIBRARY FOR RESTRICTIONS ON USE. *BOTTOM ROW, CENTER RIGHT:* THIS PHOTOGRAPH COURTESY OF THE YUBA COUNTY LIBRARY LOCAL HISTORY ARCHIVES. PLEASE CONTACT THE LIBRARY FOR RESTRICTIONS ON USE. *BOTTOM ROW, RIGHT:* COURTESY OF WESTERN SONOMA COUNTY HISTORICAL SOCIETY. *BOTTOM:* ARCHIVAR/ALAMY.

PAGE 124: *TOP LEFT:* MCKENNEY, THOMAS LORAINE AND JAMES HALL. HISTORY OF THE INDIAN TRIBES OF NORTH AMERICA, WITH BIOGRAPHICAL SKETCHES AND ANECDOTES, OF THE PRINCIPAL CHIEFS. PHILADELPHIA: J. T. BOWEN, 1848--1850. *TOP RIGHT:* COURTESY OF THE NEW YORK PUBLIC LIBRARY DIGITAL COLLECTION. *BOTTOM:* BETTMANN/GETTY IMAGES.

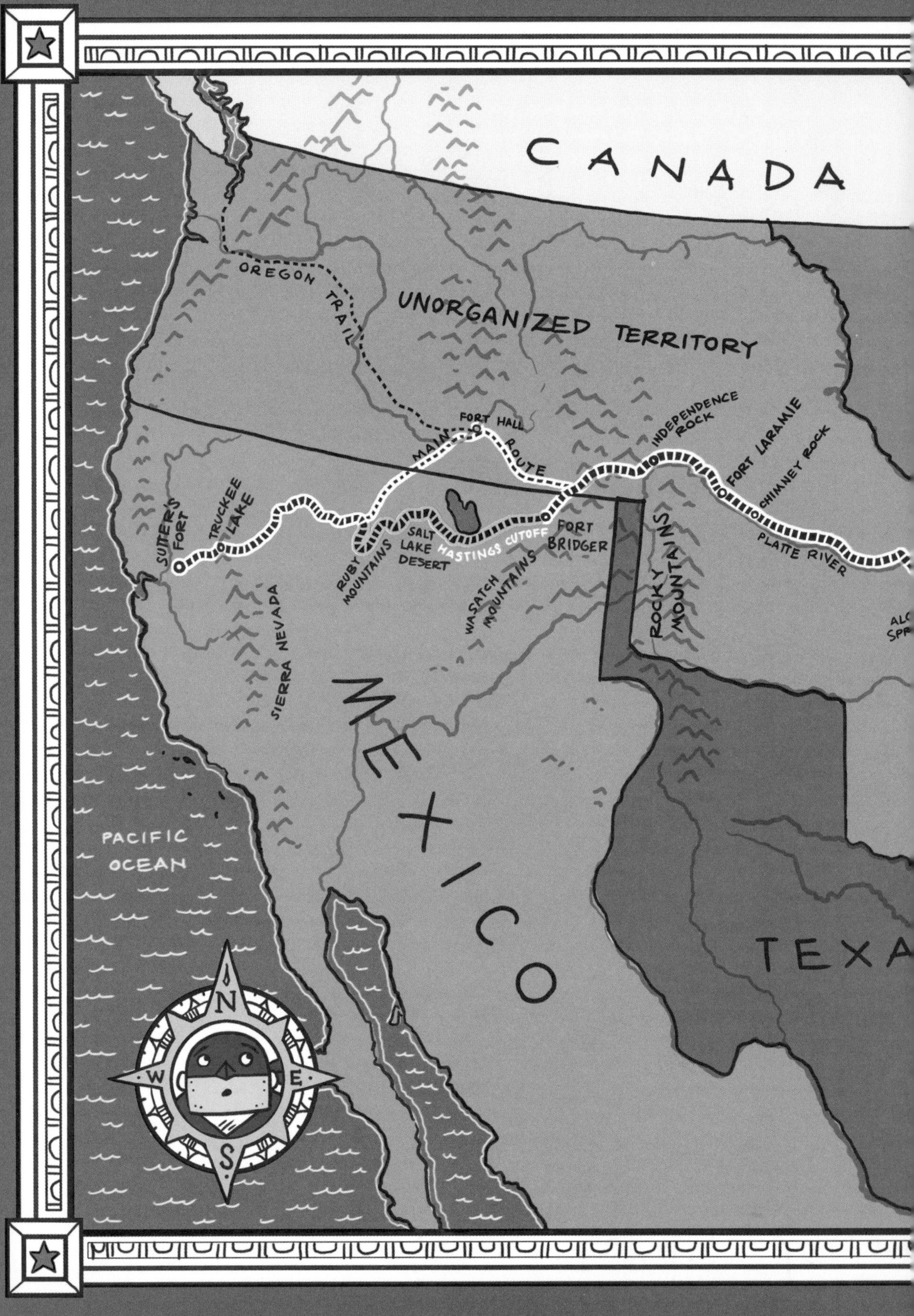
CANADA
OREGON TRAIL
UNORGANIZED TERRITORY
FORT HALL
MAIN ROUTE
INDEPENDENCE ROCK
FORT LARAMIE
CHIMNEY ROCK
PLATTE RIVER
SUTTER'S FORT
TRUCKEE LAKE
RUBY MOUNTAINS
SALT LAKE DESERT
HASTINGS CUTOFF
FORT BRIDGER
WASATCH MOUNTAINS
ROCKY MOUNTAINS
SIERRA NEVADA
MEXICO
PACIFIC OCEAN
N
W
E
S